Praise for *Social Startup Success*

"Social startup, including social business startup, success will be an important catalyst for training the next generation of social entrepreneurs on how to change the world. Kathleen Kelly Janus eloquently brings to life the best practices that all social entrepreneurs must embrace to maximize their impact. The pressing social problems we face today require creative leadership now more than ever, and this book will teach you what you need to know to be a good social entrepreneur."

—**MUHAMMAD YUNUS,** Nobel Peace Prize winner and author
of the *New York Times* bestseller *Banker to the Poor*

"Challenging inequality in the modern world demands that nonprofit leaders equip themselves with proven strategies to maximize impact. *Social Startup Success* reveals the secret sauce behind the most influential nonprofits of our time, telling their stories in memorable ways that every nonprofit leader can learn from."

—**DARREN WALKER,** President, Ford Foundation

"What *Crossing the Chasm* did for the business sector, *Social Startup Success* will do for the nonprofit sector. In this vital guide, Kathleen Kelly Janus shows how to scale an impact organization and, in so doing, change the world for the better."

—**CHARLES BEST,** Founder and CEO, DonorsChoose

"*Social Startup Success* provides both inspiration and practical advice. Based on extensive research, Kathleen Kelly Janus features some of the most important lessons that many of us have learned along our leadership journeys, so that organizations can accelerate their impact to meet the pressing social needs of today. This book is an invaluable resource for the next generation of changemakers."

—**WENDY KOPP,** Founder, Teach for America,
Co-Founder and CEO, Teach for All

"Kathleen Kelly Janus weaves brilliantly crafted stories of transformational social entrepreneurs into an invaluable roadmap of how to transform ideas and vision into execution and impact. *Social Startup Success* is an inspiring must-read, with an empathetic voice, for all of us aspiring to maximize our social value through our organizations, work and lives."

—**LAURA ARRILLAGA-ANDREESSEN,** Founder and President, laaf.org; author, *Giving 2.0*; Founder/Chairman, Stanford PACS; Founder/Chairman Emeritus, SV2; Lecturer in Business Strategy/ Philanthropy, Stanford Graduate School of Business

"Synthesizing a range of stories of leading social entrepreneurs, Kathleen Kelly Janus has created an insightful and highly useful guide that breaks down how organizations maximize their impact and create lasting change. An important contribution to the field."

—**DAVID BORNSTEIN,** CEO, Solutions Journalism Network and author, *How to Change the World: Social Entrepreneurs and the Power of New Ideas* and *Social Entrepreneurship: What Everyone Needs to Know*

"*Social Startup Success* is a playbook I wish we had when we founded Kiva! This book serves emerging and established social entrepreneurs looking to integrate cutting-edge best practices into their organizations—based on a unique account of top-performing social enterprises and academic research. When you're building an airplane as you're flying, time is precious. *Social Startup Success* provides key insights into things we all struggle with: creating a culture of innovation, measuring impact and cultivating collective leadership. Kathleen Kelly Janus takes us behind the scenes at some of the world's top-performing social entrepreneurs, providing a fun and inspiring read for anyone who cares about making the world a better place."

—**PREMAL SHAH,** President and Co-Founder, Kiva.org

"*Social Startup Success* is an important read for aspiring social entrepreneurs seeking to shift the unjust equilibria that some of the best social entrepreneurs have been fighting for years. By shedding light on the stories of inspiring leaders like Raj Panjabi of Last Mile Health, Chuck Slaughter of Living Goods, and Andrew Yoon of One Acre Fund, Kathleen Kelly Janus draws on her extensive research to pull back the curtain for those seeking to change the world."

—**SALLY OSBERG,** President and CEO, Skoll Foundation

"Written from the wellspring of technology and now social innovation in Silicon Valley, Kathleen Kelly Janus' *Social Startup Success* is a comprehensive and clearly written synthesis of the fundamental forces shaping social entrepreneurship today: design thinking, theory of change and strategic leadership, impact measurement, storytelling, new business and financial models. The 'must-read' book on social entrepreneurship for the next decade."

—**WILLIAM F. MEEHAN III,** Lafayette Partners Lecturer in Strategic Management at the Stanford University Graduate School of Business, Director Emeritus of McKinsey & Company, and co-author, with Kim Starkey Jonker, of *Engine of Impact: Essentials of Strategic Leadership in the Nonprofit Sector*

"Kathleen Janus has written a practical, inspiring, and empirically grounded guide for social entrepreneurs, drawing valuable lessons from actual stories of success and failure."

—**PAUL BREST,** Professor Emeritus, Stanford Law School, and co-author, *Money Well Spent*

"I'm always on the hunt for valuable tools and resources that tomorrow's social change leaders can use as a guide as they begin their social impact journeys. I predict that *Social Startup Success* will very quickly become a must-have for those building and scaling the best social impact nonprofits. Kathleen Kelly Janus has made a significant contribution to our field by not just focusing on the "who" but on the "how-to." She has presented all those committed to the work of the world with five practical and actionable strategies that are best practices for driving social impact. This book is an inclusive call to action that uses the inspiring stories of creative and committed social change leaders to not only educate other fellow travelers but also spark the involvement of the rest of us to get engaged with these nonprofit organizations so worth supporting."

—**CHERYL L. DORSEY,** President, Echoing Green, and 1992 Echoing Green Fellow

"*Social Startup Success* is a marvelous compilation of stories of some of the most inspiring leaders of our time. In her brilliant step-by-step process for how to make impact, Kathleen Kelly Janus shows how all of us can maximize our potential as changemakers."

—**BILL DRAYTON,** CEO, Ashoka: Everyone a Changemaker

"*Social Startup Success* makes an important contribution to the field. It's compelling, easy to read, and fills a gap in the current literature by addressing the critical first few years of nonprofit startup life. Janus covers all of the important building blocks—like having a proven model, measuring impact, and cultivating leadership—that are necessary for early stage organizations to succeed and build a strong foundation for further scale. Drawing on numerous examples of other nonprofit start-ups, Janus gives social entrepreneurs all the practical tips and advice they need to succeed. This book will no doubt help them in their efforts to change the world."

—**HEATHER MCLEOD GRANT,** Co-founder, Open Impact, and author, *Forces for Good*

SOCIAL STARTUP SUCCESS

SOCIAL STARTUP SUCCESS

How the Best Nonprofits Launch, Scale Up, and Make a Difference

KATHLEEN KELLY JANUS

Da Capo
LIFE
LONG

Copyright © 2017 by Kathleen Kelly Janus

Da Capo Lifelong Books
Hachette Book Group
1290 Avenue of the Americas, New York, NY 10104
www.dacapopress.com
@DaCapoPress

Printed in the United States of America

Originally published in hardcover and ebook by Da Capo Lifelong Books in January 2018;
Originally published in 2018 by Da Capo Lifelong Books in the USA
First Edition: January 2018

Published by Da Capo Lifelong Books, an imprint of Perseus Books, LLC, a subsidiary of Hachette Book Group, Inc. The Da Capo Lifelong name and logo is a trademark of the Hachette Book Group.

Editorial production by Christine Marra, Marrathon Production Services, www.marrathoneditorial.org
Print book interior design by Jane Raese
Set in 12-point Paradox

Cataloging-in-Publication Data is available from the Library of Congress.
ISBN 978-0-7382-1990-5 (hardcover)
ISBN 978-0-7382-1991-2 (ebook)

LSC-C

10 9 8 7 6 5 4 3 2 1

For my parents, who taught me the value of citizenship,

for Ted, forever ago,

and for Lara, Eleanor and Teddy, you are the future.

CONTENTS

INTRODUCTION

Rob Gitin never intended to start a nonprofit organization. But in college, he stumbled upon a class titled "Poverty and Homelessness in America," largely because he liked to sleep in late and the class met at two in the afternoon. The course changed his life. The students were required to intern with an organization that helped homeless people; Gitin selected a program for homeless youth, and he quickly fell in love with the work and the kids he encountered. The injustices they faced—let down at every step in their lives by the social services system—kept him up at night.

After three years volunteering or working at this program, he became determined to do something different to address the problem, and a few months after graduating, he and cofounder Taj Mustapha decided to try to create a program to reach the most disconnected youth. The well-known seed-stage funder Echoing Green supported him, and his organization, At The Crossroads (ATC), was born. He and Mustapha conducted nightly outreach with homeless youth, walking the streets of San Francisco's Tenderloin and Mission districts, often from seven-thirty until eleven-thirty at night. They were able to build trusting bonds with some of the hardest-to-reach youth and helped them build healthier, more stable lives.

The work was personally fulfilling, but after about a year Gitin and Mustapha realized that they alone could only make a small dent in the growing homeless epidemic in San Francisco. If they really wanted to make a substantial impact, they would need an army of people and money to pay them. Gitin worked hard to raise funds, and he was able to hire some staff, but he faced a number of daunting hurdles in trying to scale up. He had no idea how to hire or manage well, and there was a ton of staff turnover. He also didn't know the best methods for raising funds, and as a recent college grad with few contacts in the foundations or with high-net-worth individuals, he spent dozens of hours chasing donations that never panned out.

Despite those challenges, Gitin persevered, and he managed to grow the organization to a budget of around $800,000. But then he hit a wall; he couldn't break past that level of funding. Even after fifteen years of successful work, the organization's budget was still stuck at that level, and meanwhile the need for its services had increased several-fold, and ATC couldn't keep up with the demand. Gitin decided to make a concerted new effort to expand services and to raise more funds, launching a four-year plan to achieve an annual budget of at least $2 million. He has now just about achieved that goal, and I'll share the story of how he's done so, along with the stories of a host of other nonprofit leaders and the methods they used to scale their organizations. The struggle to scale, I have found, is the most pressing challenge for the social entrepreneurship community.

I have had a front-row view of the boom under way in social entrepreneurship. As a social entrepreneur myself—cofounder of Spark, a network of millennial philanthropic donors who raise money to support gender equality—and a lecturer in the Program on Social Entrepreneurship at Stanford University, I have watched the launch of so many exciting innovations for good. And yet, while for many nonprofits this has been an invigorating and transformative time, so many other nonprofits, like At The Crossroads, have struggled on the sidelines. Despite doing important work, many operate in constant survival mode, scrambling for the money to make payroll every month. In 2014, almost two-thirds of reporting public charities in the U.S. had an annual budget of less than $500,000.[1]

I became obsessed with understanding how nonprofits can get off the treadmill and attain organizational sustainability, which I define as reliably raising around $2 million in annual revenue. Of course, for some organizations, a small budget is sufficient to sustain their operations and be highly impactful. Scaling revenue also does not necessarily equate to scaling impact; an organization can be very good at raising money with programs that aren't really making a significant difference. But many organizations that have the potential to do a great deal more good by scaling, and that are trying to grow faster, are stymied.

I learned this the hard way in working to grow Spark. I cofounded the organization in 2004 with six friends from my undergraduate days at U.C. Berkeley. We wanted to create a membership network of young professionals to raise money for other organizations focused on issues of women's equality. As recent college grads living in San Francisco, we saw that there was no shortage of charitable galas to support, but rarely did those events educate their guests about the problem addressed by an organization or give them an opportunity to get more involved. Over drinks one night after work, my friend Maya Garcia said to me, "These events are leaving so much untapped potential on the table. What if we do something different?" Our hope was that if we could connect young people to social causes in a meaningful way early on in their careers, they would become participants in the social justice movement for life. Passionate about global women's issues, we decided to start there. We invited some other friends to join us, and the seven of us crammed into Maya's studio apartment over the course of several months, sharing several bottles of wine, to begin planning.

We held our first fundraiser in a small art gallery in San Francisco, and were elated when our promotional work led to a line around the block of people coming to donate. We had earmarked funds from this gathering for an organization of women in Rwanda rebuilding their lives after the genocide, for whom we raised $5,000. That felt like a million dollars to us. As we continued to network, we doubled our revenue every few months, and by our third year, we could afford to hire our first executive director, Shannon Farley. By then, we had over ten thousand members, but we had hit a wall.

As I witnessed other exciting new nonprofits take off all around us, we began struggling to find more growth capital. We explored creative fundraising ideas, but we couldn't bring in more than $500,000 annually. Year after year, we found ourselves spending inordinate amounts of time chasing gifts in increments of hundreds or thousands of dollars, barely making ends meet. We kept hearing about new forms of "venture philanthropy" being pioneered by leaders in the technology sector, such as Bill Gates, Pierre Omidyar and Mark Zuckerberg. But none of that money was reaching us at Spark.

In 2007, I decided to leave my job as a corporate lawyer and started teaching international human rights and social entrepreneurship at Stanford University so that I could devote myself full time to advancing social causes. Teaching with the Program on Social Entrepreneurship, where we host highly successful social entrepreneurs in residence for a quarter, I began to hear stories like ours at Spark over and over. Nearly all organizations struggle with the scaling challenges Spark faced. The difference with these social entrepreneurs was that they had somehow managed to overcome them. I wanted to understand why some social startups had beat the scaling challenge so successfully, sometimes growing to several million dollars in annual revenue within just a few years. I decided to study the nonprofit scaling challenge.

For the past five years, I have been traveling around the country, visiting the founders, leadership teams and funders of dozens of what I call breakthrough social startups. I've interviewed nearly a hundred social entrepreneurs,[2] academics and philanthropists, both newcomers and veterans in the field, including the leaders of Teach for America, City Year, DonorsChoose and charity: water, and started our conversations with a simple question: "What is the key to nonprofit success?" I've spent time at organizations and observed their operations, getting a read on the aspects of their organizational cultures that contribute to success. I've also talked to staff members and to beneficiaries, seeking to understand what it is about the approaches of these organizations that has enabled them to build highly productive teams and such strong followings among those they seek to serve. While interviewing, I also scoured the research literature, reading hundreds of articles, books, studies and reports, looking for answers.

My first discovery was that very little actual data existed about how organizations grow, especially in the early stages, despite the volumes of advice offered. To bridge the gap, I conducted a survey of early-stage organizations, drawing from the portfolios of top seed funders such as Echoing Green, Draper Richards Kaplan, Silicon Valley Social Ventures, Ashoka and the Skoll Foundation. The survey asked nonprofit leaders a host of questions about how they had launched their organizations, how they measured impact, how they managed teams, how they sought funding and how they raised awareness. I then followed up in person with one hundred of them to dig deeper into how they applied the methods they described and to get more specifics about their responses to a range of the most difficult challenges, such as measuring their impact, managing their time, developing an active board that helped grow the organization, and hiring the right people. Their answers provided a treasure trove of insights and inventive methods that every organizational leader, whether of a fledgling startup or of a large, well-established organization, can profit from.

In the pages that follow, I present five key strategies that I heard over and over again were responsible for the breakout growth of the most successful social startups. Each organization that scaled most successfully employed many, or all, of the following practices:

- *testing* **ideas** through research and development to get proof of concept *before* seeking major funding or media coverage;
- *measuring* **impact** right from the start, often with inventive metrics tailored to their specific programs;

- *funding* **experimentation** through a combination of selling products and services that were in strong alignment with their mission and employing bold strategies to raise philanthropic capital;
- *leading* **collaboratively** in a fashion that allowed them to optimize the talents of their staff, including building a strong board of directors; and
- *telling* **compelling stories** in ways that utilized the most recent innovations and tapped into others to advocate on their behalf.

What is most exciting about my findings is that the specific methods for executing on each of these, which I describe in detail, can all be readily applied to the work of any nonprofit, starting immediately. During my interviews, I kept expecting people to say success was driven by a truly remarkable idea, or by the charisma of the founder, but no one did. Not one. This isn't to say that factors like charisma, grit or brilliant ideas don't contribute significantly to success. Of course they do. But the foundation of success is this set of best practices.

In these uncertain times, when so many social problems are not only persisting, but in many cases, worsening, we need every bit of creativity and determination to find better solutions. My hope is that the stories you read in this book and the tools it recommends will help you to make your own organization, or those you are supporting, thrive. We need to spend less energy keeping organizations alive, so that we can devote more energy to spreading positive impact. This book is a guide for how to achieve that.

Social entrepreneurs are not content just to give a fish or teach how to fish. They will not rest until they have revolutionized the fishing industry.

—BILL DRAYTON, FOUNDER, ASHOKA

Social entrepreneurship is a process by which citizens build or transform institutions to advance solutions to social problems, such as poverty, illness, illiteracy, environmental destruction, human rights abuses and corruption, in order to make life better for many.

—DAVID BORNSTEIN AND SUSAN DAVIS,
Social Entrepreneurship: What Everyone Needs to Know

PART 1

TESTING IDEAS

CHAPTER 1

The Discovery Phase

Social startups face a vexing catch-22: funders want to see proof of an organization's success before offering grants, but nonprofits need funding to get their ideas off the ground. The lack of seed funding is one of the biggest differences between growing a nonprofit organization and a for-profit business. Private sector startups are often able to gain support for the research and development (R&D) phase of building their organizations from angel investors, who hope to earn a handsome return once the startup becomes profitable. For nonprofit startups, private angel funds don't exist. Most foundations are also not interested in providing financial support for testing. Typically, they want to fund organizations with a proven approach. Even at the infancy of an idea, they press for results, asking: "What is your set of early outcomes? How do we know this is going to work?"

But how can organizations improve their programs with testing and prove impact without funding at the early stage? This dilemma has left many social startups in slow-growth mode for years. The solution is to adopt a powerful set of innovation methods—a cycle of researching, brainstorming, prototyping and implementing often called "human-centered design"—that the Silicon Valley entrepreneurship community developed for creating new products and services. These innovation methods not only allow an organization to produce compelling early indications of scalable success, but also help to speed up the development process; they avoid the

3

common mistake of investing too much time and money in efforts doomed to fail. These methods have enabled much more rapid innovation at lower cost, while also facilitating the development of products and services more responsive to the needs and desires of customers. They have fueled the astonishing success of the Valley's fastest growth companies, including LinkedIn, Airbnb, Uber and Pinterest—and have driven the breakout success of many of the most exciting new social enterprises too.

A consistent theme in my interviews with breakthrough social entrepreneurs was that they had used these innovation practices to develop their models for their products or services, and had tested them *before* going out to raise capital and seek press coverage. This allowed them to develop more effective programs and products. It also enabled them to tell a persuasive story about how they had arrived at their models, impressing funders with their research and development process and their initial set of results. In the long run, adopting these practices instills a culture of continuous innovation that helps to assure that organizations keep scaling their impact— always experimenting with ways to improve and expand their offerings, while discontinuing efforts that aren't working so they can focus on new approaches.

There are three core methods to draw on. One is the lean startup approach to product development, popularized by Eric Ries in his book *The Lean Startup*.[1] Closely related but with some methods of its own is the practice of design thinking, pioneered at the Hasso Plattner Institute of Design at Stanford University (known as the "d.school") and the private innovation consulting firm IDEO. This method has been introduced in several books, including *Change by Design* by the CEO of IDEO, Tim Brown.[2] Finally, open innovation, also referred to as "cocreation," was introduced by Professor Henry Chesbrough, of the Haas School of Business at the University of California, and is described in his book *Open Innovation*.[3] Collectively, these methods can be referred to as "human-centered design." Though each has specific nuances in execution, which you can read about in more detail in the books mentioned, at the core of these

methods are three fundamental principles: that organiz
design products and services based upon an in-depth i
of the customers' needs and desires; that organizations must ..
prototypes of products and services (often very simple ones) with
customers, and further develop them according to their feedback;
and that no matter how com-
pelling an idea for a product or
service may be to a founder or
organization, if it fails to win
the approval of the targeted customers in tests, the organization
must pivot to a new approach
and consider the failures valuable learning experiences rather
than crippling mistakes.

> A consistent theme in my inter-
> views with breakthrough social
> entrepreneurs was that they had
> used these innovation practices
> to develop their models for their
> products or services, and had
> tested them *before* going out
> to raise capital and seek press
> coverage.

There is no one widely agreed-
upon strict process to follow;
organizations can either tailor
the methods to their work as
they see fit, or can follow one or
another well-established guide. IDEO, for example, has developed
a rigorous step-by-step method for nonprofits through its nonprofit spinoff IDEO.org. It offers a *Field Guide to Human Centered
Design* for free download.[4] Many other consultancies have followed
in IDEO's footsteps and developed their own set of specific procedures. Several companies and organizations have drawn on these
resources to craft their own particular processes to fit their needs.
Surveying the full range of methods, the following is a basic step-
by-step process for producing optimal results:

**1. Conduct in-depth research on the problem with the intended
"customers," who, for social innovators, we'll call beneficiaries.**
It is vital to build strong connections with the end-users in order to
better understand their needs. This must involve methods such as focus grouping or surveys, as well as going out to target communities,

observing the nature of end-users' lives and conducting in-person interviews to understand the problems they face. Prominent civil rights activist Bryan Stevenson, founder and executive director of the Alabama-based civil rights organization Equal Justice Initiative, refers to this as gaining "proximity."[5] He stresses how important it is to build understanding and empathy with communities in order to design effective programs. As he said in a recent speech: "We cannot make good decisions from a distance. If you are not proximate, you cannot change the world."[6] Proximity is also critical to getting buy-in from the communities you hope to serve.

2. Brainstorm a series of solutions for addressing the problem(s) and select a first candidate for development.

Once you have conducted interviews, discuss key findings with your team and perhaps with a range of stakeholders and outside advisors. Hold a session in which you invite unfettered idea generation about the best ways to address the problem; or for established organizations, to make changes in existing programs or products. It is imperative that everyone understands that all ideas are welcome at the table, and none should be shot down during this brainstorming. A ubiquitous practice for idea generation in Silicon Valley is scribbling thoughts on brightly colored Post-it notes, then sticking them on a whiteboard, wall or large sheet of paper.

3. Create a rough prototype and get feedback.

This should be a very simple and inexpensive representation of the product (such as a sketch depicting the product), or how the service will work (a storyboard describing how the service would operate). You can present the prototype to targeted users and gain valuable feedback.

4. Refine the prototype and launch a pilot program or product to test results.

As you observe the responses to the pilot, you will generally discover additional ways to improve it, often launching a number of

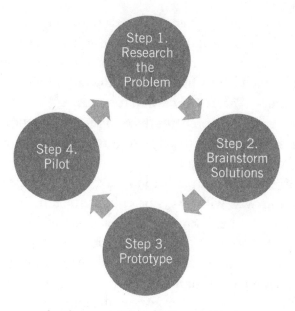

The Elements of Human-Centered Design

progressively more developed versions until you see the results you are aiming for. It is critical to have good benchmarks to measure impact during this phase to determine whether a pilot is successfully addressing the problem you seek to solve. You may find the approach simply isn't working, and that it's time to pivot to a new one.

NEVER ASSUME YOU KNOW THE ANSWER

Too many nonprofits have made the mistake of not interviewing and testing before launching their service. A number of the respondents to my survey described this as the biggest mistake they made in building their organization. One of these is Rachel Armstrong, the founder of Farm Commons, a Minnesota-based organization that serves farmers by providing them with information regarding legal issues. Her original concept was that the farmers would be clients, paying the organization for providing legal services. But after the service was launched, it turned out the farmers didn't want to pay for legal representation. What they did want was education about legal issues, and Farm Commons had to completely redesign its model, not relying on income from the farmers and developing extensive educational resources and tutorials.

Even if social entrepreneurs have direct experience with the problems they are trying to solve, research and testing with beneficiaries is invaluable. Speaking with beneficiaries and all the other stakeholders, who can either help to make one's program a success or stand in its way, will always be enlightening. It will also build understanding in the community and earn buy-in. In the nonprofit world in particular, engaging beneficiaries is essential: communities will not embrace your efforts if you do not involve them in the process of developing your idea.

Take the case of CareMessage, a multimillion-dollar organization Vineet Singal and Cecilia Corral cofounded. It provides a sophisticated web-based system that allows health clinics to send patients text and voice messages to remind, educate and motivate them to manage their disease. One target is Spanish-speaking individuals who struggle to understand the information they receive from health care providers. Corral grew up between south Texas and Mexico, and her own parents spoke only Spanish at home. She knew very well the problems these patients have with the language barrier, because she watched her parents' blank stares as they struggled to understand doctors, and sometimes even the translators.

Despite her familiarity with the problem, Corral led extensive interviewing and testing of the prototypes for CareMessage with targeted users. She sat in on meetings between Spanish-speaking patients and translators, and even enrolled people from her circle of family and friends in the program, without notice, to see how they reacted to receiving such messages. She then proceeded to question them about their thoughts as the service evolved, constantly asking, "Does this sound okay? Is it making sense?"

FROM POST-IT TO PROOF OF CONCEPT

To see how powerful this general approach of customer research and product testing can be for social enterprises, let's take a close look at the process Tipping Point Community used in collaboration with the nonprofit Aspire Public Schools (a group of charter schools) to devise a boldly creative solution to ineffective preschool education in low-income communities.

Tipping Point Community, based in San Francisco, is one of many funders supporting nonprofits to embrace human-centered design practices. Others include Google.org, the Michael & Susan Dell Foundation, the William and Flora Hewlett Foundation and the Bill and Melinda Gates Foundation. The Gates Foundation, for example, has spent hundreds of millions of dollars on R&D to test various solutions to the malaria epidemic. In a speech, Bill Gates described R&D funding as "urgent to stay ahead of emerging disease threats."[7] It is promising to see international, national and local funders recognizing the vital role they can play in dedicating significant amounts of philanthropic capital to R&D.

Tipping Point Community aims to find solutions to extreme poverty and to facilitate innovation. To promote more innovation and design thinking in its work, it established an R&D arm, called T Lab. As Renuka Kher, the founding managing director of Tipping Point's T Lab, says, "The problem is that nonprofits are held to a different standard while in the business world we call R&D spending 'infrastructure' and it sounds essential, in the nonprofit world we call it 'overhead' and it is highly scrutinized." As a result, while corporations spent $145 billion on research and development in 2015, nonprofits spent nearly nothing. Tipping Point decided to change that, making R&D spending a priority within their own organization.

Through their research, T Lab identified the lack of preschool in many neighborhoods as a key problem, leaving eighty thousand children in the San Francisco Bay area without early childhood education. The lab's research group decided to tackle the challenge.

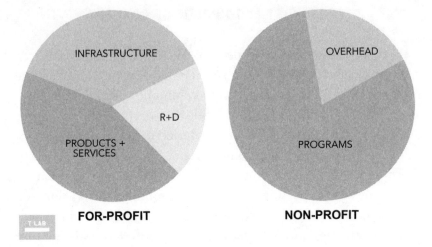

R&D Spending in For-Profits versus Nonprofits. Whereas in the business sector we characterize administrative costs as essential "infrastructure" and leave a significant portion of the budget for research and development (R&D), in the nonprofit sector we refer to administrative costs as overhead and scrutinize anything over 20 percent, leaving virtually no space for R&D. *Source:* Tipping Point.

Step one was for fellows of T Lab, a cohort of young professionals that Tipping Point trains and supports in human-centered design, to reach out to members of the communities lacking high-quality preschool options; the group asked questions about what they desired for their children in their early years, and their perspective on how to improve the situation. The fellows reached out to community-based organizations, schools and libraries to talk with parents, teachers, principles and anyone else who might have an opinion about how to solve the problem.

The team then held a brainstorming session, often called the "ideation" phase of human-centered design, and proposed a wide range of creative solutions. The team chose eight concepts, then developed a series of prototype solutions for testing. One was to convert a bus into a classroom, which was appealing because it would solve the problem of needing to either rent building space or, in many cases, construct a whole new building. They could also move

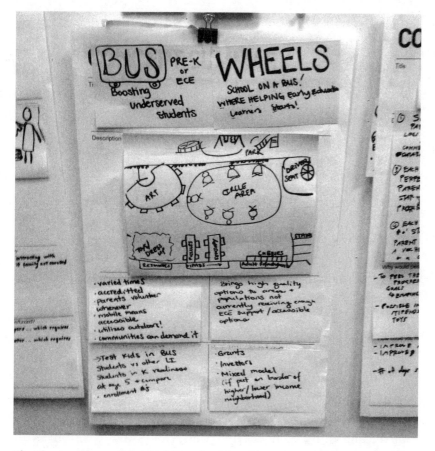

The Ideation Phase of the T Lab Preschool Bus Project. *Source*: Tipping Point.

a mobile classroom wherever needed, perhaps serving families in more than one location if scheduling permitted.

The team made a simple cardboard mock-up of a bus for their prototype, which they took to the community to ask parents, teachers and school administrators what they thought of the concept. They probed for any issues that might be important to consider. For example, they asked, "What would your concerns be if you put your children on a bus for preschool?" and "Would you be comfortable with your child being on this bus?" Many people were enthusiastic. They saw the concept as a great potential option for preschool.

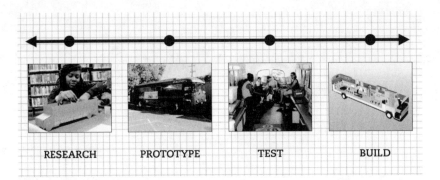

RESEARCH   PROTOTYPE   TEST   BUILD

ABOVE AND OPPOSITE: The T Lab Human-Centered Design Process for the Preschool Bus Project. *Source:* Tipping Point.

But some parents were worried about their children's safety, asking if the bus would be driving around with the children in it. They also thought that the children might not like the bus, because it might not feel as nice as a regular classroom. Overall, the feedback indicated the idea had potential, especially since the concept was to park the bus while school was in session. The next step was to build a working prototype for testing with children.

The T Lab team first used painter's tape to outline a life-sized bus in their office. They created a mock-up of the bus, furnishing the tape outline with cheap shelving, rugs, chairs and toys from IKEA to see how they could design the space. They then found a company with an old school bus for rent, and recreated their mock-up on the real bus. They got permission from Aspire to test the concept for two days at one of their elementary schools in Oakland, and invited parents to bring their children to come check it out, as well as teachers. Everyone was delighted with the result; not only were parents and teachers enthusiastic, but most importantly, the kids loved it!

With such positive responses, Aspire decided to invest further in the concept development. With $250,000 of R&D support from Tipping Point they were able to conduct a more robust five-month trial serving fourteen students. They parked the bus in the lot of an Aspire elementary school in Oakland, and invited families of Aspire students with preschool-age children to enroll. The bus was a huge

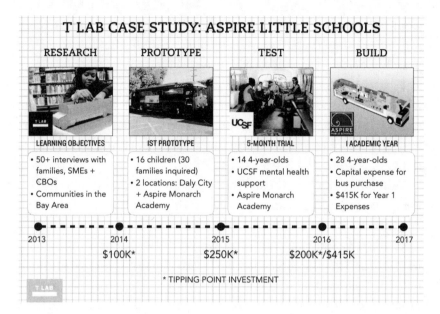

T LAB CASE STUDY: ASPIRE LITTLE SCHOOLS

RESEARCH	PROTOTYPE	TEST	BUILD
LEARNING OBJECTIVES	1ST PROTOTYPE	5-MONTH TRIAL	1 ACADEMIC YEAR
• 50+ interviews with families, SMEs + CBOs • Communities in the Bay Area	• 16 children (30 families inquired) • 2 locations: Daly City + Aspire Monarch Academy	• 14 4-year-olds • UCSF mental health support • Aspire Monarch Academy	• 28 4-year-olds • Capital expense for bus purchase • $415K for Year 1 Expenses

2013   2014   2015   2016   2017

$100K* $250K* $200K*/$415K

* TIPPING POINT INVESTMENT

hit, as described in a *San Francisco Chronicle* article, which reported that "on bench seats running lengthwise down the bus, are kids counting, coloring, laughing and occasionally throwing in a wobbly handstand on the rug at the back end, in front of the emergency exit. Outside, classmates are making noodle necklaces and building with colored blocks."[8] Following the trial, a waiting list developed for families who wanted a "seat on the bus." With such a successful trial, Aspire decided to dedicate $450,000 to conduct a pilot program for the full academic calendar year. Tipping Point provided another $200,000 grant to support their pilot. This allowed Aspire to purchase the bus and serve twenty-eight four-year-olds, offering them a full five-day school week. The pilot program was an overwhelming hit with teachers and families alike, who realized that placing children in preschool made them more kindergarten-ready, setting them up for success throughout their education.

Aspire was ready to scale the program when they ran into a wrinkle: the state of California refused to give them a license to operate more buses, saying they had failed to satisfy the state facilities code. Aspire decided they couldn't let the state's decision stop them. They went back to the drawing board, using the design of the bus class-room to redraw the classrooms in their schools, making space for preschool classes. In some cases, they decided to expand buildings. They learned that bringing the preschool programs in-house al-lowed them to serve more students than they could have with the buses. Going forward, Aspire hopes to provide all their students with preschool education, targeting a goal of serving 132 students in five classrooms by 2019.

When Renuka Kher heard that the state had shot down the bus idea, she was nervous about breaking the news to her T Lab team, who had become emotionally attached to the buses. But while they were initially sad that the buses wouldn't be deployed, they real-ized that testing the buses had been a great learning process, which helped Aspire arrive at an optimal solution. This story is a perfect example of why in human-centered design it is so important to keep the focus squarely on solving the problem, as opposed to falling in love with a particular solution.

ANY ORGANIZATION CAN FOLLOW THE STEPS

Sure, the human-centered design method worked fantastically for Aspire, you may be thinking, because it was initiated by T Lab and backed by funding from Tipping Point. But social startup seed fund-ing is still rare, despite the movement to support such R&D efforts, and most social startups can't rely on assistance from donors for the pilot phase. The good news is that organizations can conduct this process on a veritable shoestring. A number of breakthrough social innovators I met used scrappy versions of human-centered design to perfect their models, collect signs of impact and obtain funding.

One of those is Alexandra Bernadotte, founder of Beyond 12, an organization that provides technology and coaching to sup-port college students from underprivileged backgrounds. Born in Port-au-Prince, Haiti, Bernadotte's parents immigrated to the United States so she could have better opportunities for success.

Bernadotte worked hard to get into Dartmouth College, and she vividly recalled struggling through her four years there because she did not have the tools she needed to be successful, such as family members to review her resume or a network to get summer internships. Several years later, Bernadotte was working at New Schools Venture Fund, a venture philanthropy firm that supports education nonprofits, when she learned that she was not alone: by age twenty-four, only 9 percent of students from the lowest income quartile can expect to earn a bachelor's degree, versus 77 percent of students from the highest income quartile. She decided to find a way to help more low-income children succeed.

While Bernadotte had a clear idea of the population she wanted to serve, she wasn't sure how best to help them. On the one hand, a free technology platform to provide support would reach a large number of students; but on the other, a human coaching service would offer a more in-depth, personalized experience. Without funding in the bank, or a foundation willing to support her launching a formal design process, Bernadotte decided to create her own human-centered design approach to R&D. She started working with a small focus-group company to learn best practices for targeting students who were the first in their family to go to college. She ultimately did that through student groups, such as the Latino Alliance and the Black Student Union. She also got advice on the questions to ask them about their experience. With this crucial information in hand, she dove into the research phase by going to college campuses and talking with students. She set up tables at student unions, did outreach on Facebook and used word of mouth through the people she met to connect with both students who were persisting in college and some who had dropped out. Taking the student comments back to her team, she held a brainstorming session in which they came up with a variety of strategies for supporting students. They determined to test a model that combined a smartphone app, which would connect students with valuable campus resources, and individualized coaching to help them navigate personal challenges.

According to Bernadotte, this early design process was a key component of Beyond 12's success, because the organization was able to develop an intimate relationship with their target users. Meeting with students was so valuable, in fact, that her team continues to regularly reach out to them for feedback about what is working for them and where Beyond 12 can improve. This feedback loop was critical when Beyond 12 received a grant several years later to hire the design firm IDEO to lead the organization through a more formalized design process. The goal was to make the service scalable and financially sustainable. Several beneficiaries who had gone through the Beyond 12 program helped improve their model.

IDEO started by researching analogous models from the business world, such as Weight Watchers, whose model also blends live coaching with technology support. As Bernadotte recalls: "Weight Watchers was such a great example that I never would have thought of because it's not in our space, but they have been so successful at providing a very analogous experience. We were able to learn from it because it just fit with everything we were trying to do." IDEO then ran design sessions with Beyond 12 students, covering the walls of the meeting rooms with brightly colored Post-it notes suggesting ideas for features to improve the app.

The design process produced dozens of feature ideas, which were whittled down to a few that IDEO and Beyond 12 prototyped using InDesign, creating sample screenshots. The team then took the screenshots to the students for feedback. The conversations clarified that what the students most needed were resources to help them better navigate their college experience (like reminders about academic and financial aid deadlines), so the team tailored the design of new features accordingly. Because the organization had such strong relationships with their beneficiaries, they were able to tap them for additional feedback multiple times throughout the development process.

Beyond 12 is now tracking the progress of more than fifty thousand students and coaching close to two thousand students on 180 college campuses. All the testing has paid off. Of the students coached by Beyond 12 who entered college in fall 2011, 82 percent persisted into their third year, compared to 59 percent of first-generation college students nationwide.

Another example of a social entrepreneur who bootstrapped her early testing phase is Beth Schmidt, founder of Wishbone, a crowd-funding platform that sends low-income high school students to summer programs that help them pursue their dream careers. She was a high school teacher in east Los Angeles when she gave her students an assignment to write a paper about their passions. Blown away by what they wrote, she imagined founding an organization that would make her students' dreams come true. To test the idea, she simply photocopied the papers that had impressed her and mailed them to her family and friends, pleading for donations. With the money that came in, she picked seven students and arranged for them to attend summer programs. Next she built a website to experiment with growing the program. It brought in enough donations to send sixty kids to programs the following summer. She then analyzed how the model was working, and she realized that the overhead was $2,000 per student, which was much too costly to scale. In response, she asked summer programs to provide scholarships, which reduced the price significantly. With that tweak to her model, she was ready to push for growth. As Schmidt says, "You can put a bunch of kids through a poorly made machine where they don't have a great experience, and the machine is going to break down in a year and you're going to hit a plateau. Or, you can actually spend the time to explore it, get it right and do the research you need to do to create a machine that works over the long haul."

Sometimes your testing must be a little more sophisticated than using a photocopy machine and sticking some handwritten letters in the mail, but it can still be at quite low cost. Charles Best was a teacher in the Bronx when he developed his idea for a crowdfunding site for teachers. Now a $100 million fully self-sustaining nonprofit organization with celebrities like Stephen Colbert on its board, DonorsChoose is based in the heart of midtown Manhattan, with swanky offices that resemble a tech startup more than your typical nonprofit. As I waited to meet with Best, I was drawn to the flat-screen TV mounted on the wall of the waiting area showing that already that morning $87,712 had been donated to projects all over the country, including Bring Music to Our Classroom and Technology for Our Troops' Kids.

The origins of DonorsChoose were much more humble. Best got the idea one day when he and his teacher friends were talking about books they wanted their students to read, field trips they wanted to take them on and a pair of microscopes they needed for a science experiment. It occurred to him that there must be people who would help to fund these needs if they could see where their money was going.

Best was living at his parents' home at the time, so he used his rent savings to pay a web designer $2,000 to build a bare-bones website to test the idea. Today, paying a designer would not even be necessary, because so many free templates for websites, adequate for the testing phase, are available. To kick-start posting projects for funding, Best turned to his coworkers. "My mom made roasted pears for my colleagues," he told me. "When I brought them to the teachers' lounge people would pounce and I stopped them and said, 'If you eat one of these pears, you have to go to this new website called DonorsChoose and ask for whatever it is you want most for your students.'" This is how Best managed to get the first eleven project requests on his website.

Then he had to find donors. His aunt funded one of the projects, and Best secretly funded the rest using his savings. Rumors about a website where teachers could get money for their classrooms spread across the Bronx, and teachers started posting hundreds of projects. By that time, word had also spread to donors that this website would provide a chance to contribute to local schools, so luckily donations began to trickle in and Best no longer had to fund them himself. After ten months of testing his pilot site, he was able to prove the promise of the model: if you built a platform where teachers could post their classroom wish lists, people would gladly fund them. With those results in hand, Best approached foundations to seek funding; he was able to get a $100,000 grant from the Goldman Sachs Foundation to go ahead and create a more robust website and fulfillment team to launch the organization.

ADDING IN COCREATION

While interviewing targeted users and testing prototypes with them is core to all the human-centered design methods, actually engaging users in helping to generate ideas for products and services, and having them actively develop them with you, is not always included. Such direct involvement in development may not be appropriate for all organizations, but it can be a great way to make the development process more affordable, and can also speed it up. The cocreation, or open innovation, process is a method for inviting your intended users to submit ideas for developing your product or service, and maybe even take part in the development process.

The method has been used to great success by a number of companies. LEGO has implemented the method, with its LEGO Ideas platform, which offers LEGO users the chance to submit design ideas.[9] All users can then vote on the submissions; the company then produces the highest rated designs, with a small percentage of the revenue going to the designer. With the development of online crowdsourcing platforms such as Kickstarter and Indiegogo, cocreation has become even more interactive.

The Center for Youth Wellness is an example of how this approach can catapult nonprofit growth. Dr. Nadine Burke Harris, the founder, has become one of the most influential doctors of her generation, recently gaining international acclaim with prizes such as the Humanism in Medicine Award from the American Academy of Pediatrics and the Heinz Award.

When she finished medical school, Burke Harris was committed to bringing top-quality health care to poor communities. She managed to secure funding from the Sutter Health Hospital to start a clinic in the Bayview district of San Francisco, a low-income neighborhood. As she began to research the health conditions of her patient population, she came across a Kaiser study out of San Diego identifying a then little known phenomenon called "toxic stress" in children. Researchers found that adverse childhood experiences due to life traumas, such as drug problems, abuse, neglect or alcoholism, could cause disproportionate poor health outcomes down the road. She immediately realized that this was the cause of many of the serious medical problems of the Bayview community. She told me that making this connection was akin to finding a pathway to a cure for cancer. If pediatricians would screen children to discover whether they had experienced such traumas, they could more effectively target interventions to counteract the longer-term medical effects.

She founded the Center for Youth Wellness to advance that mission. In addition to spreading the word about toxic stress exposure through public advocacy, such as through a much viewed TED talk,[10] she determined that she would create an Adverse Childhood Experience (ACE) screening survey. Her hope was for the government to require every pediatrician in the country to use the ACE survey to screen patients for toxic stress exposure. Her initial plan was to use a sample survey during patient visits in her clinic in Bayview, and analyze the results over time. She wanted to test the user friendliness of the survey and perfect it before taking it to national authorities to lobby that it become a mandatory tool in pediatrics. Only after proving its effectiveness would she make the survey available for public use. But once the word that she was developing a survey got out through her TED talk, clinics and doctors from all over the world began contacting her to request it.

Burke Harris had applied for the Google Impact Challenge Award, offered by Google.org. When they awarded her a $3 million

grant to develop her survey, the Google team suggested the cocreation approach to address the immediate need. Burke Harris took
the advice and made a provisional version of the survey available
for download, fully disclosing that it was not a finished product,
including an official legal disclaimer. She invited those who downloaded it to participate in improving it. In just over a year, a thousand health providers in fifteen countries have downloaded the
screening tool and are in the process of offering useful refinements
to the Center for Youth Wellness with an online survey tool. These
doctors are now co-creators with the Center for Youth Wellness and
are poised to provide significant input on how the survey works on
their patients, what can be improved and how to help make it as
user friendly for the doctors as possible. The goal is that once Burke
Harris finally does go to national authorities to advocate for its
widespread use, the survey will have been well tested.

In my study, I encountered numerous other examples of cocreation
at work in the nonprofit world. For example, when Natalie Bridgeman Fields founded Accountability Counsel, a group of lawyers
representing communities around the world that have suffered
human and environmental rights abuses from development projects, she quickly realized that her small organization would never
be able to reach the millions in need of representation. Her team
developed the *Accountability Resource Guide*[11] to make their process
open-source, so any lawyer could read it and bring cases against the
institutions funding harmful development projects.

Countless nonprofits have used Kickstarter, Indiegogo or other
crowdfunding platforms to develop advocacy campaigns that engage their supporters not only to fund their work, but to get their
ideas about how to improve programming. SurveyMonkey and
Google Surveys are great ways to receive feedback from a targeted
audience of stakeholders. And a cocreation model doesn't even have

to be sophisticated; of course, Facebook and Twitter are easy ways for nonprofits to use social media to get feedback and constantly improve upon their programming.

STAYING CLOSE TO THE PROBLEM
AND THE BENEFICIARIES

The process of connecting with end-users and other stakeholders should be ongoing as your organization grows. As your organization hires more staff, you should implement a process for connecting new employees as well. One of the common ways nonprofits go off course is losing touch with the needs and desires of the community they are serving, thus failing to perceive new problems that might arise. Top-performing social entrepreneurs are dedicated to continuously improving their model and the services they're providing, and they find ways to stay close to their beneficiaries. For example, Dr. Nadine Burke Harris is committed to maintaining her clinical practice as a pediatrician one day a week in between speaking engagements and running her organization. Andrew Youn, founder of One Acre Fund, which provides African farmers the tools to increase their production yields, lives in Rwanda in order to be close to the populations he is serving.

> The process of connecting with end-users and other stakeholders should be ongoing as your organization grows. As your organization hires more staff, you should implement a process for connecting new employees as well.

Many of the breakthrough organizations I visited work closely with their staff to connect them to the people they serve, so they develop a deep understanding of the problem they are tackling. Charity: water, the New York–based clean water initiative, which has raised over $200 million, and in the last year brought clean water to nearly 7 million people, takes each staff member to the developing world at least once, to experience how the organization's touches the lives of its beneficiaries. Organizations also stay con. nected by hiring staff who have suffered the social problems the nonprofit addresses. For example, Jessamyn Rodriguez, the founder of Hot Bread Kitchen, a job-training facility for low-income women that helps them launch careers in food manufacturing, hires select graduates of their Bakers in Training onto their full-time staff. This allows the organization to leverage the insights of beneficiaries in administering and developing their programs.

A strong connection with the needs of your targeted users, and an open-minded commitment to listening to their input and responding to it, will gain you the support and engagement of those you seek to serve, the insights to improve your results and, in turn, the funds you need to take your organization to the next level.

CHAPTER 2

aging All Stakeholders

While the human-centered design process focuses on interviewing and testing with potential customers, or end-users, in social entrepreneurship it's vital to consult a wider range of stakeholders. One of the common mistakes nonprofits make is failing to reach out to certain important players; these players can either help craft a better approach and support its adoption, or can thwart efforts or even turn other stakeholders or the intended beneficiaries against the organization. With social innovation there are almost always governmental figures and organizations with a stake in the problem you are addressing, as well as other nonprofit organizations, and sometimes even businesses. In addition, there are often scholars who have been studying the problem. Other types of researchers, such as those working for the government or grassroots activists, may also be championing a similar or a quite different approach. The stakeholders can either help to mobilize their networks in support of your efforts—or against them.

It's important to work hard to identify and interview the full cast of characters who will play a role in the success of your organization. Listening to their opinions and insights carefully, and with an open mind, can be extremely fruitful, especially because social problems and their solutions are always more complicated than initially expected.

An infamous example of failing to consult the full scope of the stakeholders involved in understanding and solving a problem, and to take account of the information and insights they could offer, is the Invisible Children *Kony 2012* campaign. Jason Russell and two of his friends founded Invisible Children after the three graduated from film school, and in 2003 traveled to Uganda in search of a subject for a film.[1] Staying in the town of Gulu, they learned that a militia group known as the Lords Resistance Army (LRA), led by Joseph Kony, had been abducting children and forcing them to become soldiers. They founded Invisible Children to raise awareness of the problem and advocate for action to apprehend Kony and stop the LRA.

While the organization did bring attention to the problem, it was also widely criticized by many people with knowledge of the LRA and the larger conflict situation in Uganda and the surrounding Central African nations; opponents argued that it simplified the nature of a long-term conflict in which the LRA was just one party. Russell and his colleagues were accused of mischaracterizing the situation, for example, leading to the impression that the LRA was still based in Uganda when in fact it had moved elsewhere in 2006.[2] The criticisms came to a head after Invisible Children produced a thirty-minute documentary featuring the story of Jacob Acaye, whose brother was tragically murdered by the LRA.[3] The video went viral as soon as it was released on YouTube in 2012, reaching hundreds of millions of views in just days.[4] Using the video, Invisible Children galvanized action from a host of supporters, from American high school students to members of the U.S. Congress and celebrities like George Clooney, Kim Kardashian and Oprah Winfrey.

What should have been a triumph for the organization quickly turned into a travesty, as experts in Uganda and a host of grassroots Ugandan activists

It's important to work hard to identify and interview the full cast of characters who will play a role in the success of your organization. Listening to their opinions and insights carefully, and with an open mind, can be extremely fruitful.

complained that Invisible Children had irresponsibly suggested that Kony could be apprehended, although he had eluded capture for more than twenty-five years.[5] They also lamented that the video falsely suggested that Kony's elimination could solve the larger and more complex problem of violence in Uganda. If the organization had worked with these stakeholders who were deeply involved in ending the civil war in Uganda, they could have conveyed a more accurate depiction of the problem and the complexities of finding a solution. Michael Deibert, an expert on African politics, expressed the frustration of many of those with in-depth knowledge of the situation in Uganda when he said at the time: "I have seen the well-meaning foreigners do plenty of damage before, so that is why people understanding the context and the history of the region is important before they blunder blindly forward to 'help' a people they don't understand."[6] As criticism mounted, and other complaints about the organization surfaced, such as the large portion of donations that Invisible Children used to pay staff, donations dried up. Just two years after the *Kony 2012* video was released, Invisible Children was on the brink of collapse.[7]

Even organizations that work hard to engage stakeholders sometimes get it wrong, spending precious resources and often a good deal of time, only to have their efforts thwarted. Jim Fruchterman, the founder of Benetech, which promotes ways to apply technology to solve wide-ranging problems around the globe, warned about this mistake in a blog post that recounted one project he had to shut down in spite of great hopes. Before founding the organization, Fruchterman was a rocket engineer who used his technological savvy to create many innovations, such as an affordable reading machine for the blind and an open-source software application that securely gathers information about human rights violations in the field. When I arrived at Fruchterman's office to interview him, I couldn't help but notice hundreds of plastic name tags hanging on hooks behind his door, which he explained were from conferences he'd attended over the years. "Networking is key," he told me. But as he admits, it turns out even a guy who loves networking can fail to consider all the stakeholders in a project.

One of Benetech's efforts was to build a relatively inexpensive land mine detector to help prevent the massive suffering caused by bombs left in the ground in post-conflict civilian areas. In 2004, Fruchterman met the head of the land mine detector research program of the Defense Advanced Research Projects Agency (DARPA) of the U.S. Department of Defense, who told him about a new detection technology developed by a company called Quantum Magnetics. While Benetech began negotiating to gain access to the technology, Benetech simultaneously sunk considerable funds into developing the project, hiring a top engineer from Sun Microsystems and conducting field research by visiting with humanitarian land mine groups.

But the organization failed to realize that before it proceeded with development efforts, it should have ensured that one of the most important stakeholders, with the power to block its access to the technology, was on board. The Office of Naval Research, also part of the Department of Defense, had funded the development of the technology and had the authority to block Benetech's access to it. The organization became embroiled in protracted negotiations with the Office of Naval Research. By the time Benetech secured approval, another stakeholder decided to deny access—Quantum Magnetics (QM) had been purchased by General Electric, which had changed QM's management, laid off most of its technical staff and sold the rights to the technology to a British military contractor. The contractor, it turned out, was not interested in granting access to Benetech, and it had to discontinue the project.

In his "post-mortem" blog outlining the lessons he learned from the project's failure, Fruchterman made it clear that even if Benetech had secured permission to use the technology, the devices might not have been embraced by the intended users.[8] Benetech didn't anticipate pushback from stakeholders in the countries with the land mine problem. But as it conducted research in the field, the organization eventually discovered that both the governments and workers of those countries had no interest in cutting down on the number of workers needed to clear mines, which the new technology would do. Benetech anticipated that the device would, in fact, cut manpower hours by half. But the jobs of clearing the mines were hot commodities, both to employees (because the jobs paid double or triple the prevailing wage) and to politicians (who wanted to demonstrate their ability to create jobs). They viewed land mine clearance work as a jobs program. Even though people doing the work wanted technology to make land mine detection safer, no one wanted to cut the number of jobs in half. Failing to fully understand these political and economic factors was a major flaw in the early planning for the project. As Fruchterman wrote: "Historically Benetech simply waved the intelligent good-guy flag and people helped us." This time that approach fell short.

In my survey of social entrepreneurs, in response to a request to describe their organizations' biggest failures, many replied with stories of not accounting for how various stakeholders would respond to the organizations' efforts. One such story was that of Face It Together, a North Dakota organization that uses data about drug and alcohol addiction to improve treatment. The state government hired the organization to bring its model into a community that had not asked to be helped. As cofounder and CEO Kevin Kirby described: "It was like pushing a rope. We learned a hard lesson; we only go where we're invited by those with the capacity to affect transformational change." This experience exemplifies the need to evaluate the full range of players in the target community and to reach out to them to discuss any issues they may have with your plan. This is true even if other important players, such as influential funders and key government figures, are backing you.

So how can you avoid such costly mistakes? You can begin by creating a simple list of all the stakeholders in your project.

WHO CARES AND WHY?

The key here is to move beyond consideration of the immediate beneficiaries, and the most obvious people or organizations that can either facilitate or hamper your success; it is necessary to identify people knowledgeable about the broader landscape in which you will be operating and who will challenge any assumptions you might have about why your program or product will be received positively. Those people will help you to identify stakeholders you might not have considered. You can start by simply brainstorming all the players who will be directly influenced by your work, and then consider all the individuals and organizations that have any degree of control over the provision of services to your beneficiaries. This should include all government agencies, public interest groups, funders, politicians and business leaders. Also consider all players who have studied the problems your beneficiaries are facing, whether they have focused specifically on the particular issues you are addressing, or others. For example, if you are creating a drug treatment program for inner-city youth, a scholar who has studied their lives in a community much like the one you are intending to serve may offer insight about informative individuals not on your radar, such as church leaders.

Then you should begin reaching out to these people, and in the process of asking them their thoughts about your plans, ask them if they know anyone else you should consult. One social entrepreneur who used this method to great effect is Alejandro Gac-Artigas, the founder of Springboard Collaborative, which works to involve parents in underprivileged communities with their children's learning, training them to be effective literacy coaches at home. He got the idea teaching first grade in a Philadelphia school, as a Teach

For America corps member; he witnessed that the school system tended to treat the parents of struggling students as liabilities rather than potential partners in developing their children's abilities. He understood that the program he wanted to launch would benefit hugely from the support of schools. The model he ultimately developed was one of partnership with schools, and the schools paid for the service.

To hone his model and gain support from the school system, he reached out to a host of school administrators, drawing on his connections from his Teach For America network. He recalls: "I'd get on the phone in the afternoon and evening with two or three administrators a day and in each of those conversations I would ask for two more people to connect with. Then I began synthesizing their insights." By calling so many teachers, principals and superintendents, he realized that if he could offer a service that met their standards for less money than they would pay a business to develop such a program, they would come on board. Without actually talking with this range of stakeholders inside the system, he never would have been able to develop a pricing scheme that made sense for the schools.

You can also solicit the assistance of influential supporters who can help you to connect with stakeholders you might not otherwise have access to. An example is Accountability Counsel, the small human rights organization in San Francisco. It decided that it needed to better understand the leverage points for its work around the world providing a voice for grassroots communities suffering human and environmental abuse caused by development projects. For their strategic planning process, they used their board members to interview staff, experts and key friends of the organization to come up with a list of the stakeholders most important to leveraging influence on the issue. The stakeholders included people actually working in development institutions, such as the World Bank, as well as funders, nonprofit leaders and academics working at the intersection of human and environmental rights. As another example of collaboration with stakeholders, the organization has been able to create the International Advocates Working Group, which they convene on a regular basis both by phone and in person, to ensure all their efforts to support communities globally are working in harmony.

In addition, you can use the power of social media to reach out not only to members of the community you aim to serve, but also to the broader range of stakeholders. Effective actions include putting a call out on Facebook, LinkedIn or Twitter; sending cold emails to leaders at community-based organizations; posting a request for interviews in a community center; or passing out flyers at a school. This was the strategy the T Lab team that developed the preschool-on-a-bus model tapped into, posting notices at libraries, local schools and social services organizations to find teachers and librarians to talk to, as well as students and parents to interview.

A great case of incorporating stakeholder feedback is City Year, cofounded in 1988 by Alan Khazei and Michael Brown, which recruits young adults for a year of national service in high-need schools, to help students succeed. In 1988, after conducting a ten-week summer pilot for fifty initial corps members in Boston, the founders interviewed each corps member to ask what they liked and disliked about the program. City Year had been planning to launch the organization as a yearlong program, but the founders heard over and over again that they should allow corps members to have the summer off so they could get summer jobs. Though corps members received a stipend, the feedback was that the pay wasn't enough to fully compensate for summer employment. They also heard that because the work was hard, people would burn out if the program was year-round, especially because the age group involved was used to going to school, then having their summers free for work or other activities. The cofounders listened, and launched City Year as a ninemonth program conforming to the academic calendar. According to Khazei: "As a year-long program it would have been much harder to recruit our target age group." He also reflects that during the early years, the summer became a time that allowed the organization "to recalibrate as a staff and organization to learn from the previous program year, do summer training and to give the staff a break because people worked really hard during the program year." City Year has gone on to become a successful national nonprofit, even serving as a model for the AmeriCorps program, established under President Bill Clinton, which has enabled more than one million Americans to contribute upward of 1.4 billion hours of public service across the United States.[9]

CHAPTER 3

Reframing Failure as Learning

One of the key reasons that so many social startups don't break out to achieve large-scale success is that their leaders aren't willing to evaluate their programs with full honesty and to give up on ideas and approaches that aren't working. Even once an organization embraces innovation and makes R&D an integral part of its work, this is a tough challenge, for a number of reasons.

One is that in the chase for funding, the spoils are directed to those who demonstrate success. Leaders are focused on featuring their work in the best light. They fear that if word gets out that they launched efforts that failed, their judgment will be questioned and they'll be at a disadvantage with funders. Then there are worries about individual donors, who are such an important source of funds for so many social enterprises. Won't they feel let down, and that their donations have been wasted?

Another reason leaders are reluctant to shut down failed efforts is that we all tend to become intensely committed to our ideas, and it can be difficult to evaluate them dispassionately; we want to dig in and keep trying to make them work. Added to this is perhaps the most difficult aspect of program failure in social entrepreneurship: programs are meant to help people with pressing needs and problems. Discontinuing a program that's been bringing aid to people in need can feel like a betrayal of one's principles and of one's commitment to those people—and it can exact a heavy emotional toll. But the deeper truth is that an organization will

best by recognizing when efforts aren't working well
the difficult changes that will produce better results.
lately lead to greater support from funders as results
improve.

Failure, and knowing when to admit failure, are critical to the innovation process. Thomas Edison once famously said, "I have not failed. I've just found ten thousand ways that won't work." The CEO of IBM for over forty years, Thomas Watson, once said, "The fastest way to succeed is to double your failure rate."[1] In recent years, there's been a great deal of attention paid in the world of Silicon Valley innovation to the importance of teams having leeway to take more risks and to fail more often. As Richard Farson and Ralph Keyes write in their *Harvard Business Review* piece "The Failure-Tolerant Leader," these leaders "push people to see beyond simplistic, traditional definitions of failure. They know that as long as someone views failure as the opposite of success rather than its complement, that person will never be able to take the risks necessary for innovation."[2] The freedom to fail is vital to producing more creative ideas and to landing on ones that will lead to truly transformative new products and services. Hand in hand with the call for embracing the inevitability of failure has been a call for more "failure-tolerant leaders" who help employees overcome their fear of failure.

> Failure, and knowing when to admit failure, are critical to the innovation process.

My interviews with many breakthrough social entrepreneurs revealed that they embrace this failure ethos, and truly believe that failure has often been a critical element of their success. They realize that failure is a necessary corollary to innovation and that failures should be reframed as productive learning experiences. In addition, I found that adopting this ethic instills a culture of innovation that fuels faster growth.

THE REASONS FOR FAILURES
ARE LESSONS FOR SUCCESS

As Tim Brown, the CEO of IDEO, has said, "Don't think of it as failure, think of it as designing experiments through which you're going to learn."[3] This is the culture at one of the most effective innovators in the social sector, D-Rev, a nonprofit medical device company
focused on closing quality health care gaps for underserved populations. Their mission, more specifically, is to make treatment
with first-class medical devices available to those populations. They
do this by developing the products, as well as through an innovative manufacturing and distribution system by which they license
rights to manufacture their products to local for-profit producers;
they then partner with local health care providers to optimize distribution and assure correct use of the products.

Originally founded in 2007, since that time D-Rev has created
many cutting-edge products, such as the ReMotion Knee, a low-
cost replacement knee joint that allows for greater mobility than
the existing lower-cost options. The knee joint is the most expensive and complex component of a prosthetic leg, and the ReMotion
Knee is serving a great need. The numbers of leg amputations in
the developing world every year, most due to vehicle accidents, is
staggering—in the hundreds of thousands. And D-Rev reports that
80 percent of those amputees do not have access to modern quality
prosthetics.

As evangelists of the human-centered design process, D-Rev has
made it a priority to discontinue products that aren't working for
their targeted users or achieving the impact it hopes to see. Krista
Donaldson, CEO of D-Rev, stresses how important it is that rather
than frame efforts that don't work as failures, we should consider
them learning experiences and call them that. The language used
is critical to building comfort with accepting the need to change
course. "Embracing the learning always results in insights about
the problem you are trying to solve. . . . Calling a learning a failure

will discourage honesty and integrity—and hinder the pursuit of impact."[4]

A focus on building what works and retiring ideas that don't gain traction has been critical to D-Rev's success, not just in the early days of the organization, but every step of the way. For example, in 2014 D-Rev received a seed grant from USAID's Saving Lives at Birth program to develop a more compact version of the organization's flagship product, the Brilliance phototherapy device. The devices deliver blue-light therapy to infants suffering from severe jaundice, while the children lie in bassinets under intensive LED lights. Until D-Rev developed its first Brilliance device, the machines were prohibitively expensive for clinics in much of the developing world. D-Rev's first Brilliance device was so successful in delivering cost-effective treatment that, true to the continuous improvement mandate of human-centered design, the company developed two additional devices, including a "pro" version with improved functionality and usability. As of this writing, devices in the Brilliance line of products have been installed by clinics in twenty countries and have treated a reported 220,000 infants for jaundice.

USAID wanted to see if D-Rev could make a smaller, radically less expensive and more portable device specifically tailored for use in rural clinics. Treatment for jaundice is typically given in urban areas where hospitals and clinics can afford the machines, and have the staff expertise to administer the treatment. That means that many infants in more remote rural areas do not have access to treatment, and by the time they reach urban facilities they are already severely ill. The hope was that treatment could come sooner and be available in even the smallest and poorest of facilities. D-Rev developed a prototype device called Comet, which they installed in thirteen clinics in three different countries, India, Kenya and Nepal, as a pilot program for careful testing. There was no question that the device was well made; D-Rev's experience in creating its Brilliance products had taught them how to assure this. But the team also knew very well that any product had to be field-tested; unanticipated problems with design, the manufacturing process, the distribution system, or in use by clinicians would often be discovered. As D-Rev product engineer Garrett Spiegel explains: "An elegant design, however informed and beautiful it is, won't generate meaningful impact without effective education, sales, distribution and maintenance."[5]

Over the course of a year, D-Rev's investigators observed several problems with the Comet device. One was that the rural clinics did not have the necessary expertise or resources to diagnose jaundice in infants, such as with a blood test, which most of them were not equipped to administer. D-Rev would need to do something to improve the diagnosis rate in order to make the devices a worthwhile investment for clinics. In addition, the clinics had basic problems using the device, including that their power sources were unreliable and that a battery pack did not produce enough electricity to consistently keep infants warm enough throughout the several days of treatment. One clinic installed solar panels in order to try to solve this problem, but that wasn't a broadly viable option.

Although D-Rev had invested significant dollars in creating the device, and even though it built its reputation on the success of the Brilliance products, it decided to discontinue the program. Writing about the decision publicly in a blog post at the end of the trial, Garrett Spiegel was true to the firm's ethic of using the language of learning, saying, "One thing to be clear about is that Comet was not a failure. In design, everything is information for the next iteration."[6] In fact, the user testing for Comet focused D-Rev's attention on the need to improve the supply chain for the distribution of its Brilliance devices.

IT'S NOT FAILURE TO FOCUS ON OPTIMAL IMPACT

Sometimes programs simply aren't working, and when that's the case, making the call to shut them down may be quite straightforward, albeit difficult. But often the case is not so black and white. Even so, discontinuing less-effective programs is important in order to allow an organization to focus on more impactful ones. While this can be a hard decision to make, it can be the catalyst to an organization really hitting its stride and creating a distinctive identity and mission, as well as significantly more impressive results, which then attract more enthusiastic funding.

One organization that modeled how to assess the relative success of programs and focus efforts is Last Mile Health. Early on they elected to transition ownership of their programs to community members and peer organizations, but narrowed it down to the one program that was showing the best results. The organization then thoroughly rebranded itself around that program. Founder Raj Panjabi was willing to radically reconceptualize the scope of the organization's work in order to assure the greatest impact in its mission: the fight against preventable deaths in Liberia.

Panjabi was born in Liberia and was nine years old when civil war broke out there. His parents, Indian immigrants, were granted special permission to leave the country to escape the fighting. Panjabi vividly recalls the scene at the airport while his family waited for their flight: lines of Liberians begged to be allowed on a flight, then, as the hatch closed, trying to push their way onto the cargo plane his family had boarded.[7] Panjabi's family immigrated to the United States, where he eventually earned a medical degree. Shortly after, he returned to Liberia to see how he could support the health care system there.

What he learned about the medical system was astounding: there were only fifty-one doctors available to serve a country of over 4.5 million people. That was the equivalent of eight physicians serving the entire city of San Francisco. The most pressing need was to improve HIV treatment and bring it to many more people. Every day, hundreds of people with late-stage HIV/AIDS, who might have been saved if they had been diagnosed early enough, were dying on hospital doorsteps. Panjabi took a job at a hospital treating AIDS patients, and noted that many of his patients were coming from remote villages twelve or thirteen hours away, where HIV testing was not available.

Working with government officials, in February of 2007 Panjabi asked if he could pilot a program to train community health
workers to treat and track patients. Using $6000 he raised by asking
family and friends to donate in lieu of gifts for his wedding in June
of that year, he launched a community health worker program
connected to a rural clinic. Aware that the community had many
other dire needs, and eager to do all he could, Panjabi spearheaded
several projects not directly related to treating AIDS. These other
initiatives included teaching better farming methods and opening
a women's center, all while simultaneously trying to support hospitals and rural clinics. Fortunately, Panjabi did something from
the start critical to the organization's success: he made sure it had
a good system for gathering data about the effectiveness of the
projects.

After a year of operations, the data clearly showed that what
the organization was really good at was supporting HIV patients
through community health workers. In fact, 60 percent more of the
patients that workers visited survived, compared with those they
hadn't visited. The data also showed that there was a particularly
urgent need for more workers in the most remote corners of the
country. The other programs were not failures. As Panjabi says,
"None of those were necessarily bad projects." But he perceived
that the organization could have the most impact by focusing exclusively on the training of more community workers, and he was
willing to take the dramatic step of transitioning ownership of all
the other programs.

Narrowing its focus was critical to allowing the organization to
increase its budget for training; and the clear data that he could
then present, about the life-saving effectiveness of the additional
training to combat the top drivers of morbidity in the area, led to
major support from funders. Panjabi and his team were able to craft
a compelling central mission statement: "to save lives in the world's
most remote communities." They renamed the organization from
Tiyatien Health, meaning "justice in health" in a local language, to
Last Mile Health to reflect the mission more clearly.

Last Mile Health's mission has since been designed to exclusively target hard to reach communities, deploying community health professionals by giving them the training, equipment, supervision and pay they need to perform at a high level. In 2012, Last Mile Health piloted a community health worker model in the remote Konobo District, fifteen hours from the capital. This was Liberia's first community-based rural HIV treatment program, which the government of Liberia has scaled to more than nineteen sites nationally. Community health workers in Konobo District were deployed to serve forty-two communities, and for an area that previously had little to no access to professionalized health care, the quality service it provided represented an enormous step. Panjabi told me: "I would argue that we probably would have been stuck at the $50,000 in revenue barrier" if the organization hadn't recognized that spreading its efforts too thin was limiting its impact, and taken the quick action to refocus. By turning its attention to the work having the most impact and gaining significant financial support, Last Mile Health became a major force in averting a global disaster in 2014, when the Ebola outbreak hit Liberia. The organization's network of community health workers was critical to stopping the spread of the disease.

TRANSPARENCY CULTIVATES UNDERSTANDING AND SUPPORT

But how might funders perceive an organization that talks so openly about failure? Might they interpret failure as bad judgment calls? While there is no question that demonstrating success is the surest route to financial support, funders also respect thoughtful, open communication about how organizations test and monitor various approaches to maximize impact. Many foundations understand that often program failures are not in fact due to bad judgment calls, and that predicting how an effort will actually play out once it is launched is simply not possible until after the launch. Vanessa

Kirsch, founder of New Profit, the multimillion-dollar venture fund for social entrepreneurs, says that failure is something they actually look for in potential investments: "If an organization walks through our door and says they've never failed, we're skeptical. At New Profit we are equally interested in the success of the pilot as what didn't work and what they learned from it."

Thankfully, an appreciation of the value of sharing about unanticipated obstacles and disappointing results is spreading in the funding community. Appreciation is also developing within organizations, and this is in part due to some courageous pioneers who have publicly revealed the details of their stories of learnings, as D-Rev did; it even provided detailed data on its website about the numbers of infants treated in its Comet pilot, and a thorough listing of the reasons adoption of the product was flawed. Similarly, when one of its most promising pilots failed, the famously successful crowdfunding platform Kiva posted a thoughtful and highly informative explanation of why it was making the difficult decision to shut the program down.

Kiva would seem to have the Midas touch. Jessica Jackley and Matthew Flannery founded the organization in 2005, when Jackley came back from a trip with Village Enterprise Fund to Tanzania, where she had worked to help entrepreneurs build small businesses. She and Flannery, who was a Silicon Valley technology engineer, envisioned creating an online platform where U.S. donors could invest in such small-scale entrepreneurial ventures. Only two years after they launched the site, Kiva exploded when it was featured in Bill Clinton's book *Giving,* and thereafter Jackley and Flannery were asked to appear on the *Oprah Winfrey Show.* The organization received $11 million in donations in a little over twenty-four hours. Their website crashed, but crowdfunding for entrepreneurs in the developing world was born.

Kiva has been intent to continue innovating. Led by Premal Shah, who joined as president in 2006, one of the new ideas he supported was Kiva Zip, developed by Kiva employee Jonny Price. Whereas the Kiva model lent money to small businesses in the developing world through microenterprise partners, this new program would cut out the partner organization, allowing small-business owners to fundraise for their companies directly from individual lenders. It would also focus more on U.S. small businesses such as bed and breakfasts, cafes and flower shops, as opposed to small rural projects in the developing world. The organization thought this new model had the potential to dramatically increase the level of crowdsourced lending.

In 2011, it started testing the approach in two countries, Kenya and the United States. While Kiva's efforts had until that point been focused on the developing countries, the organization had learned that seven out of ten small businesses that apply for a bank loan in the United States get rejected. Kiva's impact could be greatly magnified by serving that large community. Sure enough, the model worked very well in the United States, with many success stories, such as Christina Ruiz of San Francisco, who was able to use her $5,000 crowdsourced loan to launch a mobile fashion boutique. But in Kenya, the small loan sizes, coupled with a struggle to raise grant funding to continue to pay for the pilot, posed a challenge to the economic viability of the Kiva Zip pilot.

After a careful assessment of the results, the team discontinued Kiva Zip Kenya in mid-2015. In explaining the decision, Kiva shared the insights it had gained along the way. One key problem, for example, was a widespread lack of Internet connectivity. Because many of the borrowers did not have access to the online platform, Kiva's trustees, who helped the borrowers through the process, were doing a good deal of paperwork for loan recipients. And because these trustees were volunteers, spending that much time to facilitate loans wasn't feasible for many of them. In a blog post about the closure, Kiva shared that "for the Kiva direct model to be sustainable, borrowers themselves must be digitally included at a level that is currently not common for low-income borrowers in developing countries."[8]

This public display of "failures" is gaining momentum among innovation-driving social entrepreneurs. GiveWell, an organization that looks for outstanding giving opportunities and publishes the full details of its analyses to help donors decide where to give, actually has a tab on its website called "Our Mistakes" where they detail stories about "ways in which our organization has failed or currently fails to live up to our values, and lessons we've learned."[9] The detailed table of contents proceeds to list GiveWell's "shortcomings," divided into "major issues" and "smaller issues," documenting everything from overaggressive and inappropriate marketing to diversity and tone issues.

When I asked GiveWell cofounder Holden Karnofsky whether this level of openness has put GiveWell at a disadvantage with funders, he said it's had the opposite effect: "Transparency enhances our credibility. It's about being able to share things we think based on open conversations about our experience." Some institutional funders are beginning not only to support openness about failures but to demand it. Good Ventures, for example, was founded by former journalist Cari Tuna and her husband, Facebook and Asana cofounder Dustin Moskovitz, to give as effectively as possible to maximize their impact. The foundation has supported GiveWell, and Tuna has said that the organization's openness about mistakes and emphasis on transparency were major draws.[10]

Whether the admonition of failed efforts is public or private, the most important point is that it's vital to develop a culture of recognizing failure as an inevitable part of growing an organization. And yet, research shows that only 52 percent of nonprofits feel comfortable discussing problems that occur mid-grant with a funder.[11] It is important for organizations to establish a rigorous approach to learning from those setbacks and take action to improve results. The Hewlett Foundation, under former-president Paul Brest, implemented a "Biggest Failure" competition, in which program officers competed to tell the story of their most important failed grant. Brest says he created the competition as a way to instill a comfort with open discussion of failures as part of the foundation's culture.

This is an idea that any organization can easily adopt. Leaders can also more simply share information about results, ideally with the entire staff, openly and on a regular basis. That should include discussion of what the expectations were versus the problems they encountered. They can also model frank discussion of failures by being honest about when they had mistaken views and unrealistic expectations, and what they learned in the process.

But a willingness to discuss failures openly is only one component of taking action to shut down underperforming programs and redirect resources. Good data—about what is working, what isn't, and why—is also required, and that should be both quantitative and qualitative data.

A major challenge social enterprises face is assessing which of their programs are working and which should be improved or closed down. This is because so many of them aren't collecting good data on which to base their evaluations. By contrast, a striking finding in my research is that the organizations that have scaled up most successfully prioritized developing a standard for success, then placed a strong emphasis on rigorously and frequently measuring their results against that standard. So let's turn now, in part two, to what I discovered about the best methods for measuring impact and for making the most persuasive presentation of results to funders and donors—another decisive factor in breakthrough success.

BENCHMARKS FOR SOCIAL STARTUP SUCCESS: TESTING

✓ Does your organization have an internal process for testing ideas?
✓ Does your organization dedicate a portion of its annual budget to R&D?
✓ Does your organization have strong connections with its beneficiaries and regularly ask them for feedback on its products and services?

✓ Does your organization work with its targeted users to allow them to use products and provide input as it tests them?

✓ Does your organization provide ways for staff and board members to stay "proximate" to beneficiaries?

✓ Has your organization developed a list of all stakeholders who can influence its work, directly and indirectly?

✓ Does your organization provide spaces in staff meetings, reports, blogs and/or funder meetings to have open conversations about failure?

✓ Does your organization have a process to incorporate into its programs lessons learned from failures?

✓ Does your organization regularly assess its programmatic priorities to ensure it is focusing on areas where it can have the most impact?

✓ Does your organization have a process for discontinuing programs when they are not having the expected impact?

PART 2

MEASURING IMPACT

Over the last decade, there has been a sea change in how nonprofits gather and analyze data. One report found that 75 percent of nonprofits now engage in at least some measurement of their program results, and that roughly the same number have invested significantly in measuring their impact in the last five years.[1] The impetus has come partly from funders, who now generally expect as a baseline that nonprofits will provide hard data about results in addition to the stories they tell about their programs. The demand for data is particularly strong among the up-and-coming generation of donors, many of whom made their fortunes by building data-driven technology businesses, such as Facebook founder Mark Zuckerberg and eBay founder Pierre Omidyar. But in my interviews with top organizational leaders I found that they weren't just collecting data for funders' sake; they were doing it because they genuinely cared about whether their work was producing results. They measured their impact so they could refine their programs and make them more effective. This was, in fact, the number one reason cited in my survey for why social startups conduct impact analysis.

Though it is becoming more common, impact measurement is still fraught with difficulty. One reason is that the proliferation of tools is daunting to navigate. Many organizations lack the expertise to set up a program for tracking metrics and conducting analysis. To assist with the task, the field has developed several commonly used metrics such as Robin Hood's Poverty Tracker, which creates streamlined metrics to assist the New York–based foundation's mission to fight poverty.[2] But demonstrating actual impact generally requires developing metrics specific to an organization's programs. Nonprofit leaders, who typically don't have a degree in statistics, often find creating metrics a daunting challenge. Many also lack the funding to hire specialists to set up systems for them and show them how to perform analytics. The result is that one study found that a mere 6 percent of nonprofit leaders believed they were making good use of the data they were gathering.[3] The good news in that report was that 97 percent answered that they would like to learn to use their data more effectively. The chapters in this section provide the best advice from leading practitioners about how to develop a plan for measuring impact, collecting relevant data and using it effectively to improve your programs and show your impact.

It's important to emphasize that good social impact measurement does not mean simply adopting the metrics of for-profit business assessment, such as return on investment (ROI), as some funders have advocated. Holding nonprofits accountable to the same standards as for-profits may seem like the rigorous thing to do, but it is misguided. Peter Buffet, the philanthropist son of famed investor Warren Buffet, smartly wrote about this problem: "I now hear people ask, 'what's the R.O.I.?' when it comes to alleviating human suffering, as if return on investment were the only measure of success."[4] I can't agree more. Pursuing social change is categorically different from selling widgets.

In general, the impact of nonprofits should be measured quite differently from for-profit business success. As Albert Einstein reportedly once said, "Not everything that can be counted counts, and not everything that counts can be counted." The most effective formula for nonprofits is a combination of hard-data metrics, some of which are commonly used and others that are specifically tailored to the organization's work, and qualitative assessments, such as those made through surveys of beneficiaries. Developing such strong combined measures can lead to major improvements in programming and breakthroughs in attracting funder dollars.

Take the example of New Door Ventures, a San Francisco–based organization that provides paid work internships to at-risk youth between the ages of sixteen and twenty-four by running two businesses: a T-shirt printing company and a bicycle repair shop. The mission is to help their clients obtain education, employment and the social support they need to make a successful transition to adulthood. Founded in 1981, the organization spent nearly two dozen years stuck with an annual budget of under $2 million. According to former board chair Alexa Cortés Culwell, a key factor holding back growth was that the organization had not collected hard data about its success.

Then in 2003, New Door hired Tess Reynolds as CEO. She had worked for two decades in the computing industry, having codeveloped the first presentation software, Harvard Graphics, as well as running her own management consulting firm. She completely transformed the organization by making impact assessment and continuous improvement a core focus. She started by hiring outside experts to help her clarify the organization's goals and develop a theory of change: a detailed description connecting their social intervention with the ultimate impact they hoped to achieve. She then successfully applied for a grant to buy a data system and hire a data analyst, which was unheard of at the time for such a smaller scale community-based organization. She credits the growth of the organization's annual budget to $6.5 million largely to the new data-driven approach. As of this writing, New Door Ventures is serving nearly four hundred clients annually and can demonstrate that 87 percent of their graduates can obtain higher education or a job after their internship.

While Tess Reynolds was able to hire experts to assist her, the wealth of resources now available to organizational leaders allows for any organization, no matter how small and budget strapped, to vastly improve their impact measurement. It's also possible to work with consultants on a pro bono basis. In the chapters to come, I will not dive into the weeds about which tracking and analysis programs to use and the details of the kinds of data analytics to conduct. In Appendix C, I offer a set of resources that provide that kind of more detailed, hands-on assistance, such as links to free downloads. Here I present instead a set of fundamental guidelines for getting up to speed with the best practices for impact measurement and creative approaches that a number of breakthrough organizations have developed. The competitive landscape demands that all nonprofits consider these approaches. Indeed, all the leaders of top-performing social startups I interviewed reported that impact measurement was a core part of their organizations' DNA, central to driving their operations, as well as to their fundraising. If organizations don't embrace these practices, they are at high risk of losing funding and stagnating in low- to no-growth mode.

CHAPTER 4

Crafting a Compelling Theory of Change

One of the biggest problems nonprofits face in trying to scale up is showing funders that their programs are having a powerful positive impact on their beneficiaries' lives. A key reason for this difficulty is that organizations often limit their measurement of impact to what are commonly called "outputs," rather than the more persuasive measures of long-term impact, or "outcomes." What exactly is the difference? Outputs are best defined as the basic measures of an organization's activities, such as how many people have attended trainings, have used services or have received goods. While such statistics are vital measures of the number of people an organization engages, they are not adequate indicators of the actual impact on those participants' lives. Just because someone participates in a program, it does not mean their life changes. And just because their life changes, it does not mean there is a causal link between the change and an organization's services. Funders have generally begun demanding proof of such impact.

In order to assess true impact, organizations must develop measures to track outcomes. For example, if an organization offers education programs, instead of measuring only how many students it tutors, it should find ways to track students' test scores. Job training organizations, rather than counting only how many people they train, should determine how many people actually get jobs, and

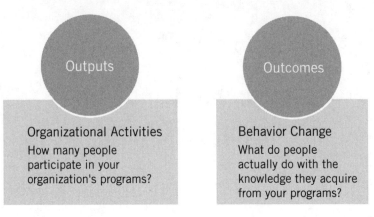

Definition of Outputs versus Outcomes

even better, how many of them still have those or other jobs two years later. Of course, the reason organizations so often resort to measuring outputs as a stand-in for outcomes is that data about outputs is so much easier to compile. If your long-term goal is to help improve teacher training, while measuring how many teachers participate in your program is a breeze, what about measuring their progress in the classroom over time? Or how your program impacted their preparation and whether they are still teaching ten years later?

Even large organizations with long experience have grappled with the challenges of moving from tracking outputs to formulating measures of actual outcomes. The Nature Conservancy, for example, learned the value of measuring long-term outcomes after over fifty years of operation.[1] With the goal of trying to preserve the diversity of plants and animals by protecting the habitats of rare species, the organization measured its success by metrics they called "bucks and acres": how many dollars it had raised and how many acres of land it had purchased. Those metrics had the benefit of being clear; program managers knew how their performance

> In order to assess true impact, organizations must develop measures to track outcomes.

would be judged and donors could see the progress of purchases. By 1999 the conservancy was able to raise close to $800 million in annual income and had protected many millions of acres of land in the United States and twenty-eight countries around the world. But the organization's leadership began to realize that those metrics actually provided zero indication of progress in its mission to protect species. In fact, judged by the standard of biodiversity preserved, the Nature Conservancy had been utterly failing: the extinction of species had reached its highest rate since the extinction of the dinosaurs 65 million years ago. The organization had to completely shift gears to develop an impact measurement system that included a much more sophisticated set of outcome indicators, such as biodiversity health.

YOU NEED A COMPELLING "WHY"

The other major obstacle organizations face in attracting funding is offering a compelling story about *why* their programs are having the impact their data shows. The strongest cases combine hard data about outcomes and a well-articulated argument as to why their approach is working.

Take the case of Springboard Collaborative, an organization that provides training workshops to parents about the importance of reading to their children. Founder Alejandro Gac-Artigas crafted an argument for the program so compelling that he was able to convince schools to fund it and run it on their premises. He got the idea for the training workshops by digging deeply into the well-documented problem that students from lower income families often experience a regression in their reading skills during the summer break from school. He knew research showed that when young children's parents read to them at home, their abilities improved. When he dug further, he learned that the parents of the children experiencing the slide were not reading to them at home as much, if at all, as the parents of more privileged children. And from his own teaching experience, he knew that school personnel did not generally engage actively with low-income parents; but his experience of growing up in a low-income neighborhood assured him those parents would respond positively to outreach. He formulated a theory that if schools reached out to the parents of the affected children, explained the problem and offered training in reading to their children, many parents would be receptive and would in fact begin reading to their children. Schools backed him because he had such a well-articulated argument for the program's efficacy. Years later, he has ample data that proves the concept.

The "theory of change" process is an increasingly popular practice in the nonprofit sector for assuring that nonprofit programs are effective and leaders have the data they need to make a strong case for their effectiveness. A number of large funding organizations, such as the Ford Foundation, the W.K. Kellogg Foundation and the Annie Casey Foundation, as well as government and non-govenmental agencies, have been adopting the method in evaluating programs.[2] I have engaged in the process with many organizations, and I can attest that it is not only an effective method but also an enjoyable and stimulating process.

WHAT IS A THEORY OF CHANGE?

Just as with the variations in the approaches to human-centered design, from the lean startup approach to design thinking and open innovation, there is no one completely agreed upon definition of what a theory of change is and the best method for developing one; different proponents offer moderately different descriptions. In short, a theory of change is a tool showing the causal links between an organization's vision and its programmatic activities, detailing the intermediate outcomes and assumptions that must occur to achieve success.[3] The concept arose in the 1990s from the work of a group of researchers affiliated with the Aspen Institute Roundtable on Community Change; they wanted to help organizations improve their outcomes and articulate more clearly the causal link between their programs and their ultimate vision.[4] One of the leaders of the roundtable, Heléne Clark, founded the New York City–based social enterprise ActKnowledge in 2000 to create guidelines for developing a theory of change. Out of that grew the Center for the Theory of Change, which on its website offers a free downloadable software tool and a webinar to help organizations learn about the process and actually conduct it.[5]

A *theory of change* is the empirical basis underlying any social intervention—for example, the belief that a young person's close relationship with adult role models can reduce his susceptibility to violence, or that regular visits by registered nurses to first-time pregnant women can improve parenting skills and children's outcomes.

—Paul Brest, "The Powers of Theories of Change," *Stanford Social Innovation Review,* Spring 2010

The theory of change method addresses the problem that, too often, nonprofit organizations have set forth a very broad organizational mission, such as to raise children out of poverty or to combat global warming, without breaking down their goals into steps that can serve as benchmarks toward success, along with metrics that allow them to measure and demonstrate their intermediary progress. The theory of change process facilitates describing the mission with more specificity, as well as a detailed path of "mini-steps" to success organizations can use to set very clear target goals.

The process of designing your theory of change starts with outlining your organization's long-term goals. You might start by asking, "What does success look like?" You then work backward to identify the intermediary outcomes you must see to achieve the ultimate goals, and the program activities that will facilitate progress. Your theory of change should show exactly how your organization's activities will help you achieve your final goal, either in narrative form or with a diagram, such as the ones on pages 56, 57, and

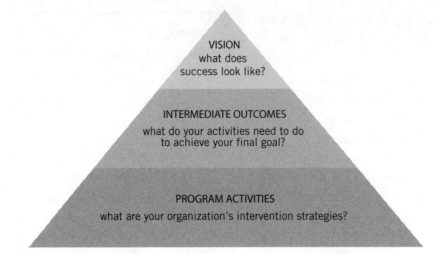

There are many ways to visually represent a theory of change. One of the simplest is the "planning triangle," which outlines how an organization's activities cause intermediate outcomes that lead to the final goal. *Source:* "Developing a Theory of Change," NPC and Clinks.

61 or combining both. The document you produce is a powerful teaching tool for staff as well as funders. Finally, you establish the metrics you should use to monitor achievement, sometimes called "key performance indicators" (KPIs), and a dashboard to measure your progress over time. The theory of change process can be quite simple, for example, involving only the founder and the leadership team and three or four meetings, or more elaborate, bringing together much or all of the staff, the board and outside stakeholders and conducted over a longer period of time.

THE PROCESS IN ACTION

One organization that has become a champion of the theory of change process is Arbor Brothers, a funder of social enterprises founded by Scott Thomas and Sammy Politziner in 2009. They focus on supporting what they call "second-stage" organizations,

Program Theory

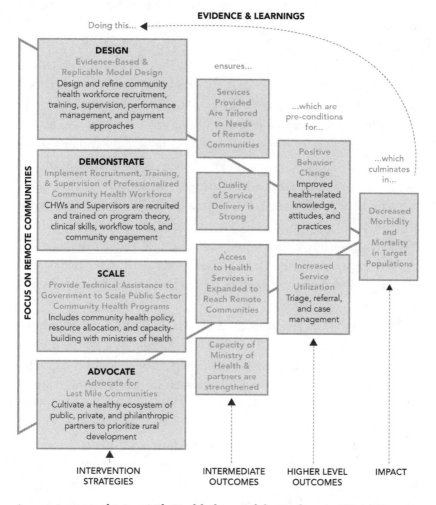

EVIDENCE & LEARNINGS

Doing this... ◄- -

FOCUS ON REMOTE COMMUNITIES

DESIGN
Evidence-Based & Replicable Model Design
Design and refine community health workforce recruitment, training, supervision, performance management, and payment approaches

ensures...

Services Provided Are Tailored to Needs of Remote Communities

...which are pre-conditions for...

DEMONSTRATE
Implement Recruitment, Training, & Supervision of Professionalized Community Health Workforce
CHWs and Supervisors are recruited and trained on program theory, clinical skills, workflow tools, and community engagement

Quality of Service Delivery is Strong

Positive Behavior Change
Improved health-related knowledge, attitudes, and practices

...which culminates in...

SCALE
Provide Technical Assistance to Government to Scale Public Sector Community Health Programs
Includes community health policy, resource allocation, and capacity-building with ministries of health

Access to Health Services is Expanded to Reach Remote Communities

Increased Service Utilization
Triage, referral, and case management

Decreased Morbidity and Mortality in Target Populations

ADVOCATE
Advocate for Last Mile Communities
Cultivate a healthy ecosystem of public, private, and philanthropic partners to prioritize rural development

Capacity of Ministry of Health & partners are strengthened

INTERVENTION STRATEGIES | INTERMEDIATE OUTCOMES | HIGHER LEVEL OUTCOMES | IMPACT

As you can see in this Last Mile Health theory of change from its FY17–FY19 strategic plan, what is key in depicting the theory of change is to show in very specific terms the causal links between the intervention strategies (i.e., community health workforce recruitment), the intermediate and higher outcomes (i.e., services to remote communities and improved health-related knowledge) and the long-term impact (decreased morbidity and mortality rates).

meaning those that are beyond the launch phase but have not yet scaled their impact. Thomas and Politziner had been best friends for over twenty years, since their days attending the University of Michigan in Ann Arbor (hence the name Arbor Brothers), and had both participated in Teach For America. They had moved on to jobs on Wall Street, but hearing of the struggles of many friends they'd made through Teach For America who were starting education nonprofits, they decided to quit and put their energies toward the social sector. They perceived a huge funding gap for organizations between the shiny new seed stage and the stage of having proven models and a well-established infrastructure. In the process of meeting with a wide range of people in the philanthropic, academic and nonprofit communities, trying to figure out how they could be most helpful, they also learned that many of those organizations needed to lay a stronger foundation for growth. As Thomas says, "Those leaders don't just need more gas for the car, they need a better engine."

As a part of their research, they met Mario Morino, the cofounder of Venture Philanthropy Partners and author of *Leap of Reason: Managing to Outcomes in an Era of Scarcity,*[6] which focuses on methods organizations can use to increase their impact. Marino is an advocate of the theory of change process. They also met David Hunter, the author of *Working Hard, Working Well,*[7] a guidebook to theory of change development. Hunter and Morino influenced them to incorporate the process into their work with organizations, helping them to do a better job of their analysis. According to Thomas: "Anyone can slap a theory of change together, but to be useful it needs to be rigorous, measurable and plausible."

With this in mind, Thomas and Politziner always start the process by clearly identifying the goal. They ask the basic question, "How will you know if you're successful?" which helps them "design with the end in mind." The team then works backward to help organizations refine their models and metrics. For example, if an organization is saying, "We're trying to help low-income kids between the ages of eighteen and twenty-four find jobs," they work to identify more detailed characteristics of the kids the organization is trying to serve, such as the level of their household income, whether they have graduated from high school and whether they are attending post-secondary school, as well as more specifically indicating the kinds of jobs they are trying to help them find. They then help to establish intermediary indicators, such as targets for what percentage will graduate from the program, what percentage will find jobs and what the minimum salary will be, and the best measures of ultimate success, such as what percentage will retain those jobs over time. Finally, they help the organization to create a better dashboard for monitoring its progress toward these benchmarks and refining its programming.

An example of an organization that Arbor Brothers helped this way is the Coalition for Queens (C4Q), a nonprofit founded by Jukay Hsu and David Yang based in Queens, New York. C4Q's flagship program, Access Code, is a ten-month software development course that trains high-potential adults from underserved populations to become programmers. When Arbor Brothers selected the organization as a grantee, the C4Q founders were still in their early days, having completed an eighteen-month pilot program with twenty-five young people. Conversations with Thomas and Politziner forced them to get much more specific about the outcomes they hoped to see; they were then able to more clearly map the causal links between their work and their goal: a more robust Queens tech ecosystem. For example, they didn't just set a goal of increasing their participants' starting salaries; they did extensive research to figure out living wages and starting salaries in New York City for engineers, so that they could set specific targets. Today, they can say with specificity that 85 percent of their participants will graduate, and that within six months of graduation 70 percent will secure a technical career-track job earning a minimum of $85,000 per year.

Having so clearly charted the population C4Q was serving, their program activities and their metrics for success, Hsu and Yang were able to see that some of the ways the organization had been devoting their time and resources were misplaced. For example, C4Q had been hosting regular events to create a technology community

---

THE STEPS TO CREATE A THEORY OF CHANGE

1. *Identify your goals and assumptions:* start by asking the question "How do you know if you're successful?"
2. *Map backward* to think through the steps toward achieving the desired outcomes.
3. *Identify interventions,* meaning all the things the program must do to achieve the outcomes.
4. *Craft the indicators of progress,* such as identifying what changes in the behavior of beneficiaries you are seeking, and how much change over what period of time.
5. *Create a figure* to summarize the above and write a narrative description of the theory.
6. *Develop a dashboard* to track your key performance indicators, test your assumptions and measure your progress over time.

Source: Adapted from the steps outlined in "Theory of Change Basics: A Primer on Theory of Change," ActKnowledge.

---

in Queens; however, those events weren't contributing directly to any of the intermediary indicators of success that would lead to achieving their goals for their program participants. Instead, they reframed the goal of those events as important to understanding the community's needs, marketing and outreach.

YOU CAN FACILITATE THE PROCESS YOURSELF

What if you aren't so lucky as to have partners like Arbor Brothers working with you? There are many consultants skilled in helping nonprofits facilitate a theory of change workshop. But even without outside help, any organization can implement the process. When Accountability Counsel engaged in a workshop, the San Francisco–based human rights organization was struggling with how to better evaluate its progress toward its goals. Accountability Counsel's

Access Code - Theory of Change

Access Code recruits diverse cohorts of underserved young adults, equips them with in-demand computer programming skills, and places them in middle-class, career track jobs.

Target Population

Underserved Young Adults
- Cohort median age 20 – 28 years old
- Cohort average annual earnings at or below poverty-line ($24,000)
- 50%+ hold Associate's degree or less; balance hold BA from a non-selective college

From Diverse Backgrounds
Reflecting Queens, cohorts target:
- 50%+ underrepresented minorities
- 50%+ women
- 50%+ immigrants

Recruiting and Selection

"Broad Funnel" Recruitment
Uncovering non-traditional candidates at:
- CUNY + NYC community colleges
- Nonprofit referral partners
- C4Q Meetups, Hackathons and community events

Basic Skills
Application process tests:
- English proficiency
- Basic computer literacy
- Basic problem-solving aptitude

Performance Potential
Interviewers select for:
- Passion
- Grit
- Able to apply learning to new contexts
- Teamwork

Program

Comprehensive Technical Training
Intensive course in mobile development
- Fundamentals of coding and mobile app development through classroom-based study and group projects
- 6 modules taught over 9 months of evenings and weekends (40 hours/week involving 4 days of class, HW & office hours)
- Lead instructor + volunteer teams yield 5:1 student-teacher ratio

Industry Immersion
Continuous exposure to tech ecosystem
- Company site visits
- Guest speakers (VCs, founders, etc.)
- Hackathons and product showcases

Job Placement and Support
Ongoing assistance for participants from instructors and previous program graduates
- Resume prep and interview coaching
- Frequent and candid informational interviews within volunteer network
- Matching with employer partners

Outcomes

High Persistence Rate
- 90%+ of entering participants will graduate

Demonstrable Skills
- 100% of graduates launch an application in the app store
- 100% of graduates pass an internal test of technical skills, industry knowledge, and soft skills

Career Launch
Within 6 months of graduation:
- 70%+ of graduates will secure a technical, career-track job earning a minimum of $60,000 per year
- Additionally, up to 10% of graduates will enroll in a BA / graduate degree program in a programming-based field

Career Growth
Two years after graduation:
- 75%+ of graduates will remain employed at technical, career-track jobs earning at least $70,000 per year
- Additionally, up to 10% of graduates will have completed a BA / graduate degree program in a programming-based field

Vision

A Robust Queens Tech Ecosystem
Our network of graduates will:
- Actively contribute to the local tech community through teaching, mentoring or organizing
- Earn salaries at or above the industry median
- Launch companies at rates comparable to similar-sized technology hubs (e.g. Austin)
- Increase the diversity and inclusivity of the tech workforce and founders of companies in Queens

Coalition for Queens, Access Code Theory of Change

mission is to amplify the voices of communities in order to protect their human and environmental rights. It supports complaints at the grassroots level where communities are demanding justice for abuses in development finance. Their policy work advocates for complaint offices to be fair, independent and effective. They also foster a network to support the global movement for accountability. Their cases often take years to see a resolution, as does their policy advocacy work. Founder and executive director Natalie Bridgeman Fields realized that the organization could benefit by firmly grounding its work in a well-developed theory of change, so they could better track their progress. As board chair, I worked with Fields to organize a full-day retreat with board and staff to hammer it out.

Advance planning was critical to making the most of our day together. For example, we wanted to be sure to incorporate the views of a wide range of stakeholders, but we also wanted to keep the conversation at our retreat intimate. So we made a list of academics, policy makers and directors of other human rights organizations whose views we wanted to consider; we divided them up among board members, to interview them about key topics, asking questions such as "What is your understanding of what Accountability Counsel does?" "What is your view of where our work sits within the human rights field?" "What are our greatest accomplishments?" "In what areas do you feel we could be more impactful?" "How would you define success?" "What are the biggest challenges we face in achieving success?" After completing the interviews, we compiled the findings and circulated them to the board and staff ahead of time, along with some "homework" to brainstorm three to five ideas for each of the components (ultimate impact, intermediary outcomes, immediate outcomes, day-to-day activities) of the theory of change.

For the day of the retreat, we recruited an executive from Intuit, who enjoys helping nonprofits with their strategic planning on a pro bono basis, to help facilitate; this made it possible for everyone on the staff and board to be participants, rather than anyone needing to take a leadership role. We dove deeply into how, specifically, our activities were impacting our clients and policy makers, then produced a working draft of our theory of change, which the staff of Accountability Counsel has been able to refine over time. What once felt like a lofty, intangible goal—creating a more level playing field in disputes between grassroots communities around the world and large corporations and institutions—is now divided up into a well-detailed report of performance indicators that each staff member updates in a dashboard on Google Docs. The dashboard is available to everyone internally to update regularly (color coding all indicators by green for on track, yellow for slow progress and red for no progress) and track each goal in the theory of change.

This tracking process has been critical to the organization in prioritizing and focusing its efforts in order to generate optimal impact. As Fields recounts: "It's not that we weren't measuring before; it's just that we were guessing about the types of things we should measure. After going through the theory of change process, we understand why we're measuring and how we can measure better." For example, the organization always tracked how many complaints it supported, but now it can connect the dots to measure which types of complaints achieve the best impacts for client communities, and under what circumstances they have achieved those victories; it can then more strategically allocate resources based on the evidence. Fields says this has created a much stronger causal link between their work and their goal, explaining: "It's about following the flow of activity to the ultimate impact. The activity itself is not enough to measure; it's the impact of that activity which makes the metric so meaningful."

Once you start to rigorously track indicator data and connect it to impact, you too will fall in love with the power of good analytics; you will want to keep diving deeper so you can maximize both the discoveries you make and the case you present to funders. Doing data analytics well doesn't require that you hire an expert or become one. In the next chapter, we'll see how a number of founders, none of whom had data science expertise, have been remarkably creative in using data to get funding and improve their results.

THE ELEMENTS OF A SUCCESSFUL
THEORY OF CHANGE WORKSHOP

1. *Obtain stakeholder input* on the strengths, weaknesses, opportunities and threats to your organization.

2. *Assign participants (board and/or staff) homework* for pre-workshop reflection.

3. *Recruit an outside party* to facilitate (preferably on a pro bono basis).

4. *Start by brainstorming the vision:* How do you define success?

5. *Work backward to brainstorm outcomes and activities* using Post-its to cluster ideas by category.

6. *Take notes and develop ideas* into a draft theory of change illustration.

7. *Solicit feedback from participants* and revise.

Source: Adapted from "Developing a Theory of Change," NPC and Clinks.

CHAPTER 5

Maximizing Use of Data

After developing a plausible theory of change, the next step is to turn each of your intended outcomes into measurable goals you can track regularly. The key here is making sure the data you collect is easy to understand and that the causation between your work and the outcomes is clear. One acronym the nonprofit world has adopted from business is SMART, the idea of making your measurements specific, measurable, attainable, relevant and timely, introduced by George Doran in the 1981 *Management Review* article "There's a S.M.A.R.T. Way to Write Management's Goals and Objectives."[1] Nonprofits have used SMART goals for tracking everything from communications to fundraising to programmatic outcomes.[2] Even nonprofit leaders with very little experience collecting data can use these guidelines to track their organization's impact.

One of the people I interviewed who had little impact assessment experience but who marshaled its power brilliantly was Aimée Eubanks Davis, founder of the education nonprofit Braven. Eubanks Davis's passion is to open up economic opportunity for people from underprivileged backgrounds. Before launching Braven, she devoted herself for thirteen years to that mission by working in senior-level roles at Teach For America, including as the chief talent officer during the organization's enormous growth years. In considering what kind of program she should offer, she conducted extensive research, determining that she wanted to create more opportunities for people from low-income backgrounds to transition

---

DEVELOP S.M.A.R.T. GOALS

Make sure your key performance indicators are as follows:

- *Specific:* there is a clearly defined goal.
- *Measurable:* there is an objective calculation of the goal such as "how much" or "how many."
- *Attainable:* the goal is realistically achievable.
- *Relevant:* there is a connection between the work and the intended outcome.
- *Timely:* there is a realistic timeframe to achieve the goal.

Source: Adapted from G. T. Doran's "There's a S.M.A.R.T. Way to Write Management's Goals and Objectives."

---

into better jobs once they graduated from college. She wrote a research paper outlining the problem, estimating initially that over a hundred thousand young people were falling through the cracks; they were missing out on opportunities in the job market because they did not have access to a specific set of skills, personal networks and experiences necessary for success. What the research couldn't tell her was whether her programming should start in kindergarten or college. So she embarked on a testing process to use data to determine the most effective intervention.

She developed a proposal requesting funding for four pilot programs to launch simultaneously, three with K–12 students and one with college students, to see and understand the continuum as quickly and efficiently as possible. One of those for K–12 was for fifth and sixth graders, for whom she created a science, technology, engineering and math (STEM) curriculum to test whether it would inspire them to become self-starters and embrace projects to do on their own, such as writing their own code or building robots. Another program aimed at college students was based on the hypothesis that university students from lower income backgrounds often didn't optimize their potential to find a good job after school; this happened because they lacked access to many of the "soft" skills and networks more privileged students gained organically through their parents and social circles, such as how to network with people who could get you a job. Eubanks Davis's strong presentation of the theories behind the approaches, and her plan to launch pilots to test them, won her a coveted grant from the Chan Zuckerberg Initiative, which allowed her to go ahead.

In evaluating the effectiveness of the pilots, she looked for answers to three primary questions: (1) Does strong content help students learn better? (2) Can a coach and a team of peers help take learning to a new level? (3) Were they able to shift the broader system with the program? After about eight to nine months, while all the programs produced good results, the data clearly suggested that Braven's college program would be the most innovative and impactful. Eubanks Davis learned just how desperate college students were for such programming and also how little funding existed in this area. The lack of funding might have been interpreted to mean the idea was too risky and funds would be hard to come by, but she instead saw a serious gap in services that Braven could help fill. Additionally, Eubanks Davis discovered the need was far greater than for a hundred thousand young people. Each year, three out of four of the 1.2 million low-income and/or first-generation college students are ending up either unemployed or underemployed.

Eubanks Davis decided to start by launching two programs, one at San Jose State University in California and the other at Rutgers University in Newark, New Jersey. The programs admitted primarily sophomores and transfer juniors as fellows, offering a semester-long course teaching both hard and soft skills, such as project management, how to use data to help solve problems, how to communicate strongly using email, how to network and how to build inner confidence. Groups of five to seven fellows were assigned to leadership coaches, volunteers from the workforce whom Braven had recruited and trained. As part of the course, fellows found and applied to high-quality internships to get experience that would help them learn about the workplace and enhance their resumes.

From her time at Teach For America, a data-driven organization, Eubanks Davis knew she should develop strong metrics, from the beginning, for assessing how the programs were working. With this goal in mind, one of her early moves was to hire John Hsu, a former colleague from Teach For America focused on strategic analysis, to help her develop metrics and a performance management dashboard for tracking and reporting on them. They divided their performance measures into three categories: (1) overall growth in skills and mindsets of fellows, (2) the coaches' assessment of the individual students and (3) the strength of the content to engage students; they then created an evaluation rubric for tracking a number of metrics on a monthly or weekly basis. The methods of measuring were very refined. For example, for the student assessments, one measure was whether the students could write a compelling cover letter. To "grade" the students' performance, Braven had teaching assistants, just as in other college courses, that she provided with achievement-detailed rubrics on which assignments were scored across eight different categories on a ten-point scale. One of the most important benchmarks was whether the coaches said they would recommend the students to people within their network, because such recommendations were so important in job placement. Eubanks Davis also wanted to be sure she could track students' progress well after they finished the course, so her team created alumni surveys and is using data from LinkedIn to follow their career progress. Former participants are encouraged to share job opportunities with each other on the Braven LinkedIn and Facebook communities. She also invites former students to alumni events, surveying them every time they get together.

A particularly impressive aspect of Braven's impact measurement is that it also establishes a way to compare the performance of its participants vis-à-vis student peers who did not participate. Too many organizations fail to find a way to create such comparative data, which is necessary to make a truly compelling case about impact. Otherwise, you can't be sure that your programs in particular are the cause of the results you're tracking. You also must be sure your results aren't just a figment of a skewed selection of beneficiaries. For example, say two nonprofits are offering very similar support services to low-income high school students, with the aim of helping them enter college. Nonprofit A reports a college matriculation rate of 99 percent and Nonprofit B reports a rate of 65 percent. Well, what if Nonprofit A has a more rigorous application process and only accepts top-ranking students—but Nonprofit B works with recently arrested, academically unscreened participants? And further, what if statistics indicate that 85 percent of mainstream students with the profile Nonprofit A is working with go to college anyway, whereas only 5 percent of participants with the profile Nonprofit B is working with attend college? All of the sudden, Nonprofit B's work looks much more impactful.

The gold standard for comparative evaluation is the randomized control trial, in which a researcher randomly assigns people into two groups, one of which receives whatever service or treatment is involved and the other doesn't. But such a formal study of program effectiveness is extremely costly and has limitations.[3] Eubanks Davis creatively devised a low-cost and highly effective alternative. The organization reached out to students at the same campuses, who were demographically similar to its participants, to form a comparison group, and gave them a $15 Amazon gift card in exchange for agreeing to respond regularly to surveys about how prepared they felt for the job market, how they were accessing networks and whether they were obtaining internships and eventually jobs.

Due to her diligence, after less than two years of program operation, by the fall of 2015 Braven was able to show that 96 percent of their inaugural spring 2014 fellows and 100 percent of their 2014–15 fellows were persisting in college. This was not Braven's ultimate goal, but a promising early indicator that their students were on track to graduating. Additionally, 73 percent of the fellows agreed that Braven greatly increased their chances of getting their desired job, and 88 percent of leadership coaches said they would professionally endorse Braven's fellows to their own network of friends and colleagues. Perhaps most important, based on its comparative data, Braven can show that its participants are two times as likely as their peers to get internships, which the organization's theory and external research argues is a good intermediary indicator of progress toward the ultimate intended outcome of the fellows obtaining good jobs after graduation.

When Eubanks Davis met the with Peery Foundation in 2015, the program staff awarded her $50,000 because they were impressed by her background and passion for innovation, her conviction in why the program should result in higher rates of employment and the strong proxy indicators of impact, even though the organization had no hard data at that point about actual employment rates.

TAP OUTSIDE SPECIALISTS

While Eubanks Davis was able to hire a data specialist, many of the tools she used could be implemented with or without an expert; for example, developing a rubric for tracking how your individual beneficiaries are progressing, creating a comparison group and hosting an online forum on Facebook or LinkedIn to facilitate tracking the progress of beneficiaries over time. Many outside resources are available to help you develop strong metrics. Hiring a part-time consultant can be a way to achieve good results at a fraction of the cost of bringing in a staff member. For our first ten years at Spark, we made the mistake of not doing sophisticated impact measurement because we didn't think we had the resources to devote to the job. We relied on simple metrics, like how many members we had and how many people attended events, which told us nothing about how those events were helping improve the organizations our members supported. Eventually, we were able to hire a consultant for $15,000, funded by one of our donors. We now have an impact measurement strategy that collects good information about results.

Another source of assistance with developing a metrics strategy is students, who are eager to work with organizations actually doing the social change work they study in the classroom. Most organizations are in the vicinity of at least a few colleges, many of which have programs in business management or statistics. Reaching out to these programs and asking for students' assistance to craft metrics with you is a win-win solution; the schools will be pleased to be asked, and they may even be able to fit the work into class assignments.

Gemma Bulos started the Global Women's Water Initiative, which trains women in East Africa how to provide access to water and sanitation for their communities. She enlisted graduate students at Stanford University to develop a survey tool to track water quality and sanitation interventions implemented by the women the initiative trained; improvements in hygiene and in sanitation knowledge; the financial and health impacts in families and target groups; and the women's sphere of influence in their communities. Several students were able to get funding from the university to travel to Africa to administer the surveys and offer workshops in data collection, and they came back to analyze the results for her, using sophisticated statistics software and translating it into compelling infographics. The survey data not only allowed Bulos to prove her impact but also to make continual improvements in her programming. Additionally, the data helped reframe the traditional narrative of women as passive recipients of water projects, and provided evidence of significant impact when women were trained as water providers.

Many struggling organizations get help from experts for free. Of the social entrepreneurs surveyed who are measuring their impact, 25 percent rely on a pro bono consultant (usually an expert from the nonprofit field willing to donate their time) to assist with that work. In addition, pro bono aggregator organizations, such as Volunteer Match and the Taproot Foundation, help find highly qualified volunteers.

More and more funders are also helping grantees with impact measurement. Tipping Point, for example, the San Francisco–based foundation I mentioned chapter 1, works closely with its grantees to create customized measurements that suit their organizational needs.

BE CREATIVE ABOUT YOUR
INDICATORS OF PROGRESS

Aimée Eubanks Davis and John Hsu brilliantly devised ways to obtain strong intermediary data. This is possible for all organizations to do, at any point in their development, even if the number of beneficiaries they serve is quite limited, and even if proving substantial ultimate impact will require many years. Another great case of applying creativity to this task is the metrics developed by Rob Gitin, cofounder of At The Crossroads (ATC), the homeless youth outreach organization based in San Francisco discussed in the introduction. Gitin and his cofounder, Taj Mustapha, did not approach establishing the organization in the research- and data-driven manner Eubanks Davis followed. It was quite the opposite. As I described in the introduction, they started out as recent graduates of Stanford University, and they saw the organization as a two-person operation, having no larger vision for scaling its impact. Gitin told me that he had never expected to get involved in counseling work until he and Mustapha won an Echoing Green fellowship to start the organization.

To start out, Gitin and Mustapha began reaching out to community organizations and doing street outreach in various neighborhoods in San Francisco to ask young people questions and identify the level of need in each area. The street outreach was so effective that they built their entire program around it, holding one-on-one counseling sessions in restaurants and cafes. Gitin and Mustapha always knew that their favorite clients would be those who were the hardest to reach: the youth who had fallen through the cracks of the city's traditional social services and were in desperate need of support. But they were also the ones who took the most effort to convince to come in for discussions. These kids had been disappointed at every turn—by their parents, by the foster care system and by society at large. Often the organization had to encounter the kids many times out on their nighttime outreach walks before earning their trust.

Gitin slowly learned that with funders looking for strong metrics of success, targeting the most challenging cases was a recipe for lots of funding rejections. The number of clients the organization served was much lower than that of organizations tackling the low-hanging fruit cases. Gitin attributes this to what he calls the "creaming effect," whereby nonprofits are incentivized to target easy-to-reach populations in order to boost their metrics. The other funding challenge At The Crossroads faced was that the founders didn't want to impose their own goals on their youth, such as that clients would find employment and a place to live. But that philosophy cut against the grain of funders' expectations. "The traditional way of tracking outcomes didn't work for us," Gitin explained, "because our whole mission is centered around not focusing on predetermined outcomes, instead letting every single kid we work with determine the things that they want to focus on and supporting them in that."

Finally, after many agony-filled late-night conversations, the founders came up with a solution for how to stay true to their mission and their values, while also strengthening the way they evaluated the effectiveness of their programs. They realized their solution would not only assist greatly with fundraising, but also allow them to constantly improve upon their model by developing a better understanding of what practices worked best. They decided to create a set of phases of achievement: the thinking stage (e.g., "I want to get off drugs"); the planning stage (e.g., "I am signing up for rehab"); the acting phase (e.g., "I have been clean for a week"); and the maintenance phase (e.g., "I am still clean"). For each phase, they created eight categories of progress, such as housing, education, job networks, health, mental health and others. For example, for housing the first phase would be a client deciding that he wanted to get off the streets; the second phase would be working with ATC to plan a pathway to finding a place to live; the final phase would be that the client was continuing to live in permanent housing months and years later. This allowed ATC to track each client's progress according to a wide range of outcomes and many mini-steps. They also tracked extensive qualitative data documenting the clients' individual stories, their counseling conversations and progress toward accessing the services they needed to improve their lives. This way ATC could use both quantitative and qualitative data to work together in harmony with their clients to figure out how their programs were working and how they could be better.

More than fifteen years later, Gitin and his team have grown the organization on their own terms, attracting sufficient funding by being able to present both a compelling set of data and persuasive stories of individuals' successes. The organization is not large, with a staff of fourteen working out of one office, but large scale was never their aim. Depth of connection and quality of intervention were the goals, and on those terms ATC has succeeded admirably, having counseled thousands of kids. Its current goal is to increase the number of clients they can counsel in one-to-one meetings from 60 to 150 per week. Gitin reports that the method of impact measurement the organization devised has given him total confidence in speaking to donors about how ATC is achieving its goals and why it takes an intensive approach. As Gitin says, "Our vision is centered around the idea that unconditional support transforms lives. If you don't believe that, don't fund us. And we are really okay with that."

CREATIVELY LEVERAGING EXISTING RESEARCH

Another great model for developing creative metrics is the method Row New York used to demonstrate positive impact, which drew on extensive educational psychology research in how the characteristic known as "grit" contributes substantially to academic and life success. The organization pairs rigorous athletic training with tutoring, and other academic support, to empower young people from New York's underresourced communities by getting them involved in the sport of rowing. Amanda Kraus had been a competitive rower in college and fell in love with the sport. In 2002, with a borrowed boat and eight rowers, Kraus started Row New York to share her passion with others. Like many early-stage founders, initially she tracked the organization's progress with the most obvious measures; in this case, the number of participants in the program, the growth in their fitness levels and how many of them were graduating from high school or college. But core to Kraus's concept was that the rigorous program, which involved a demanding six-day-a-week rowing regime, offered to participants for up to six years, was developing their grit. She began to explore how she could prove that, and she came up with a number of inventive measures. For example, by keeping track not only of attendance but of the daily weather conditions, the organization can show which participants are showing up and rowing even when it's 38°F or pouring rain and which are not. By measuring things that indicate grit, Row New York has been able to make a compelling case that its programs are contributing to kids' propensity not only to get into college, but to succeed while there.

Mining research data can produce remarkably persuasive support for an organization's approach well before the organization can produce any strong intermediary measures of impact. Take the case of SIRUM, which redistributes unused pharmaceuticals from pharmacies and nursing homes directly to community clinics serving individuals who cannot afford to purchase them. When Kiah Williams and her cofounders started SIRUM, they struggled to make a compelling case about their impact. To do so was vital not only to obtaining funding but to getting partners to participate in the program. They were facing a catch-22: without enough drugs to distribute, they couldn't have impact, and without proof of success, they couldn't get enough drugs.

At first they tracked how many people registered on their site, thinking organizations that registered would always donate; but they weren't tracking whether those organizations had actually donated medicine. Their metric was essentially meaningless, so they had to start tracking their sales funnel much more closely; this included registrations, first and subsequent medicine donations and the actual amount of drugs donated. Once SIRUM did this, they saw that their numbers still weren't very high. If they wanted to get the attention of funders, they would need to show they were on track toward bigger impact. They realized that they could strengthen their case by drawing on broader research conducted by government, academia and other nonprofit organizations. A survey had shown that producing just one kilogram of an active ingredient in medicine generated up to 200 to 30,000 kilograms of waste.[4]

By redistributing rather than making new medicine, and calculating how many pounds of medicine they were redistributing, SIRUM could also talk about their impact in terms of reducing waste. With that information, SIRUM has been able to make a strong case that their redistribution programs have prevented up to 72,300,000 pounds of waste. In addition, by drawing from a National Institutes of Health study showing that one in two personal bankruptcies involve substantial health care debt,[5] SIRUM was able to make the case that the access to medicine it provides benefits the economy as a whole, as well as the health of its registrants.

AS YOU BUILD UP YOUR COLLECTION OF DATA, KEEP DIGGING DEEPER

The longer you are in operation, the more demanding funders will be about proof of impact, and the more demanding you should be about what your data can tell you, so you can continue to improve your model. Demonstrating that you are driven to probe ever more rigorously into how your programs can achieve the greatest effect is a powerful way to build stronger relationships, not only with funders but with all stakeholders, as well as to provide rocket fuel for continuing growth.

Rey Faustino is an exemplar of the payoffs of this ongoing commitment to an intensive interrogation of data to refine programs and boost results. Faustino is the founder of One Degree, a Yelp-style website guide to social services. As the son of Filipino immigrants, he grew up watching members of his community struggle with how to access social services; starting as a young child, he often acted as an intermediary to help them navigate the complicated webs of local community resources and state and federal benefit programs. He developed the One Degree site to help those in need to help themselves. The idea was strong enough that he was able to get sufficient initial support from funders to build the site. Before long, he could boast that an impressive forty thousand people had visited it. But he saw that as just a "vanity metric." It wasn't really a measure of how many people the organization was actually helping to get services, let alone how their lives were being improved because of gaining access. Even digging deeper into the site visitation data to examine what types of services visitors were searching for and then clicking on, and whether they downloaded an application to receive government benefits, wasn't giving him the information he wanted. He was determined to gather data about how many of the site's visitors actually accessed services and, even more challenging, to discover how by having done so, their lives were positively affected.

> Demonstrating that you are driven to probe ever more rigorously into how your programs can achieve the greatest effect is a powerful way to build stronger relationships, not only with funders but with all stakeholders, as well as to provide rocket fuel for continuing growth.

Luckily, when Faustino received funding from Tipping Point, one of the first things he did was to sit down with their data analytics team, who had a lot of experience seeing organizations move from tracking outputs to tracking outcomes. Together they plotted how best to use One Degree's rich well of data. They developed a funnel to visualize a beneficiary's path from visiting the site to seeing an improvement in their quality of life, and tracked all the metrics indicating movement along the path, from inputs (finding relevant resources) to outputs (accessing benefits) to outcomes (reporting on their experience) to impact (lives improved).

One Degree has continued to refine its impact measurement system, now tracking regular progress on goals such as the number of new resources they add to the site, the number of users and the total number of people who have used One Degree, which they review as a team on a weekly basis. They've also refined the service they provide; users can personalize their experience with a "My Plan" page that allows them to receive personalized resource recommendations, and build a list of providers who can help them access resources. Finally, the system allows users to report on their experiences accessing services. Not only have these refinements provided better service, but they have allowed One Degree to track individuals' specific paths toward outcomes, and ultimately to provide better services for their users by personalizing their recommendations.

DEVELOP STRONGER OUTCOME DATA
BY SUSTAINING RELATIONSHIPS

The longer organizations stay in touch with beneficiaries, gathering information as to how the services provided have assisted them in their lives, the more and more powerful a case for impact they can make, and the better and better they can refine their programs. But how can organizations develop ongoing relationships? Some organizations find great ways to allow past participants to continue to connect with the work, such as creating opportunities for them to mentor current participants, hosting reunion events where they can reconnect, or offering ongoing services to help keep them afloat once they complete the program.

One organization that has done a masterful job of developing strong ties with its beneficiaries is Genesys Works, which offers a work-training program for high school students that places them in internships at major corporations during their senior year in high school. The organization has rigorously kept tabs on the success of their graduates over time. At a high level, Genesys Works tracks two levels of outcomes: (1) college attendance and persistence and (2) success in the workforce. Eventually, they want to be able to quantify the mindset shift as a result of participating in the program, measured with metrics like grit and perseverance. The first one, whether they attend and graduate from college, is easy to measure through National Student Clearinghouse data. They could not, however, gauge the long-term work success of their students or the grit and perseverance they picked up from the program without continuing input from the students. When the organization was small and they had serviced only a couple of dozen students, keeping in touch with them and asking how their careers were progressing was relatively easy. But as they grew to serve nearly three thousand students per year, such personalized follow-up became impractical. So the organization developed an annual survey that it sends to former participants, including those who are many years out, and elicits a remarkable 63 percent response rate. The response rates nonprofits generally report for such surveys are in the 10 to 20 percent range.

According to founder Rafael Alvarez, the reason Genesys Works gets so many responses is that it has formed such a strong ongoing connection with its beneficiaries. It does this in many ways, such as continuing communication with alumni through a texting platform; inviting them to alumni programming events to hear speakers talk about job readiness and letting them know the organization is there to help during college if they need job advice or help with their resumes; and helping them make connections by introducing them to potential employers in the Genesys Works network. Their surveys show that Genesys Works alumni feel a strong emotional connection with the program, which the organization believes is largely due to these forms of continued outreach.

BE HONEST WITH YOUR DATA, AND PRESSURE TEST IT

Nonprofit leaders often fear being honest with funders about their impact data when it isn't as strong as they might like, worried donors will pull their funding. But what I heard from many of the leaders of breakthrough organizations is that transparency about results, even when they are disappointing, has the opposite effect, if they are demonstrating that they are taking a rigorous approach to evaluation and using their findings to improve their programs. And that's not only true regarding early-stage organizations and pilot programs, such as D-Rev's admonition that its pilot to develop a lower-cost phototherapy device failed.

One person adamant about the importance of working hard to verify the validity of results and being fully transparent about findings is Nick Ehrmann, the founder of Blue Engine, a New York–based organization that partners with schools to create better support for teachers through an apprenticeship model; its ultimate goal is to improve the quality of the classroom experience for students and teachers alike. Instead of pushing out success metrics in a vacuum, he is obsessed with "developing the counterfactual," as he puts it, by which he means finding ways to evaluate whether or not a program is *actually* driving results.

He learned the importance of this style of probing early in his career, when he was finishing up his PhD dissertation research. He was comparing the academic experience of the students who had participated in a scholarship program he developed as a fifth-grade teacher in Washington, DC, with the experience of students who had not. He remembers sitting at his desk, in the summer of 2008, hitting ENTER for his statistics software. He learned that when it came to academic achievement, absence rates, pass/fail rates and credit accumulation, the scholarship students had fared no better than the students who hadn't participated in the program. "My stomach hit the floor," he recalled. "That experience laid bare the assumption that good intentions and real results go hand in hand: oftentimes, they don't."[6] What made that moment even more difficult was knowing that students were reporting positive gains from participating—just not in the way he'd set out to measure the gains. At that point he became committed, and built an organization around the principle that energy and resources should increasingly flow to places truly driving positive, aligned outcomes in the lives of young people.

At Blue Engine, which has grown into a $6+ million organization with twenty-six staff serving eighty-six teaching apprentices, Ehrmann has set a standard of transparency about all its results, with an annual release of data on 100 percent of students served, and no cherry-picking of data or narrow reliance on uplifting positive anecdotes in the absence of hard data. Blue Engine regularly sends out impact statements to its funders, saying where they think they've done well in addition to where their efforts have tanked. Even when they obtain positive results, they dive deeper to try to determine for sure that they are due to Blue Engine's intervention. For example, in one year 65 percent of the class passed a certain standardized test, and the next year 75 percent passed. Rather than patting themselves on the back, the organization hired a statistics consultant, for $100 an hour, to use districtwide data to craft an analysis of how individual students would have performed without participating in Blue Engine's apprenticeship, based on their prior test scores and demographics. Blue Engine also works hard to obtain student-level feedback so they can blend real, qualitative assessments of their program; they also interview the teachers who conduct the apprenticeships and the school principals to get their insights. Ehrmann has infused the organization with a healthy blend of deep student-facing belief and data skepticism, and is convinced this culture of probing and commitment to improvement has been critical to Blue Engine's growth, credibility and trust with key stakeholders.

Reporting persuasively about results is not only a matter of transparency, of course. It requires mastering the art of powerful data presentation, so that the data tell a clear and impressive story. We'll next learn about inventive ways to achieve this.

CHAPTER 6

Making Your Data
Tell a Story

With an arsenal of great data showing the incredible impact of your work, you have to show it off. But one big problem is that foundations request all sorts of different kinds of reports from grant applicants and awardees. As a result, nonprofit leaders often spend an awful lot of time and money doing one-off reports to satisfy grant requirements, which often don't actually help them improve their services or tell their story to a broader audience.

While nonprofits can't change the way funders request data from them, what they can do is get their own data house in great shape to make both their internal reporting and review, and their public reporting, as efficient and effective as possible. As a widely read *Stanford Social Innovation Review* article titled "Drowning in Data" highlighted a decade ago, the push for better impact analysis and data reporting has left many organizations feeling overwhelmed by unwieldy masses of data they've gathered.[1] But masses of data are in no way a bad thing in themselves.

Though there has certainly been much hype about the wonders of "big data," the fact is that the tools to analyze data are becoming ever more powerful and easily applied. So if you're not collecting rich data now, you may well find yourself down the road unable to perform important analyses that you have developed the capacity to do, or to pay someone else to do. What's vital is to carve out of the masses of data only what you really need to regularly track and report. Many organizations I studied have developed exemplary practices for making data reporting more impactful and less crazy-making.

MAKE LESS INTO MORE

One of the most powerful things you can do in reporting to the public is to pare down the data you highlight to bite-sized portions that people can easily digest. An organization that does this masterfully is Room to Read, which is so committed to data gathering and analysis that it has a full department dedicated to the task. The organization has come a very long way since founder John Wood made a 1998 life-changing visit to a school in the Himalayas. He was an executive at Microsoft at the time, and on a trek in rural Nepal he came upon the school, which he discovered taught 450 children but had only a handful of books. The school director challenged him, saying, "Perhaps, sir, you will someday come back with books." When Wood returned home, he solicited donations from friends and family and bought three thousand books for the school. A few years later, Wood left Microsoft to start Room to Read, which is now a large nonprofit with a $50 million annual budget. Its programs have reached over 10 million children in ten countries in Africa and Asia over the past twenty years.

The organization collects key data from thirty-five hundred sites annually and has invested in randomized control trials to prove their intervention is having a measurable impact on its beneficiaries. But even with so much impressive data to marshal, the presentation of impact statistics on its website is streamlined and easy to follow. The main page focuses on just one number: the 10 million children and their communities that have benefited. For each of its two programs, one in girls' education and one in literacy, the organization offers two simple and graphically appealing dashboards,

Our Literacy Program aims to tackle this challenge and help children become *independent readers* — with not only reading skills but also a habit of reading that will serve them throughout their lives.

2015 RESULTS [1]

9,232
TEACHERS & LIBRARIANS TRAINED

7.8 MILLION
BOOKS CHECKED OUT

1,127
NEW LIBRARIES ESTABLISHED

1,222
SCHOOLS IMPLEMENTING ROOM TO READ LITERACY INSTRUCTION

CUMULATIVE RESULTS

9.9 MILLION
CHILDREN BENEFITED

18,699
PARTNER SCHOOLS

1,300
ORIGINAL CHILDREN'S BOOK TITLES PUBLISHED

18 MILLION
BOOKS DISTRIBUTED

An Example of a Room to Read Literacy Dashboard. *Source:* Room to Read Global Monitoring Report, 2015.

each highlighting six additional statistics the organization has determined offer the best snapshot of the impact achieved. Cofounder and CEO Erin Ganju advises: "It's really important that you boil down, for each program, the two or three things that people want to know about the most."

The website does offer a wealth of additional data, tucked away and accessible through tabs for clicking through to take a deeper dive. This includes free downloads of numerous videos and research reports, which are also models of succinct and engaging reporting, free of jargon and effectively highlighting the most important findings. Overall, Room to Read has figured out how to make vitally clear that measuring impact is a critical focus of the organization, while also assuring its presentation of data helps to tell a great story.

If you feel it's important to display a fuller set of impact measures on your website, you can still do so in a manner that leads people through the information in a captivating manner, telling a longer story but still a highly engaging one. An organization that does this well is New Teacher Center (NTC), based in Santa Cruz, California, which is dedicated to improving teacher effectiveness through mentorship and new teacher induction programs. When Ellen Moir first started the program as director of Teacher Education at UC Santa Cruz, she was seeing all her top students go into teaching and then leave after a year or two. They complained about being overwhelmed with classroom management and developing curriculum, and of lacking the resources they needed. Moir imagined, what if we could pair these new teachers with mentors to help support them when they run into challenges? Would that result in them staying? Within six years, upward of 97 percent of the mentored teachers stayed in Santa Cruz County, compared to an overall state retention rate of just 50 percent. Today, NTC can show that teacher retention

NTC ADVANCES TEACHING PRACTICE[1]

88% of teachers enrolled in the New Teacher Induction Program report a direct impact on student achievement as a result of their mentorship relationship. NTC-supported teachers demonstrate a higher capacity for analyzing student work and adjusting their teaching practice accordingly.

 90%
OF NEW TEACHERS

agree that work with their NTC mentor influences their practice and meets their needs as a growing professional.

 87%
OF ADMINISTRATORS

believe NTC influenced their district's growth in advancing teacher practice.

NTC INCREASES TEACHER RETENTION[2]

When new teachers had strong support from school administrators as well as other teachers, they were 3-4 times more likely to remain in their school district.

 30%
INCREASE IN RETENTION

New teacher retention increased by 30% after just 2 years of NTC support.

 90%
OF NTC TRAINED MENTORS

in Hillsborough County Public Schools remained committed to the district after five years.

Citations

1. Induction Survey, 2015. Over 4000 Beginning teachers responded across 21 sites.

2. NTC Analyses, 2015. Comparison study conducted in a southeastern district.

Source: "Our Impact," New Teacher Center; available at https://newteachercenter .org/our-impact/.

increases by 30 percent after just two years of support; as a result the program has been adopted widely in California and expanded across the country, with an annual budget of $40 million.

While teacher retention is still the organization's most important metric, Moir hired a data team to collect all sorts of data about teacher effectiveness and student achievement levels as well, and the website presents a compelling scroll of impressive graphs comparing the student achievement and teacher effectiveness of NTC-mentored teachers versus those who didn't participate. As rich as the information is, it can be easily absorbed in just seconds.

STREAMLINE INTERNALLY TOO

Narrowing down your key indicators is important for your internal reporting and assessment also. Mike Dugan, executive director of Domus Kids, told a cautionary story of drowning in data. The Stamford, Connecticut–based organization helps children living in poverty create a path to success in school and life. With such a challenging mission, involving so many factors in children's lives, it's certainly understandable that the organization had developed a wild proliferation of indicators. Dugan said, "At one point I think we had eighty-nine indicators that we were tracking, which as I look back were really just a bunch of numbers on a piece of paper that made us feel good. We thought, 'Oh we have data, we have outcomes, we can report that to funders,' but really now we look at them and we realize that it wasn't very rigorous, and if we hit a mark or didn't hit a mark, we didn't really do anything with it."[2] After going through a theory of change process, Domus Kids narrowed their focus down to just four indicators that are sharp and directly connected to changing the trajectory of the kids' lives: (1) improved attendance; (2) improved behavior; (3) improved social and emotional growth; and (4) improved literacy skills. Their research showed these were the factors that really got in the way of kids succeeding.

Certainly, program evaluators must dive periodically into the full range and depth of an organization's data, but for day-to-day operations, a tight focus on key indicators facilitates clarity about the progress toward goals. Creating an effective data dashboard, made widely accessible around the organization, is the best way to harness your data so you are in command of it rather than it commanding you.

MAKE YOUR DASHBOARD A LIVING DOCUMENT

Data dashboards have become ubiquitous in the nonprofit world, and I won't belabor in discussing them. But a few key points are important to highlight.

While elaborate columns of data can be oppressive, a dashboard really can be as remarkably powerful a tool for internal tracking and program improvement as it is for external validation. Many organizations I interviewed develop a standard two- to three-page deck of indicators that they use to update their results on a quarterly, monthly or even weekly basis to make sure they are on track toward achieving their impact goals, and to be on top of any red flags that might arise. The key to making the

> Creating an effective data dashboard, made widely accessible around the organization, is the best way to harness your data so you are in command of it rather than it commanding you.

process easily manageable is to develop a disciplined approach to updating it, and to make it widely accessible, so the staff responsible for having a detailed command of various elements of the data can consult it, and perhaps also update it independently.

An organization that has led the field in dashboard management is BELL, which offers summer and after-school tutoring and mentoring programs nationally to pre-K through eighth-grade students from underprivileged backgrounds. CEO Tiffany Cooper Gueye has been vigilant about using a data dashboard to help improve the organization's performance. When Gueye and her team started measuring outcomes nearly twenty years ago, they were doing it on a shoestring budget, using homemade surveys they administered themselves during site visits. Eventually, they purchased a standardized achievement test to track student performance using a validated tool. As they began to collect more and more data, they migrated it to Salesforce.com, which offers its cloud-based database services for free to nonprofits. BELL then developed a system to automate the collection of their data.

To make the most efficient and effective tool for seeing what the data has to reveal, BELL created a regional performance quarterly dashboard that lists BELL's goals with respect to student service, philanthropic donations, sustainability and long-term impact. The

Regional Performance Measures – quarterly dashboard

REGION X - JOHN SMITH

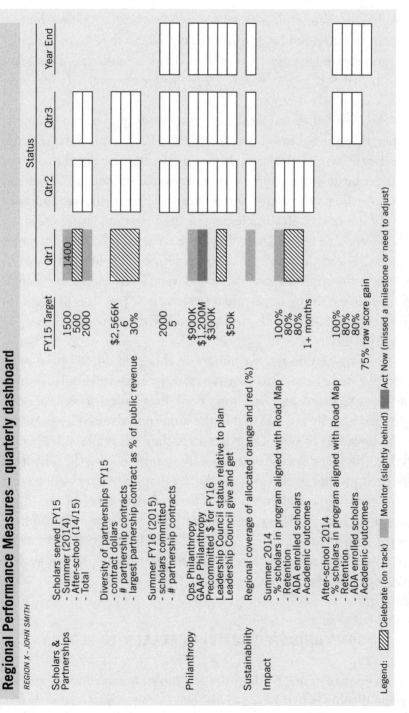

	FY15 Target	Status			
		Qtr1	Qtr2	Qtr3	Year End
Scholars & Partnerships					
Scholars served FY15					
- Summer (2014)	1500	1400			
- After-school (14/15)	500				
- Total	2000				
Diversity of partnerships FY15					
- contract dollars	$2,566K				
- # partnership contracts	6				
- largest partnership contract as % of public revenue	30%				
Summer FY16 (2015)					
- scholars committed	2000				
- # partnership contracts	5				
Philanthropy					
Ops Philanthropy	$900K				
GAAP Philanthropy	$1,200M				
Precommitted $ for FY16	$300K				
Leadership Council status relative to plan					
Leadership Council give and get	$50k				
Sustainability					
Regional coverage of allocated orange and red (%)					
Impact					
Summer 2014					
- % scholars in program aligned with Road Map	100%				
- Retention	80%				
- ADA enrolled scholars	80%				
- Academic outcomes	1+ months				
After-school 2014					
- % scholars in program aligned with Road Map	100%				
- Retention	80%				
- ADA enrolled scholars	80%				
- Academic outcomes	75% raw score gain				

Legend: Celebrate (on track)   Monitor (slightly behind)   Act Now (missed a milestone or need to adjust)

Sample Performance Dashboard from BELL Showing Key Performance Indicators results are color coded green for the "celebrates," yellow for the "monitors" and red for the "act nows" (where they missed a milestone and need to adjust). This allows the senior management team and board of directors to quickly see where the organization is on track and where it is not.

This dashboard has facilitated many discoveries. For example, when they started to collect more rigorous academic data from the students participating in their programs, BELL realized there was quite a bit of variability in outcomes across school sites. They did some further surveys and found this was due to the variability in how each of the sites implemented the program. Using the data, they were able to see where they were achieving the best outcomes and why, and then use those strategies across other programs to create more consistencies. It also led them to develop a more comprehensive training department to share best practices in program delivery, and as a result they started seeing more consistency in their outcomes.

Creating an effective dashboard of this kind doesn't have to be complicated or expensive, with so many free services available, such as Google Sheets and Salesforce.com. Purchasing more elaborate options may also be worth it in the long run. Many colleagues told Tess Reynolds of New Door Ventures they thought she was crazy when she spent $70,000 on a software system to track the outcomes of their programs. She told me that by that point they were paying an analyst almost as much to do manual data entry of their program surveys, so the expense made good sense, even in the near term. And it has ultimately reaped much richer rewards as the organization has been able to perform analysis on data in their system dating back nearly ten years.

COMMUNICATE YOUR DATA PERSON TO PERSON

With so many great communication tools available for live conferencing, some organizations have been capitalizing on the ability to communicate with funders and donors about results on a more personal level than through a written report. Leila Janah of Sama-source has taken a page from the business world and hosts "quar-terly learnings" calls (her version of quarterly earnings reports) in which her impact measurement team communicates about whether they are hitting their target numbers and, if not, their hypotheses about why. Scott Warren of Generation Citizen Year communicates with his foundation supporters using a webinar format. According to Warren, this is not only wonderfully efficient, allowing all his funders to receive the information in one place at one time, but it also facilitates getting real-time feedback from donors, engaging them in the process and making them feel even more invested in the work.

Of course, reporting persuasive data is only one part of the challenge of seeking funding. With competition for grants so fierce, and with so many organizations for individual donors to choose from, nonprofits must be highly strategic and creative about their approaches to generating financial support. In the next part, we'll dive into an exploration of a wide range of funding approaches organizations have used to break through the $500,000 barrier.

BENCHMARKS FOR SOCIAL STARTUP SUCCESS: MEASURING

✓ Have you brought together your staff, board and/or external stakeholders for a theory of change workshop?
✓ Does your theory of change clearly articulate the causal links among your program activities, your intermediate outcomes and your vision?
✓ Do you have an illustration of your theory of change to provide to partners, donors and other supporters?
✓ Have you developed SMART (specific, measurable, attainable, relevant and timely) indicators of progress you hope to see as a result of your programs, such as changes in behavior?

✓   Have you developed a plan to track your indicators, such as by surveying beneficiaries or using proven assessments?

✓   Have you developed a dashboard using a platform like Google Sheets and/or Salesforce.com to track your key performance indicators and measure your progress over time?

✓   Have you considered bringing in an outside consultant to assist you with developing and/or pressure testing your theory of change work?

✓   Do you have a plan to be honest with your data if it is not showing you the results you hoped for?

✓   Have you distilled your performance data into bite-sized chunks supporters can easily digest in a few seconds?

✓   Do you have ways of communicating your impact data internally to staff and board, such as through a quarterly dashboard summary report?

✓   Do you have ways of communicating your impact data externally to supporters, such as through an annual impact report or quarterly impact calls or webinars?

PART 3

FUNDING EXPERIMENTATION

Attracting funding is by far the biggest barrier to scale. In fact, 81 percent of the social entrepreneurs I surveyed identified access to capital as their most pressing problem. Nonprofits at all levels struggle to get noticed by new funders. What separates the best organizations is a culture of testing a variety of funding streams to figure out what works. By purposefully experimenting with revenue, they discover a funding model both authentic to their mission and effective at raising money.

Earned income such as selling products or services is fertile ground for experimentation. My survey revealed that successfully developing an earned-income strategy was one of the ways organizations broke through the $2 million annual revenue barrier. The responses showed that while organizations typically start out with mostly philanthropic support, with just 8 percent of their budget coming from earned income, as they grow past $2 million in revenue, they are more likely to report that a higher percentage of their budget is covered by earnings; on average about 30 percent. These findings indicate that testing earned-income strategies should be a key ingredient of efforts to scale. But my research into how non-profits generated earned income also highlighted that the process is fraught with challenges, and is more viable in some subsectors, such as education and health care, than others.

And caution is advised. The argument that nonprofits should function more like businesses, and even that a for-profit business approach is preferable for tackling some social problems, has often been pushed to the extreme. As the Bridgespan Group's William Foster and Jeffrey Bradach wrote in their *Harvard Business Review* article "Should Nonprofits Seek Profits?": "Many philanthropic foundations and other funders have been zealously urging non-profits to become financially self-sufficient and have aggressively promoted earned income as a means to 'sustainability.' . . . Despite the hype, earned income accounts for only a small share of funding in most nonprofit domains, and few of the ventures actually make money."[1] Social entrepreneurs are, by definition, working to solve problems resulting from market and government deficiencies. A purely market-based approach cannot always work. If bringing clean water to the 800 million people who don't have access to it, or selling mosquito nets to the 200 million suffering annually from the scourge of malaria, were profitable ventures, private companies would be doing it. Expecting social entrepreneurs to figure out how to devise profit-making solutions to such problems, when even the behemoths of modern-day capitalism can't do so, is misguided wishful thinking.

My survey indicated that earning income is much more viable in some subsectors than others. Although, on average, earned income accounts for 30 percent of the budgets of the larger organizations I surveyed, 78 percent of those organizations earned only 10 percent of their income. My sample size wasn't large enough to make broad generalizations, but it does reflect a broader trend that earned income typically works better in certain sectors, such as education, where 48 percent of nonprofits have earned revenue that accounts for over 20 percent of their budget, followed by health (27%), global development (24%) and youth development (22%). On the flip side, in my experience human rights, criminal justice and environmental organizations are particularly unlikely to find sources of earned income, whether because their clients cannot afford to pay fees or because making any sort of profit from the work is widely considered inappropriate.

For years, some funders suggested that Accountability Counsel, the San Francisco–based organization representing grassroots communities globally in human and environmental rights cases against big companies, try to figure out ways to generate earned income; for example, by charging fees for their expert advice. Founder Natalie Bridgeman Fields was clear from the start that these strategies would not work because of inherent conflicts of interest between serving their clients and being paid by corporations or other large institutions. But with this clarity, today Accountability Counsel has broken through the $2 million in annual revenue mark by relying primarily on foundation funding. In chapter 9, we will explore how they did it.

For organizations like Accountability Counsel that can't rely on earned income, revenue testing focuses more on attracting philanthropic capital through foundations and individual donors. Here, finding more effective ways to reach out to funders and developing better leveraging opportunities to meet funders and potential individual donors are vital skills to build. We will consider a number of innovative strategies breakout organizations have employed for bringing in more philanthropic funding as well.

The vast majority of organizations under $3 million in annual revenue will rely on a combination of funding sources to come up with a model that fits their unique mission and values. In one of the most widely read *Stanford Social Innovation Review* articles, titled "Ten Funding Models,"

While organizations that want to scale substantially should be driving toward finding one or two primary sources of reliable ongoing revenue, they should get there by testing a good diversity of approaches as they're growing.

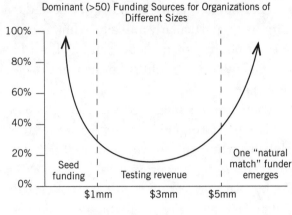

Dominant (>50) Funding Sources for Organizations of Different Sizes

Dominant (>50%) Funding Sources for Organizations of Different Sizes. *Source: Adapted from William Foster, Ben Dixon and Matthew Hochstetler, In Search of Sustainable Funding: Is Diversity of Sources Really the Answer?*

William Foster and his Bridgespan colleagues reveal that of the 144 nonprofit organizations created since 1970 that have grown to $50 million a year or more in size, each grew by more narrowly pursuing sources of funding, typically concentrating on one particular source: what they call the "natural match."[2] For example, the Sierra Club relies on membership fees.

A key point to highlight, however, is that their research also shows that organizations typically do not begin to transition to dominant funding sources until around $3 million in annual revenue.[3] This underscores the point that while organizations that want to scale substantially should be driving toward finding one or two primary sources of reliable ongoing revenue, they should get there by testing a good diversity of approaches as they're growing. The chapters in part 3 offer a wealth of strategies for this testing.

CHAPTER 7

Laying the Foundation to
Experiment with Earned Income

Many of the organizational leaders I interviewed remember the great recession of 2008 like it was yesterday. Virtually overnight, foundations that had promised multiyear grants reneged on their funding because their endowments had tanked along with the Dow Jones. Earned income was critical to many of them in order to stay afloat. Beyond providing a financial cushion, earned income helps bridge the gap lying before so many organizations: the funding they're able to raise versus the amount they need in order to invest adequately in growth. Another benefit is that demonstrating your capacity to generate reliable income appeals to funders, many of whom have come to see earned revenue as a vital part of the "path to sustainability." But before an organization begins playing with potential earned-income streams, it must establish the right expectations.

IF YOU BUILD IT, THEY MAY NOT COME

Building a paying client base or a market of retail customers takes every organization, whether for-profit or nonprofit, substantial effort and time. Many, many entrepreneurs have run headlong into the "if you build it they will come" trap. They've launched their businesses, maybe even with a grand promotional flourish, and found that virtually no paying customers have shown up. Studies of for-profit startups have shown that in general they earn relatively minimal revenue, if any, for two to three years, even those that go on to become runaway successes. In the nonprofit sector, finding paying customers can be even more challenging because so many who are the most likely targets, the beneficiaries of programs, can't afford to pay, or can pay only a minimal amount. More about that shortly.

Experimentation is crucial when it comes to earned income, and organizations for the most part should expect some failures along the way. Honing products or services to generate an appreciable base of paying clients or customers can take substantial time and effort. Those launching an organization with a business venture as a core part of its model, or launching a service or product line for an existing organization, should plan on philanthropic funding covering a significant portion of operating expenses for at least a couple of years, if not more. And even once revenue is coming in and a venture is thriving, it is likely that earnings will not be sufficient to totally cover the organization's expenses, or all the services it wants to provide, no matter how appealing and well-devised the products or services are.

Take the case of successful Hot Bread Kitchen, a training facility for low-income women who want careers in the food industry, founded by Jessamyn Rodriguez. She smartly played to her strengths in conceiving the organization, after having worked for a decade in international development before she came up with the concept. A passionate foodie, she landed an internship in renowned chef Daniel Boulud's kitchen. That happened by serendipity. She was interviewing for a job at a microfinance organization called Women's World Banking, when a friend misheard her as saying Women's World Baking. The idea of an international women's baking collective struck her, and it is now located in the heart of Harlem in La Marqueta, a historic produce market dating back to 1936, which had fallen into decline until the organization redeveloped it. The space is divided into three separate areas of operation: a kitchen that hosts a six-month job-training program for low-income women, an area where they bake bread products for sale and an incubator where small-business owners in the food industry can rent space to make products they sell throughout the city, from grocery stores to markets.

Rodriguez told me the key reason the business has been successful is that they don't sacrifice quality despite the fact they are mission driven, and after tasting their multigrain pepita bread I can attest to that. In fact, the organization sells its bread to a number of major retail outlets, such as Whole Foods and JetBlue, as well as some of the top restaurants in New York City. But even with a top-quality product and a strong personal network for building the market, she initially overestimated the extent to which profits from bread sales would support the organization. While at first she envisioned a model where her bread sales and cafe operations would cover close to 100 percent of her operating expenses, she realized quickly that goal would be hard to accomplish. She had underestimated the costs of the training, and overestimated the profit margins on selling bread. She was forced to reset her expectations, and had to go back to her donors with a new model that would continue to rely on philanthropic donations to support 35 percent of the program budget. Rodriguez told me that "in talking with our donors, I realized that people were attached to our strong outcomes and that was most important, not being 100 percent sustainable. Over time, my understanding of the economics of the business have changed a lot," she told me, "and I realized that there is actually a huge benefit that comes from philanthropic funding that allows us to do more for the women we serve, such as providing child care during the classes."

Foundations and donors, and organizational leaders themselves, must not put organizations under unrealistic pressure to fund more and more of their operations by selling products and services. Recall that in my survey, most of the organizations that had scaled to over $2 million in annual revenue reported that earned income accounted for 30 percent, which therefore is a reasonable target for many organizations to shoot for during the initial phase of growth.

The bottom line: plan on grants and donations to almost entirely sustain your efforts for at least the first couple of years, as you experiment with building your revenue stream.

The bottom line: plan on grants and donations to almost entirely sustain your efforts for at least the first couple of years, as you experiment with building your revenue stream.

THE HYBRID IDEAL AND MISSION DRIFT

One of the ways the social entrepreneurship community has sought to facilitate earning more funds through business ventures is by developing the hybrid organizational model. The concept has become so popular, Echoing Green reported that in 2016 nearly half of all applications for its fellowships were from organizations proposing for-profit and hybrid business models.[1] But just exactly what they are has become a somewhat murky subject. Gaining clarity about hybrid organizations and the challenges of operating them is important, especially given how much interest there is in starting them, and the mistakes that can be made. The good news is that many good models have been developed.

The term "hybrid organization" originally arose to describe social enterprises that paired a charitable 501(c)(3) organization, which could receive tax-deductible donations, with a for-profit "arm" that could take investment capital and pay investors a financial return, while also earning unlimited (theoretically) income. The concept was that this hard division into two separate operations allowed mission-driven organizations to break free from constraints on sources of funding and the portion of earned revenue 501(c)(3)s were subject to. (In essence, in order to claim tax-exempt status, 501(c)(3)s could not earn a "substantial" portion of their income from activities unrelated to their mission. The details are more complicated, and organizational leaders must learn about them in detail.) Nonprofits were also not allowed to issue equity shares to investors, which of course limited their funding pool substantially.[2] Another perceived benefit of the dual structure was that the for-profit part of the organization could donate some of its earnings to the nonprofit part and claim tax exemption (up to a point) for the donation; in turn, the nonprofit part could purchase goods or services from the for-profit (subject to the regulation that they be purchased at reasonable cost), which in theory could help the for-profit business to thrive.

The hybrid model is ingenious, but it's proven quite difficult to manage, with the complexity of the legal issues alone being very arduous. This can put organizations at a disadvantage when they approach foundations, which may perceive that their money is better spent going to organizations unable to support themselves with earnings.[3] Running a for-profit business also means you are under more intense competitive market pressures. For these reasons, over time, most nonprofits seeking to earn income have not gone this route, and as a wider menu of options for combining nonprofit and for-profit operations has emerged, the meaning of hybrid has evolved to a much looser term that refers to any nonprofit organization that has revenue generation, regardless of its legal structure.

We won't dive deeply into the details of all the legal structures, as there are plenty of resources to help nonprofits navigate them. For one, Rob Wexler, a prominent lawyer in the field of social entrepreneurship, wrote a very thoughtful piece called "Effective Social Enterprise—A Menu of Legal Structures," available free online, in which he includes the brilliant table on the following pages describing the options.[4] Even this chart does not fully reflect all of the various hybrid legal structures that could come from combining the various forms. What's most important is that organizational

Legal Structure	Tax Factors	Management and Control	Sources of Capital	Distribution of Funds Not Used for Programs	Liquidation
For-profit corporation	Taxed on net income	Shareholders elect a board of directors, which delegates to committees and staff	Investment capital from shareholders and sometimes program-related investments (PRIs) from foundations in the form of equity or loans	Dividends to shareholders; charitable contributions deductible up to 10% of net income	Net assets to shareholders, after paying creditors
Limited liability company (LLC)	Items of income and expense passed through to members	Management committee or single manager, typically elected by the members	Investment capital from members; possible PRI funding	Distributions to members; charitable contributions deductible on members' own returns	Net assets to members, after paying creditors
B-Corp (a for-profit corporation with a social mission)	Same as for-profit corporation above	Same as for-profit corporation above	Same as for-profit corporation above; may be in a better position to attract PRI money	Same as for-profit corporation above	Net assets usually to shareholders, but also possibly to charity
L3C (LLC that is formed as a low-profit limited liability company)	See LLC above	See LLC above	See LLC above; plus set up to accept PRI money more easily	Distributions to members and grants for charitable purposes	Net assets to members and 501(c)(3) charities

Nonprofit corporation 501(c)(3)	Not taxed on income unless it is unrelated business taxable income (UBTI); can offer tax deductions to donors	Board of directors controls	Charitable contributions and grants; easily eligible for PRI money	Grants for charitable purposes	Net assets to another 501(c)(3) charity with like exempt purposes
Nonprofit corporation 501(c)(4)	Not taxed on income unless it is UBTI, no tax deduction to donors	See 501(c)(3) above	Nondeductible contributions, grants; possible PRI money	Can make grants for charitable and social welfare purposes	Net assets to another 501(c)(4) or to a 501(c)(3), in either case with like exempt purposes

Social Enterprise Legal Structures. Note that tax laws in this area are constantly evolving, so organizations should seek formal legal advice to determine which structure is most appropriate for their needs. *Source:* Adapted from Robert Wexler, "Effective Social Enterprise—A Menu of Legal Structures," *Exempt Organization Tax Review,* June 2009.

leaders considering earned-income strategies learn the details of these different structures, and get professional legal and tax advice as they pursue options.

The differing strategies pursued by two highly successful organizations—Embrace, the developer of a low-cost baby warmer for hypothermic infants in developing countries, and Hot Bread Kitchen—illustrate some of the considerations organizations face when deciding on their legal structure. After operating for some time as a 501(c)(3), Embrace decided to transition to the classic hybrid dual structure, creating a for-profit company to further develop and sell its warmer.[5] A key reason it did so was that the development of the warmer required so much capital, and the constraints of raising money as a nonprofit were holding back development. Creating the for-profit allowed the organization to pursue funds from venture capital firms and impact investors, and speed up R&D. Founder Jane Chen highlights, though, that making the transition was difficult and the complexity of managing two different operations was a real challenge. By contrast, Hot Bread Kitchen elected to incorporate as a 501(c)(3) because as Jessamyn Rodriguez tested her model, she discovered that the size of her market and the earnings she could bring in were not sufficient to cover costs, and she was going to need donations and grant money to supplement her revenue from the bakery and incubator. In addition, in the early years the administrative burden, such as the legal costs of operating a hybrid organization, were too great.

However you decide to structure a hybrid, execution can be fraught with complications. A big problem is "mission drift," meaning the tendency that running the business part of the organization will pull focus and resources away from your core purpose: the social impact you are striving to achieve. Many of the social entrepreneurs I interviewed cautioned about an inherent tension between maximizing impact and maximizing profits. A thought-provoking article on the hybrid model in the *Stanford Social Innovation Review*, titled "In Search of the Hybrid Ideal" by Julia Battilana and Matthew Lee of Harvard Business School and John Walker and Cheryl

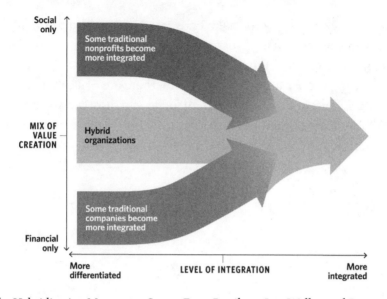

The Hybridization Movement. *Source:* From Battilana, Lee, Walker and Dorsey, "In Search of the Hybrid Ideal."

Dorsey of Echoing Green, showcased this danger.[6] In it they make the case that the best way to limit the tug of mission drift is to run a business venture directly related to your social mission and integral to furthering it. Hot Bread Kitchen is offered as an exemplar of this "hybrid ideal." Teaching the beneficiaries to bake bread and help run the for-profit part of the organization is at the very core of its mission to provide women with job skills that will facilitate their obtaining gainful employment. New Door Ventures is another case in point. Their T-shirt printing and bicycle repair businesses provide valuable job skills, as well as income to the beneficiaries; earnings from the ventures help pay for other skill building and support for the beneficiaries, such as educational tutoring.

It's important to appreciate, though, that even when the business venture and the mission are in good alignment, managing the tensions of mission drift can be difficult. Hot Bread Kitchen founder Jessamyn Rodriguez told me that, at first, when the business was not as profitable as she would have liked, she tried cutting hours, keeping people in the program longer to increase efficiency, and anything else that could make ends meet. But as she did that she realized she was making cuts at the expense of the mission. That's when she decided to put more emphasis on grants and donations.

Keeping these cautions top-of-mind, there are a number of great methods for earning income that social startups can experiment with. We'll dive into them next.

CHAPTER 8

Testing
Earned-Income Strategies

Organizations have many potential sources of earned income: from beneficiaries, the general public, other organizations (whether nonprofit or for-profit businesses) or government. The media has directed lots of attention in recent years to innovative products developed by social enterprises, like the Embrace baby warmer, but that is not the most common strategy—selling services is.

SELL YOUR SERVICE EXPERTISE

The vast majority of the nonprofit organizations with earned-income streams I interviewed are raising money from service delivery. Some of them are able to charge their beneficiaries, while others rely on third-party payers, such as government entities like schools, but also private firms.

While some organizations' beneficiaries truly have no money to pay up front, some can pay a moderate fee and will readily do so as long as you convince them there is real value in your service. For example, Planned Parenthood charges for its services using a sliding scale based on household size and income. Other organizations like National Public Radio operate using a voluntary donation model, where users can decide whether they want to give and how much.

Professor Gregory Dees, one of the leading pioneers of the discipline of social entrepreneurship, addressed this topic in a wonderful chapter he wrote with colleagues for *Strategic Tools for Social Entrepreneurs*.[1] Titled "Developing Viable Earned Income Strategies," this is the best single source I have found about basic approaches to try and challenges to be aware of. He and his coauthors argue that charging appropriately calibrated fees to beneficiaries can be empowering to them, affording them the dignity of paying. They also highlight that it can be productive in helping to screen out those not getting much value out of the program, allowing you to focus better on those who are finding it more helpful. It can also increase beneficiaries' commitment to your services, because they have some financial skin in the game; and because they are paying, they may also be more forthcoming with feedback, which can be so important to improving your offerings.

Third-party payers are often willing to pay for services largely because they have an interest in the mission's success. We saw this with CareMessage, which partners with hospitals to offer follow-up care via mobile technology to its patients. Hospitals are willing to pay CareMessage because they have a financial stake in patients showing up for their follow-up appointments. The government can also be a third-party source of earned income, particularly in the education, health and youth development sectors, which we will discuss more later in this chapter.

Many of the issues nonprofits address are also relevant to the challenges of private sector firms. Laura Weidman Powers, cofounder of Code2040, smartly capitalized on negative publicity about the low percentage of minority workers in many Silicon Valley companies. The organization's fellowship program places black and Latinx college- and graduate-level students with excellent technical skills in summer jobs in tech companies in San Francisco and Silicon Valley; this helps them develop the work skills and build the networks they need to succeed. When Google released dreadful diversity numbers, highlighting the recruitment and retention problems of minority staff in Silicon Valley, and creating a mountain of bad press,

Powers seized the day. The executives in many tech companies began scrambling to increase their hiring of minorities, and Code2040 was there to help them.

When Powers first hatched her idea with cofounder Tristan Walker, she was very clear about pitching the pipeline problem to companies: blacks and Latinx earn nearly 18 percent of computer science bachelor's degrees, but make up only about 5 percent of the technical workforce at top tech companies. She also very smartly pitched the business case to companies, showing them that by failing to have a more diverse work environment, they were missing out on top talent that could help boost profits; they were also falling prey to expensive employee turnover. Powers shrewdly realized that by asking tech companies to pay for partnerships with Code2040, not only would she obtain significant funding, but their willingness to pay would send a strong message to other firms, as well as to funders and donors, about the value of the service. It would also make them more invested in creating a more diverse and inclusive workforce.

It took Code2040 a few years to figure out their precise revenue model. The first year they did not charge because they were running a pilot, though they explicitly told tech companies this was a limited-time offer. In year two, they began charging companies whatever amount they decided to pay; Code2040 wanted to test what range of fees seemed viable. Based on the results, they developed a tiered pricing structure, with fees dependent on the size of the company and its capacity to host interns. For example, at one point they developed a sliding scale where a "bronze sponsor" hosted one student for $5,000, a silver sponsor could host up to three for $15,000 and so on. In addition, the companies paid the students' salaries directly from their payroll. The services Code2040 provided include vetted and trained candidates, talks to the company and manager trainings about diversity and inclusion, and volunteer opportunities for their employees. The companies also got branding and marketing benefits from getting to say they were working with Code2040. Tech companies have snapped up the service, and in just five years Code2040 has become an $8 million a year organization working with Silicon Valley leaders such as Twitter, Pandora and Airbnb.

Another organization that has seized the opportunity to earn revenue by providing a service to corporations is Genesys Works, the national organization that places disadvantaged high school students in internships at major corporations during their senior year in high school. When Rafael Alvarez founded the organization, he was determined to support the program with revenue from companies that would partner with Genesys. Integral to his pitch is that the organization provides the service for less money than other for-profit service providers. "Our model works," Alvarez told me, "because we are providing a cost-effective solution to businesses, while affecting people's lives forever." As a result, Genesys Works served more than twenty-eight hundred students in 2016 alone, resulting in a college enrollment rate of 94 percent.

COMBINE FREE AND PAID

One of the biggest challenges of charging fees is that you may be lured away from serving the neediest clientele in favor of those who can afford to pay. This is one reason that adopting the "freemium" model of offering a free service with add-on premium services at cost can be a good idea for nonprofits. It allows you to offer your service for free, or perhaps for a very moderate fee, to those who can't pay, and at a greater cost to those who can. This also solves another common problem organizations run into. Lance Fors, an expert on social entrepreneurship who has successfully helped a number of social startups scale, points out that organizations too often start out by offering all their services for free. "Nearly everybody wants to give their services away in the beginning. They see a problem, they're passionate about the cause, and they want to get it out there, but they price it as if it has no value." If an organization later imposes fees, it can provoke a backlash. Many technology startups have also struggled with this problem; because they initially offered their products for free, working out how to earn revenue became a major stumbling block. That was the motivation for the innovation of the "freemium" model, employed to breakthrough success by leaders in that sector such as LinkedIn and Dropbox.

The Open Media Project is making good use of a version of the model. Their mission is to make government proceedings transparent by providing users with software that searches online efficiently through the morass of available proceedings data. It charges on a sliding scale, offering the software free to municipalities serving populations of five thousand or less and for $6,000 annually to larger communities of over fifty thousand; it also offers a number of add-on services, such as training sessions, for fees ranging from $900 to $3,000.

In deciding on your fee scale, it's important to keep in mind that even if you don't cover the total costs of your services this way, covering part of them can be a vital complement to your philanthropic income. You should feel free to set your prices according to a combination of market demand and ability to pay, not according to the profit standards of private business. You can also decide to "compete on price" by charging somewhat less for your service than for-profit competitors, or perhaps nonprofit competitors, are charging. This is one of the real advantages nonprofits have in competing for customers; because they receive income from grants and donations, and they don't have to be concerned with shareholder value, they don't need to price according to for-profit standards.

OFFERING SERVICES ON A LOAN BASIS

Microfinancing has paved the way for this earned-income strategy. Core to this model is that you are providing some means for your beneficiaries to eventually repay you, ideally by training them in skills or providing them with equipment that allows them to improve their income. Microlenders such as Kiva have discovered that many of those who seek funds respect the principle that once they have benefited and can afford to, they should begin to pay outlays back. As a result, Kiva's loan repayment rate is 97.1 percent for all borrowers. Beneficiaries may even prefer to receive assistance on a loan basis.

One Acre Fund is an excellent example of making this model successful. Founder Andrew Youn was visiting a nongovernmental organization (NGO) in a remote village in western Kenya when he started talking with farmers about their challenges growing enough food for their families. He became really interested in how people could learn to sustain themselves on an acre of land; so when he was there he launched a pilot to see what kinds of resources would be helpful to them. He came back to the United States and while attending business school, developed a business plan for the organization, envisioning a world where all farmers had the skills and resources they needed to lift themselves out of poverty. He was interested in building a nonprofit that could sustain itself for the long term, so he crafted a model that drew on a bundle of services, including financing for the purchase of farm capital; direct distribution of seed and fertilizer; training in techniques for increasing yields and negotiating favorable terms for sales; and direct assistance in taking goods to markets.

As of this writing, One Acre Fund serves half a million families per year. One of its beneficiaries is a woman named Ruth, a hardworking farmer and mother of eight from western Kenya. She was only able to raise enough corn to fill a few small bags each year, not enough to feed her children. So she would buy a bag of potatoes from her village and travel to the nearest market to sell french fries, earning about $5 per week, just barely enough to sustain her family. In her first planting season after she started working with One Acre Fund in 2009, her crop yielded ten bags of maize, enough to feed her family for an entire year, with some left over to sell. With the money she made she was able to pay for her eldest son to attend high school, the first in the family to do so.

She has paid back One Acre Fund their initial loan for her farm supplies, which funding they will use to help another farmer, multiplying their impact. In fact, 99 percent of the farmers working with One Acre Fund have paid their loans back, covering 73 percent of its direct program operating expenses. Grants and donations cover the remainder of program costs. The organization hopes to eventually sustain the programs entirely through farmer repayments, by implementing cost-cutting measures and taking advantage of economies of scale. This goal has also been critical for raising additional money from foundations, which are eager to see sustainable financial models in the organizations they support.

RETAIL INNOVATIONS

Chuck Slaughter was a successful businessperson, the founder of TravelSmith, which he grew to $100 million in sales and sold in 2014, before he decided to launch a social venture. The organization he founded, Living Goods, is pioneering one of the most successful retail innovations ever developed in the nonprofit sector. As Slaughter had traveled around the world and learned how poverty affected so many people, he began looking for ways to leverage his business skills to tackle the problem. One issue that struck him was the lack of medicines. "Children under the age of five were dying in the developing world every day for lack of medicines that cost less than a cup of coffee," he told me. "It was hard for me to look at these children and not see my own children." While advising the Health-Store/CFW shops, a chain of drugstores in Kenya that was struggling to get people in the door, he had an ah-ha moment. Hold on, he thought, there is a hugely successful retail model that doesn't require getting people in the door—Avon.

As he began researching the idea of applying the Avon model to medicine delivery, Slaughter learned that Avon, a $10 billion business operating in a hundred countries, had actually started in rural

America in the 1880s as a response to poor access to quality goods in small towns. Living Goods, which he launched in Uganda in 2007, recruits and trains community health entrepreneurs to go door to door to sell life-saving products; this creates a cost-effective supply chain and distribution system to the rural poor in Africa, delivering goods such as drugs to combat the leading diseases killing children; family planning; fortified foods; and money-saving tools like solar lights.

The organization uses its buying power to reduce costs to consumers and saves families valuable time and money by delivering to the home. The organization has also created successful products of its own, such as a fortified porridge called Healthy Start that provides children with vitamins in which they are badly deficient. These branded products are Living Goods' best sellers. Meanwhile, the community health entrepreneurs earn a percentage of the margin of profit from sales, providing much needed income that is transforming the lives of their families and communities. The model doesn't just sound good, independent research proves its substantial impact. In a randomized control trial of eight thousand families from more than two hundred villages conducted over three years, Living Goods reduced child deaths by 25 percent. And due to the income the organization earns, the net cost is less than $2 per person reached. As Slaughter says, "That's an unbeatable value in public health."

One reason Living Goods community health agents have been so successful is that they use digital enabled distribution. Digital technology has positively disrupted virtually every other sector, from books to travel to taxis. Now a kind of Uber of health delivery, Living Goods is taking the power of digital enabled distribution to increase health for the poorest, providing every agent a smartphone with their ground-breaking Smart Health™ app. The app's intelligent algorithm automates diagnoses of the three diseases killing the most kids. This ensures accuracy and consistency, enabling the organization to deploy capable health workers at a fraction of the cost to train a nurse or doctor. Like Uber, the app uses big data to optimize agents' efforts, sending them to the highest risk patients each day. It enables any manager to see the performance of any agent in real time on any device. And also like Uber, Living Goods empowers an army of independent entrepreneurs to rapidly scale networks.

Living Goods took on one of the biggest challenges of any business: distribution. As venture capitalist Peter Thiel says in his book *Zero to One*, "Superior sales and distribution by itself can create a monopoly, even with no product differentiation. The converse is not true. No matter how strong your product—even if it easily fits into already established habits and anybody who tries it likes it immediately—you still must support it with a strong distribution plan." The Living Goods model is one brilliant solution. Benetech experimented its way to another.

Benetech hit product distribution challenges from the start. Founder Jim Fruchterman was working at a tech company called Calera Recognition Systems when he helped invent the first successful machine that could read just about any printed text. Fruchterman and his team used this technology to develop a reading machine for the blind, a transformative product in 1989. He founded Benetech as a nonprofit to sell the product at a low cost. The organization almost failed to take off because of a misguided distribution strategy. According to Fruchterman: "We started out doing direct sales [to users], when we realized it would be much more cost effective and impactful to sell the product through dealers and distributors. When we made that change, they sold the hell out of our product and our venture went from zero to $5 million in sales in just three

> Nonprofits may be able to tap the existing mechanisms of for-profit retail rather than create their own sales operations, even though they're selling products at costs favorable to consumers.

years." The lesson here is that nonprofits may be able to tap the existing mechanisms of for-profit retail rather than create their own sales operations, even though they're selling products at costs favorable to consumers.

TEACHING BENEFICIARIES TO FISH

If you decide to sell a product that does not itself provide a social good, then per the earlier discussion of mission drift, the best practice is to follow the "teach a man to fish" philosophy, and create a business that provides truly valuable work and life skills to your employee beneficiaries. Key here is assuring that the types of skills the business will allow you to train people in will in fact facilitate their obtaining employment elsewhere.

New Door Ventures has operated according to this model, and their experience highlights that organizations should expect some of the businesses they attempt to create will be much more successful than others; they should run pilots in order to focus on those that will work best and have the greatest impact before launching them full-scale. New Door Ventures initially created several businesses in addition to the screen-printing business and bicycle shop it runs now, such as restaurants and a resale shop. When Tess Reynolds became CEO in 2003, she decided to focus on their most successful enterprises. She performed a cost-benefit analysis that involved not only an assessment of how much demand there was for the business's products or services and their profitability, but their benefits to the youth employees they were training. They scaled down to just the two businesses they run today. They can boast that both have strong revenues that pay for most business costs; that 89 percent of its program graduates are employed and/or in school six months after completing training; that 91 percent of them had retained stable housing six months after the program; and that 96 percent had not reoffended six months after the program.

COLLABORATE WITH GOVERNMENT AGENCIES

Government agencies and affiliated organizations are one of the biggest sources of income, especially in certain sectors, such as education and health services, in which federal, state and local government agencies are mandated to spend certain amounts of money on issues many nonprofits are tackling. Many government agencies also have extensive experience in partnering with nonprofits.

For many of the organizations I studied, government partnerships were critical to scaling. BELL, the organization that provides after-school programs to underperforming students, is one of these. Founded by Tiffany Cooper Gueye in 1992, it showed strong results in its first ten years of operation, but by 2002 it was funded purely on philanthropy, and the leadership began to consider earning income in order to grow faster. Around the same time, President George W. Bush came into office and championed the No Child Left Behind Act, which provided vouchers to support underperforming elementary and secondary school students. One provision was that low-performing, high-poverty schools could spend up to $1,500 per child on tutoring at the government's expense. As an organization that provides tutoring, BELL decided to explore whether it could access any of this new funding.

The organization hired an expert in government grants to evaluate its eligibility. When the consultant told them that hands down the organization's work was not a fit because college students were doing the tutoring, whereas the bill required tutors with college degrees, BELL was determined to overcome that obstacle. By hiring certified teachers to deliver instruction, BELL successfully made its case to the government. In one fell swoop, the organization grew, in New York City for example, from serving two hundred kids on a Friday to serving eleven hundred kids the following Monday, and it has continued to grow from there.

Gueye cautions that obtaining government funding requires "tedious, compliance-oriented applications about technical aspects of your programming, such as how many vendors you employ and whether they are minority and women friendly." She recommends hiring a technical expert to help navigate the process. It is important to think outside the box about how to partner with governments to tap into sources of earned income. As she points out: "No government bill is written with your name on it. You have to think creatively about how to make them work for you."

One way you can do this is by actually working with government bodies to understand their needs and convince them to write policy into law to fund your operations. Raj Panjabi has done this brilliantly in Liberia with Last Mile Health, which, as you will recall, trains community health workers. Since 2007, Panjabi has worked hard to develop connections within the government. He felt the ministry of health needed to hear the harrowing stories from the front lines about how the lack of access to basic health care was affecting the population, particularly with regard to the AIDS epidemic. So he chronicled people's stories in a document he sent to the minister of health, highlighting how bad the distribution of medicine was, and the devastating implications.

Later that year, with the country in crisis, the government held a meeting, organized by the Global Fund for HIV/AIDS, to determine how to distribute antiretroviral drugs. To Panjabi's surprise, during the proceedings ministry of health officials actually cited the patients he had written about by name, proclaiming how desperate they were for treatment. Realizing that he had gained credibility with the government, he approached officials and suggested they support a pilot in a government hospital testing the use of community health workers to treat patients. The hospital had only one physician, who alone could not administer treatment to all its patients. The program was wildly successful, and as a result Last Mile Health partnered with government to fund its work. As Panjabi recalls: "We thought if we could get paid to do valuable work, but we also were then helping the ministry of health write its national health policy to reflect this model we had tested together which actually worked, it was a win-win." It most definitely was. Having then expanded from hospitals into ten districts in rural areas over the next five years, ultimately the community health care workers were invaluable in stopping the reach of Ebola during the 2012 crisis.

Many of the most successful social entrepreneurs in the United States have partnered with government and helped shape programs. The youth service programs run by City Year were so successful, for example, that they helped inspire the federal program AmeriCorps, which has eighty thousand members serving in 21,600 unique sites across the country.[2] In 2015, federal AmeriCorps funding represented approximately $33 million of City Year's $142 million annual budget.

CAREFULLY PLAN YOUR STRATEGY

If you decide you want to experiment with earned income, you should undertake a rigorous strategic analysis and a pilot program. Gregory Dees and his coauthors lay out this five-step process for developing a viable earned-income strategy I highly recommend:[3]

Step 1. Reaffirm your organization's mission.
As we've discussed, earned-income strategies work best for nonprofits when they are highly aligned with their mission. To assure that ideas are serving the mission well, Dees and his colleagues advise performing an assessment of how clear your mission is by asking five or so people (a mix of staff and other stakeholders such as a board member and a funder) to describe the mission, without referring to your website or materials describing it. You could do this with a simple email request or perhaps by calling them. The responses will tell you whether or not you should spend some time aligning everyone on the objectives of the organization. Going through the theory of change process outlined in part 2 is another way to ensure you have clearly articulated your organization's goals.

Step 2. Brainstorm your options.

Bring together your full team (staff, board and even external stake-holders) to brainstorm a variety of potential sources of income, and whittle them down to just a few to evaluate further. Think about the various categories of revenue. Can you charge your beneficiaries for services you already provide? Is there an invested third party such as a company or a government entity that might be willing to pay for those services? Does it make sense to launch a new business venture? What other types of revenue relationships can you form in your network?

Step 3. Assess total mission impact.

Evaluate whether the proposed activities are likely to enhance or detract from the pursuit of your goals, and assess the potential net financial gain (or loss) of each idea.

Step 4. Evaluate feasibility.

Analyze the internal capacity of your organization to conduct the required activities, considering whether you have the human re-sources and necessary experience, the financial stability and the appetite for the risk involved, as well as the likely demand for your products or services. Then assess likely funder support, which might involve making some calls to trusted funder advisors.

Step 5. Develop an action plan.

Develop a design for a pilot program, following the steps for testing introduced in part 1. Solicit feedback about the design from profes-sionals with experience in nonprofit earned-income programs as part of your testing process, perhaps by working with a paid or pro bono consultant, and also be sure to seek the advice of an attorney to assure you fully understand the tax implications.

CHAPTER 9

Optimizing Fundraising Efforts

Across the board, my survey revealed that the largest source of capital, an average 43 percent of annual revenue, for nonprofit social startups is grantmaking foundations. For organizations below $500,000 in annual revenue, the proportion of their budget coming from grants is even larger, at 52 percent. Individual donors also make up a critical percentage of income, coming in at about 20 percent overall for the organizations I surveyed.

Optimizing the time, resources and energy you spend on applying for grants and soliciting individual donors is vital, but also a very tough challenge. That's especially true for smaller organizations, given the odds they're up against. A great deal of philanthropic capital goes to larger, well-established organizations that have strong relationships with the people allocating resources. Fledgling organizations generally don't have those connections to program officers or major donors. In fact, when asked to name their top challenges in raising money from foundations, 71 percent of my survey respondents reported difficulty gaining access. Challenges with individual donors were similar: two-thirds of organizations cited securing large donations as a top challenge and 61 percent said it was getting noticed.

The methods for soliciting contributions, pursuing grants, awards and prizes are generally quite well known, even if executing well on them inevitably requires experiencing some hard knocks, and a lot of learning. Many good books and online resources that survey the landscape of foundations and competitions are available; they offer detailed guidelines for effective grant proposal writing and pitching, and strategies for individual donor outreach. Rather than offer a broad survey of best practices, I will focus here on a few key recommendations that came out of my study about how to improve results.

A number of particularly vexing difficulties came to the surface. One of the trickiest issues is deciding how much to diversify efforts. Organizational leaders can easily find themselves spread too thin, chasing after more and more grants they've discovered or trying to finish with demanding grant proposal processes while also going through the hoops of a competition, all the while working on an annual campaign soliciting individuals. On the flip side, some organizations reported nearly disastrous cases of having focused too much on one source. One of these is NBA Math Hoops, which seeks to help low-income students improve their math skills by playing a board game in which they learn the statistics of their favorite NBA and WNBA players; they form their own teams, progressing through a series of tutorials about the importance of statistics to a winning team-building strategy. As founder Khalil Fuller recounted: "We lost a funding opportunity we had been pursuing for eleven months and had every indication was going to go through." This is an all too common story. Another organization, Reach Incorporated, a nonprofit that trains teens to serve as elementary school literacy tutors, described a rocky road of having three times lost funding from one major source. The CEO told me: "We had to be honest, regroup and seek new opportunities." They then diversified their fundraising plan.

> It's important to have clear conversations with your prospective donors about whether or not you are on a path toward getting funding.

These stories underscore that it's important to have clear conversations with your prospective donors about whether or not you are on a path toward getting funding. It's also important to carefully guard yourself against wasting time in unproductive meetings with prospects. This is a particularly common problem in approaching foundations, which can often take many years to commit to a new grantee. To avoid this dance, one founder I met, Carmen Rojas of the Worker's Lab, has established a "two meeting rule" for herself. In her second meeting she asks directly whether or not the relationship is likely to lead to funding, to set expectations on all sides. We'll cover more about how to make the "ask" later in this chapter. But first, for wrestling with the diversification of your efforts, you need a good plan.

DEVELOP A MULTIYEAR STRATEGIC FUNDRAISING PLAN

All organizations in the early growth phase should surely be pursuing multiple funders, and doing so is always going to be something of a juggling act. The best way to make sure you're not overextending yourself, and that you plan your time optimally, is to develop a detailed road map that plots your efforts out by the calendar; ideally this should be a two- or three-year plan. This will help assure that you have enough prospects to yield the funding you need to meet the organization's budget goals.

Making the plan multiyear also helps with getting out of a mentality of yearly "restarts" to the fundraising cycle and of being on a relentless treadmill. Though longer-term funding can be quite difficult to secure, by at least mapping out a multiyear strategy to grow your budget, you will be better able to step back from the day-to-day grind and spot opportunities. One founder I talked to had a memorable way of discussing this issue. In 2010, Abby Falik started Global Citizen Year, which is reinventing the "gap year" between high school and college as America's launch pad for global leaders. It has raised over $15 million and grown the organization's budget to over $4 million in that time. She told me: "Most people approach nonprofit fundraising as though they're filling a bathtub spoonful by spoonful until the end of the year. And when January 1 arrives? You drain the bathtub and start over. This mentality leaves many of us constantly chasing dollars. To break this cycle, I've focused on building a revenue engine that doesn't require starting from scratch every time we hit a new year."

Typically, a process for developing a fundraising plan looks something like this:

1. Target strategically. The most successful fundraisers concentrate intensively on funding directly devoted to their mission goals, as opposed to chasing after sources that require them to bend over backward to meet funder priorities.

2. Rate your prospect list. Your list of prospective funders should include all the foundations and individual donors you've researched, and should be divided into categories by whether they are "hot" (you have had more than one meeting and they seem interested in your work), "warm" (you have had an initial conversation and need to follow up) and "cold" (no initial contact and/or connections to the funder).

3. Create a realistic gift table. Break this down into the amount of money you think you can realistically raise based on your relationships with foundations and donors and their level of resources. This is a powerful device for staying alert to not focus too much on one or another type of source. A well-diversified group of prospects might break down as in the table on the next page, with the ratios of anticipated gifts to the number of prospects based on a well-established norm that, assuming you have a compelling mission, model and pitch, you can expect to receive around one in three of the gifts you solicit.

4. Plan your outreach calendar. A general rule of thumb is that it takes six touch points throughout the year to cultivate a donor, ranging from high-touch contacts, such as an in-person meeting, lunch or hosting an event, to lower-touch, such as an e-blast, a video release, an impact report or an end-of-year letter. Develop a personalized outreach plan for each of your prospects that calendars each of the six touch points. With this disciplined basic game plan, you can step back to consider trying out a number of innovative approaches to fundraising.

Gift Level	# of Gifts	# of Prospects	Amount
$100,000	1	3	$100,000
$50,000	2	6	$100,000
$25,000	4	12	$100,000
$10,000	8	24	$80,000
$5,000	15	45	$75,000
$1,000	45	135	$45,000
TOTAL			**$500,000**

Sample Gift Table. *Source:* Adapted from *Fundraising Fundamentals*, Section 6.4, Higher Education Funding Council for England; available at http://www.case .org/Publications_and_Products/Fundraising_Fundamentals_Intro.html.

CONSIDER COLLABORATION, *CAREFULLY*

In recent years, the concept that nonprofits should collaborate to apply for grants has been widely promoted. The idea is that crafting collaborations in programming allows organizations to optimize their impact while also optimizing the cost-effectiveness of foundation money. This trend toward collaborative funding has risen hand in hand with the theory of collective impact, which argues that organizations cannot change the larger economic and political factors behind social problems, unless they work together with a common agenda and engage in mutually reinforcing activities.

Championed in an influential 2011 *Stanford Social Innovation Review* article titled "Collective Impact," by John Kania and Mark Kramer of the FSG consultancy, the argument has inspired many organizations to try new forms of collaboration.[1] And funders are taking notice. Grantmakers for Effective Organizations argues, for example, that "grantmakers achieve far greater impact by partnering with other organizations in pursuit of common goals and providing grantees with support for collaborative efforts."[2] A 2014 survey about nonprofit collaboration conducted by the Bridgespan Group found that "both nonprofit and philanthropic leaders expressed a great deal of appetite for participating in or supporting future collaborations," and that evaluations by nonprofit CEOs of collaborations their organizations engaged in, as well as those of funders that backed collaborations, were quite positive overall.[3] The authors of a report on the study write that "the most surprising finding was the overwhelming success that CEOs ascribed to the collaborations they participated in and that foundation officers ascribed to those they funded—70 percent or better in both cases."[4]

But caution is advised. The reason the authors say the findings were a surprise is that collaborations can be fraught with complications. Looking into opportunities to secure grant money through collaboration is definitely advised, but organizations should do so very strategically, and must go into collaborations with eyes wide open about how hard they can be to manage.

One collaboration that navigated the complexities of partnership with ultimate success was the effort among California Pacific Medical Center (CPMC), the Center for Youth Wellness (CYW), the San Francisco Child Abuse Prevention Center (the Prevention Center) and Tipping Point Community (Tipping Point) to create an integrated center for children's health, wellness and advocacy.

The concept launched in 2008 when city leaders asked the Prevention Center to lead an initiative to create a children's advocacy center for victims of child abuse: a center that would promote justice and healing by conducting forensic interviews in a child-friendly and safe location, embedded with mental health and victim advocates to avoid repeated trauma to the child. In some communities, the welfare system required victims to report their story repeatedly, sometimes to more than a dozen parties—their teacher, a school counselor, a child protective services social worker, the police, a doctor, a nurse, a mental health professional, the district attorney, the city attorney, their own lawyer—before these various agencies could develop a plan to ensure the safety of the child. City leaders and the Prevention Center envisioned a "one stop shop," a national best practice, where children could tell their story directly to a trained and licensed expert in the privacy of a specifically designed, developmentally appropriate setting, while the other agencies that needed to hear the child's story listened behind a two-way mirror. The children would receive everything from immediate health care treatment to mental health support in one place. The idea had been developed for decades, but the Prevention Center needed the right time to rally the necessary funding and community support to achieve such an audacious goal.

At the same time, Dr. Nadine Burke Harris was envisioning a new center to promote the wellness of children living in San Francisco's Bayview neighborhood who had been impacted by adverse childhood experiences (ACEs). Through her pediatric practice, Burke Harris had been caring for children whose life expectancy and health were negatively impacted when the adversity they experienced—abuse, neglect, exposure to violence in their homes or on the streets, drug use, incarcerated parents, loss, grief, or the simple fact of poverty—led to the chronic overactivity of their biological stress response, a condition called "toxic stress." Having founded CPMC's Bayview Child Health Center, a pediatric clinic to support Bayview families, she was now working to launch the Center for Youth Wellness to focus on averting the long-term health consequences of childhood adversity.

Later that same year, then–San Francisco district attorney Kamala Harris brought together Prevention Center executive director Katie Albright and Burke Harris, suggesting they collaborate. District Attorney Harris knew kids needed a safe start in life to ensure they succeeded in school, avoided risky behavior and stayed out of jail. Albright and Burke Harris had not worked together in the past, but shared the common goal to keep children safe from trauma. They decided to partner.

Albright and Burke Harris, along with their colleagues, spent hours envisioning what an integrated children's wellness and advocacy center, which joined the pediatric focus of the Bayview Child Health Center, the trauma-focus of the Center for Youth Wellness, and the healing and justice focus of the Children's Advocacy Center, might look like. They calculated that it would require millions of dollars in seed funding and massive collaboration, not only among their organizations but also with the local hospitals, other government agencies and funders. They determined that the best way to secure funding would be to partner with an existing funder who would champion their project. They turned to Tipping Point, which had funded both programs and was invested in improving the lives of underserved children in San Francisco. CEO of Tipping Point Daniel Lurie was immediately drawn to the joint project and led his organization to raise an extraordinary $4 million from individual donors at its annual gala event.

Within two years, the partners successfully opened the dream center they had envisioned. The warm, welcoming and vibrant community space was child-centered and family friendly. The Bayview Clinic and the Center for Youth Wellness occupied the second floor, working together to provide coordinated health care for all children in the community; and the Children's Advocacy Center occupied the light-filled third floor to provide state-of-the art, one-stop services for kids who had had an acute experience of abuse or neglect. At the grand opening, Lurie issued a warm welcome to attendees including the mayor, the chief of police and health care executives.

This milestone event came on the heels of the partners' navigation of substantial challenges behind the scenes. Though they had come together to create an integrated center, the organizations themselves were not operationally integrated. The partners realized that while they held similar values and a shared agenda to keep children in San Francisco safe from violence and trauma, they had very different immediate goals. The CYW was focused on the national agenda of how to treat ACEs and, as a startup, was in the process of raising additional seed money to launch its organization. The Prevention Center, an established organization serving San Francisco's community for decades, was focused on local partnerships and the best practices of running a children's advocacy center. This led to conflicts regarding timelines and priorities. Though the partners had done extensive planning on fundraising and communications for their shared agenda, creating a one-stop health and wellness center for families, they hadn't agreed on how best to make it clear to external stakeholders and donors when they were communicating about the partnership and when they were talking about a specific agenda for their individual organization.

When a new funder came calling, how was it determined whether they should be directed to the partnership, and what were partners to do if it seemed like the donors' interests were more aligned with the initiative of an individual organization? When news media came calling, which program would be spotlighted? Perhaps the biggest challenge became apparent in the area of donor stewardship; the groups had been so successful at creating a united front that donors ended up confused as to which organization they were supporting, a key question in San Francisco's relatively small community, where organizations often relied on funding from many of the same donors. This lack of clarity became problematic when Albright and Burke Harris later approached donors for their individual fundraising efforts.

To carry them through these sometimes challenging issues, the two organizations kept their end vision in mind: providing best-in-class pediatric, mental health, forensic and advocacy programs under one roof; ensuring excellent services to families and the community; and launching a national agenda to focus on raising awareness about the impact of adverse childhood experiences.

Albright and Burke Harris ultimately decided to cease joint fundraising and communications efforts to avoid confusion among donors and key stakeholders. Each developed messaging to help donors clearly understand the scope of their work, so donors could clearly understand what each organization was offering. Though the partners continue to collaborate on some core functions, they do so via "back office" partnerships, with members of their staff working closely to ensure that families have a seamless experience, and fund these initiatives from their individual operating budgets.

Despite the challenges, they have accomplished much of their original vision. Their work and collaboration serves as a national model. In 2016, the Prevention Center secured additional funds to purchase their building and secure a permanent home for their collective work.

While they know that their work is not done, they could not have gotten this far without working together. As Albright stated: "The Children's Advocacy Center and our haven for children in the Bayview is more impressive and more visionary than I could have imagined because our two organizations, with the support and guidance of Tipping Point, pushed each other to dream big." Their partnership ultimately led to bigger funding sources to support their visionary idea, which they would not have been able to pull off on their own.

To consider organizations that might be especially well-suited collaborators, you can start with a competitive analysis. Organizations are generally very well aware of who their direct competitors are, both in seeking funding and in serving beneficiaries; considering more broadly the landscape of organizations that have overlapping missions, and particularly those offering complementary services, is a good mechanism for organizations to identify the ones with whom they can develop jointly beneficial programs. One way to start is by looking at other organizations in your domain that your existing funders are also funding, as the Center for Youth Wellness and San Francisco Child Abuse Prevention Center did with Tipping Point.

Before entering into an agreement, both organizations must carefully consider the value each is adding, and create a plan for dividing up the work, which should include detailed written expectations of everyone's role, including whether the organizations plan to have joint decision-making authority or whether one organization, often referred to as the "backbone organization," will take that lead role.[5] Finally, organizations should create a plan for fundraising both individually and collaboratively going forward to avoid confusing their donors.

> The range of funders is so vast, and their priorities differ so much, that organizations simply do not need to see each other as inherent competitors; they should feel free to share advice and connections.

SHARE FUNDER INTRODUCTIONS

The challenges of formally collaborating with people at other organizations may not appeal to you, but you can still gain a great deal of assistance from them; leaders at peer nonprofits can be a font of valuable information regarding funders to pursue, personal introductions, and ideas for successful strategies they've employed. The range of funders is so vast, and their priorities differ so much, that organizations simply do not need to see each other as inherent competitors; they should feel free to share advice and connections. While those in the nonprofit sector involved in fundraising have learned very well that they have to make the "ask" to foundations and private donors, many are not optimizing the opportunities to ask one another for creative problem-solving assistance in pursuing grant money.

Correcting this omission is a goal of Natalie Bridgeman Fields, founder of Accountability Counsel. As a veteran Echoing Green fellow, having won a fellowship in 2009 that helped her start her organization, she has taught an Echoing Green workshop to incoming and seasoned fellows on the importance of maximizing peer relationships to help connect them to funders. She divides twenty-five classroom participants into groups of five based on the issue areas they support. She then tells them to look to their left, look to their right, and recognize that these are the people who are going to be their biggest fundraising allies. Fields then asks everyone to find a partner sharing issue overlap and have a discussion reviewing their current funders, exchanging their views of which might be good prospects for the other person, for example, if the funder is supporting a related aspect of their peer's work. Following her example, as you do this, in addition to tapping your existing network of organization founders and staff, you can also check foundations' portfolios to see if you know people at other funder organizations who may be good candidates for offering recommendations.

In her workshops, Fields encourages the fellows to limit their requests for introductions to one or two funders, to minimize the work they're requesting, and that they include a brief explanation of why they think the funder would be a good fit. Note that such explanations may be the basis of a pitch template you can largely cut and paste into an email to the funder. Perhaps most important, those making the ask should always offer to reciprocate, and in fact be proactive in doing so. In cases where people demure, perhaps telling you they don't feel comfortable recommending a funder, or that they have a delicate relationship with the funder you're asking them to help connect with, it is important to respect their preference and not push them further.

Another method of building up a network of peer support is to create a team of peer executive directors in your issue area and meet with them once a month to compare notes about new funding opportunities, and successes and failures and creative approaches others have taken. Your current funders are also your best allies in providing introductions to other funders in their circle who may be interested in hearing about your work. If they fund you already they are likely to be some of your biggest champions.

In short, you do not have to be so alone in the fundraising endeavor, but the onus is on you to surround yourself with people who can help you.

GETTING COMFORTABLE WITH THE "ASK"

One of the hardest aspects of approaching funders is that personal relationships with donors, which many young leaders do not have, are so important. Additionally, there is an unwritten set of "rules of the game" that more experienced organizational leaders and those who have developed strong connections, perhaps by getting a degree in the field or through family, can leverage. Author Chris Rabb writes about these personal resources in his book *Invisible Capital: How Unseen Forces Shape Entrepreneurial Opportunity*, which I highly recommend.[6] He discusses how success in entrepreneurship, whether in the private or public sectors, can be largely attributed to the ability to tap such a set of connections; being well versed in the unwritten rules; and having a high level of comfort with making pitches, because of that web of connections and general savvy. Women and people of color are particularly disadvantaged when it comes to "invisible" capital; in fact, data from Echoing Green 2016 applicants shows that male-run U.S.-based organizations that have reached a proof of concept stage report raising twice as much money as those run by women.[7] This trend is also displayed when comparing U.S.-based organizations run by self-identified white and black applicants: in 2016, 56 percent of white applicants had already raised funds at the time of application, whereas only 36 percent of black applicants had reached the same milestone.

This is a key reason why fellowships and competitions, such as those sponsored by Echoing Green, Draper Richards Kaplan, Ashoka and so many others, are valuable. They go way beyond the monetary support provided, offering not only top-quality coaching but greatly helping to open the door to other funders. I think a less appreciated aspect of their rewards is that they also introduce recipients to a network of peers, whether in the current group of recipients or those from past years; these peers can be wonderful resources for advice about the challenges of growing an organization (e.g., how to get introductions to funders and learning how to make a good "ask"). As Cheryl Dorsey, the CEO of Echoing Green, says, "The gaps in capital and in the perception of who is fundable are a reality that entrepreneurs face that slow social progress. To mitigate some of that, we leverage our network and facilitate peer-to-peer learning and support among our fellows. Our role is to not only to support the ongoing development of our fellows, but also to build out this social innovation ecosystem where these barriers are confronted, understood and dismantled to give these leaders their best chances to achieve."

Those fellowships and awards are, of course, extremely competitive. There are over three thousand organizations applying for just twenty-five spots in the Echoing Green seed-stage fellowship, for example. And even experienced social entrepreneurs who have made it into these networks through winning a fellowship or prize may continue to struggle with a lack of invisible capital.

One founder who generously shared about her challenges with this issue is Gemma Bulos, who cofounded A Single Drop for Safe Water. The organization provides technical and organizational expertise to help villages and municipalities identify, design, build and manage their own community-driven water projects. Bulos showed enormous courage in building the organization. She had no intention of becoming a social entrepreneur when she got the idea, and had no training or special connections in the field, but she acted vigorously to capitalize on a serendipitous turn of events.

Bulos was a preschool teacher in New York City by day and a jazz singer by night. On September 11, 2001, she was supposed to be at the World Trade Center for a meeting, but she called in sick. In response to the tragedy she wrote a song called "We Rise," inspired by the way New Yorkers came together and celebrated their goodness and generosity. Then she quit her jobs and began traveling around the world to build the Million Voice Choir, eventually mobilizing voices from a hundred cities and sixty countries to sing "We Rise" at a designated time on September 21, 2004, to celebrate the UN International Day of Peace and the Global Cease Fire Day. Because the song uses the metaphor "it takes a single drop of water to start a wave," it became her rallying cry to bring people together in peace, and Bulos began getting calls to present at water conferences, including the UN Water for Life Conference.

At the time, she knew virtually nothing about the water crisis afflicting so many communities around the world. But as she discovered the importance of developing strong water, sanitation and hygiene practices (WASH), she learned how to build simple clean water technologies. She went back to her native Philippines to help develop a training program for women about water, sanitation and technology. She drew on her personal connections there for early support, and within a year was able to win an Echoing Green fellowship, as well as contracts with the Canadian embassy, UNICEF and OXFAM, even though she didn't know anyone at any of those organizations. She had simply cold-called them and asked, "Who should I talk to about my project?" The work of A Single Drop of Safe Water continues to touch the lives of tens of thousands of people annually.

After four years, Bulos left the organization in the Philippines when it reached the milestone of no longer being dependent on charitable aid; she set her sights on taking the training model to communities in Africa and cofounded Global Women's Water Initiative. Even though she followed all the right steps, launching pilot programs with groups of women in Kenya, Uganda and Tanzania, and producing strong data about their effectiveness, this time the fundraising was much more difficult. She didn't feel as comfortable approaching funders in the United States as she had in the Philippines. She told me that as a Filipina American she "felt personal insecurities about being brown around rich, white people, and about not having a relevant college degree," despite the numerous social entrepreneur awards she's won and the significant impact her programs had had. Her immigrant parents had instilled in her the values of being hardworking, self-reliant and not asking for help. Help equaled "begging" in her mind, and that affected her view of fundraising. She told me that she had trouble thinking of herself as a "fundraiser" and said, "I know that I could be a good fundraiser if I wanted, but I haven't been able to click into it, and I'm still figuring out how to approach it without feeling like I'm begging."

While Global Women's Water Initiative is going strong and having enormous award-winning impact on the communities they work with in East Africa, fundraising remains a challenge, and Bulos still isn't able to pay herself a salary, prioritizing program delivery over a paycheck. She works a separate day job to sustain the organization, which she runs in the evenings and weekends.

So many founders deal with the same kinds of insecurities and discomfort about fundraising that Bulos felt so deeply, despite her astonishing success and the courage with which she made those early cold-calls to funders. There are numerous psychological and emotional challenges nonprofit leaders face when forced to ask for money, which stem from societal taboos associated with discussing money, fear of rejection, power imbalances and embarrassment about "being in need," to name a few.[8]

In her popular Harvard class Exponential Fundraising, Jennifer Mc-Crea promotes a mental shift by nonprofit leaders to begin thinking differently about their relationships with money and with donors. As McCrea told me, most people start by infusing money with values like scarcity and control. With this mentality, money becomes a dark, scary thing. McCrea explains: "If you grew up in a family that equates money with safety, when you ask people for money you may feel like you are asking them for their safety." To solve this problem, she suggests "recasting fundraising as a dynamic relationship between organizations and their philanthropic partners that is designed from the start to be cocreative and generative." She encourages nonprofit leaders to start thinking of foundations as part of their philanthropic team of "partners" as opposed to donors—a way to shift the power dynamic, putting the work at the center of the relationship as opposed to the money. After all, everyone has the same goal of making social change, and arguably the nonprofit leaders have an even more critical role in that journey than the funders.

Even once you make that mental shift, you can't get around having to make the ask of donors for their financial support. McCrea provides some examples of tips she gives to make the ask less scary, including things like making one ask a day to develop the asking "muscle." As she says, "An ask simply requires twenty seconds of courage, so just try it."

Another of her tips is to think about resources in terms of abundance. It's so easy to say that social entrepreneurs must be bold in asking for financial support, and of course it's a whole lot harder to do, especially when pitching the biggest name funders. But it must be said that working hard to develop your confidence in asking for introductions and making pitches is likely to pay off in spades. Again and again in my meetings with breakout organizational leaders, I was impressed by their spirit of fearless determination and their attitude that financial resources are plentiful if you are bold enough to go after them with confidence.

One such founder is Abby Falik. When I asked her how she's been so successful in growing Global Citizen Year to over $4 million in annual revenues so fast, she insisted it is because she approaches her work from a perspective that founders have to be bold and committed to scaling their impact to the size of the problems they're trying to solve. She says that when she sits with very early stage social entrepreneurs, she can usually spot those who seem likely to "break through" based on their ability to think and act, without constraints.

Laura Weidman Powers, the cofounder of Code2040, told me that from the very beginning, she felt Code2040 was "a huge organization living in the body of a small organization," and that this mindset affected every interaction she had from the start. A great example is that after Google and Apple released their abysmal diversity numbers, Powers asked a board member for an introduction to Jeff Weiner, the CEO of LinkedIn, and invited him to dinner so she could discuss Code2040's approach to inclusive hiring. He agreed. She told me: "My mentality has always been that of course I should be going out to dinner with people like Jeff Weiner, because we are on the forefront of a movement that is much bigger than ourselves." This confidence also led her cofounder Tristan Walker to ask high-powered venture capitalist Ben Horowitz of Andreessen Horowitz to be on the board of Code2040. He agreed, and Horowitz has been instrumental to the organization's credibility, access and growth.

Jennifer Pitts from the founding team at Tipping Point told me: "When you ask an organization, 'What would you do if you had $10 million?' there's a big difference between the CEOs who can give you an immediate answer and the ones that get stuck. At Tipping Point, our job was to really push people to think big, because this is where the exciting stuff comes out."

Such a confident mindset is second nature to some social entrepreneurs, of course, but for those who struggle with boldly making
the ask, it's vital to develop the muscles. This mindset shift has been
incredibly helpful to Gemma Bulos. She now realizes that one reason she was spinning her wheels was that she was mostly chasing
smaller donations in the $5,000 to $10,000 range, which took much
too much time. Meanwhile, she knew they weren't going to get her
over the funding hump to scale the organization to sustainability.
She has begun to ask for bigger grants, which she finds makes donors take her more seriously, and results in bigger payoffs.

GET OTHERS TO MAKE THE ASK FOR YOU

When someone mentions a nonprofit fundraiser, we immediately
conjure up an image of people sitting around banquet tables in a
downtown hotel eating dinner or looking at their watches as they
listen to a program where people talk far too long, albeit about
important social issues. The top-performing social startups have
turned this kind of "rubber chicken" fundraising dinner into a
thing of the past. Fundraising 2.0 involves a much more creative approach to raising money from individuals that taps into a broader
audience, increasing organizations' pie of donations. For example,
John Wood, the founder of Room to Read, developed a model where
other people would actually become actively involved in fundraising for Room to Read.

John Wood has become a fundraising legend. Some of the social
entrepreneurs I interviewed even said they try to channel Wood in
their meetings with individual donors, asking themselves, What
would John Wood do in this situation? How much money would
he ask for? Wood's success in breaking the mold of nonprofit fundraising is perhaps attributable to his roots in the corporate world,
as a former executive at Microsoft. When he first described his idea,
many people told him his model would never work, that it wasn't

sustainable to try to raise money from individuals for libraries. He insisted that he was selling something donors wanted, and that if he packaged it in the right way, to create a one-to-one connection between the donors and the individuals they were supporting, they would eagerly respond. According to Room to Read's cofounder Erin Ganju, that packaging was really important to the organization's success with individuals. "We started a model where you could support a school, you could support a library, you could support a local-language book being published in Nepal or Vietnam, and you knew exactly where that $5,000 or $10,000 check was going, and even got a couple of reports back throughout the year with photos of the school library being set up in that school or children reading those books." This approach made donors feel strongly connected to the mission and the results.

Room to Read's supporters felt so connected, in fact, that they wanted to do more. The organization started setting up chapters across the country and around the world to engage their supporters in raising even more money for the organization. These volunteer fundraisers commit to participating in geographic chapters based in cities around the world. Each chapter has a couple of leaders that go to San Francisco every year, at their own expense, for a leadership conference where Room to Read helps them develop their annual plan for their individual market. For example, they decide how many events they want to do, who their target audience is and how much money they plan to raise from them. In addition, Room to Read uses the gathering as an opportunity to energize these champions, much like a corporate annual sales conference, sharing motivating stories about the organization's impact they can take back to their chapters, and revealing the organization's key objectives for the year. The chapter model has been so successful for Room to Read that they now have chapters in over sixteen countries in over forty cities, which in close collaboration with their staff help raise about 25 percent of the organization's $50 million annual budget.

INCREASE THE PHILANTHROPIC PIE

Another way you can try to increase donations from individuals is by being responsive to the skepticism many potential donors feel about how nonprofits would spend their money. This was a key to the success of charity: water, which builds wells and other water projects to bring clean drinking water to people in developing countries. Charity: water's New York City gala events, which raise millions of dollars in one night, have become the envy of many in the nonprofit world. But a vital early strategic choice founder Scott Harrison made about soliciting funds was a lynchpin to early growth.

At the time he was starting the organization, Harrison learned a startling statistic: 43 percent of Americans distrust charity. When he asked friends about their views, many said, "I don't know where my money goes" or "Charities are black holes, and very little money actually reaches the people who need it." This inspired him to innovate a new funding approach with which to target that 43 percent of nongivers, one where a few major donors or board members covered operating expenses so that other donor contributions went directly to cover program expenses, like building water wells; this left no doubt as to how their money would be used. This form of fundraising is now commonly called the "100 percent model."

Harrison also innovated by applying the standards of for-profit advertising to building the charity: water brand. His first hire after a program officer was a creative director. While many people in the sector balk at spending money on nonprofit marketing, Harrison sees it as a necessary way to engage people in the cause. "A junk food company can spend hundreds of millions of dollars on marketing food that is killing us," he told me, "and the most important life-saving causes in the world have these anemic brands, ineffective websites and a poverty mentality that they can't look too good, or else people will think they are spending the money unwisely." It wasn't that the organization was pouring significant money into marketing, but by being scrappy and creative, while also being conscious of branding, charity: water was able to achieve enormous success from word of mouth.

Harrison has continued to innovate, also developing creative ways his donors could get other people to give. For example, with the birthday donation program, donors can ask their friends on Facebook to donate the amount of their age ($35 for a thirty-five-year-old) in lieu of throwing a big party or accepting gifts. They also host an annual gala called charity: ball. One feature, which drew a great deal of press coverage a few years back, was asking guests to walk down a fashion show–like catwalk, referred to as the "waterwalk," with two yellow five-gallon jerry cans of water to simulate what it's like for those who have to walk miles a day with these jugs to provide water for their families. More recently, they made five hundred virtual reality headsets available at their event so that all five hundred guests could experience "being" in Ethiopia together at the same time. Collectively, these efforts have allowed the organization to raise over $240 million in the ten years since their founding.

Scott Harrison is certainly not alone. Every single organization I spent time with during my study has brought great creativity to raising money. Harrison has helped raise the game in a number of ways, and all organizations can apply that kind of ingenuity to doing the same.

BENCHMARKS FOR SOCIAL STARTUP SUCCESS: FUNDING

✓ Does your organization have a clear mission that your staff and board can easily describe?

✓ Have you gathered your staff, board and/or external stakeholders to brainstorm potential earned-income sources?

✓ Have you tested charging your beneficiaries for services you already provide?

✓ Are there any third parties—government entities or companies—invested in your case that might be willing to pay for services you already provide?

✓ Do you have a multiyear fundraising plan?

✓ Have you assessed your organizational capacity to ensure you have the capacity within the organization—human resources, financial stability, appetite for risk—to achieve your fundraising goals?

✓ Is your funding model consistent with your organizational mission and values as opposed to detracting from them?

✓ Have you engaged an attorney to explore potential legal structures (i.e., nonprofit, for profit or a hybrid combination) to accomplish your goals?

✓ Have you created a realistic gift table with a corresponding prospect list?

✓ Have you developed an outreach calendar with a personalized outreach plan for each prospect on your list?

✓ Have you considered collaborating with other organizations to pursue joint funding?

✓ Have you connected with peers and/or existing funders to brainstorm foundation introductions they may be able to make for you?

✓ Have you assessed your plan to make sure you are dreaming big?

✓ Have you, your staff and/or your board practiced making an ask with trusted colleagues?

✓ Have you considered other champions for the organization who may be willing to fundraise on your behalf?

✓ Have you considered fundraising from potentially untapped sources?

PART 4

LEADING
COLLABORATIVELY

One of the trickiest challenges in scaling any organization is that you suddenly have to start managing people. A founder usually works like a whirling dervish to get things off the ground, either alone or with a partner, playing all roles: program director, publicist, fundraiser, finance manager and receptionist. But before long, to keep growing, it's imperative to start hiring people and creating a management structure. My study showed this was the area in which most founders believed they had made the most mistakes. Probing into the problems they reported, I discovered there were three key errors they made: (1) continuing to play too dominant a role in the messaging about the organization and in running it; (2) failing to hire people with the right expertise at the right time; and (3) appointing the wrong people to the board. The leaders of breakthrough social startups had done a better job of managing these challenges, though many of them had also made these mistakes at first and had to make course corrections. In this set of chapters, we'll explore the leadership approaches and specific methods of team building that allowed organizational leaders to free up their time so they could focus on top priorities such as fundraising and strategic planning. We'll also learn how they hired the right people to do the right jobs at the right time, and fostered a high level of engagement and commitment to the mission. Finally, we'll see how some leaders created truly active boards, with expertise the organization needed, and how invaluable that can be in navigating leadership challenges.

CHAPTER 10

Cultivating Collective Leadership

One of the liabilities of starting a social enterprise is succumbing to the pressures of the "cult of the social entrepreneur." Founders have become a new type of celebrity. Think about Teach For America's Wendy Kopp and Toms Shoes founder Blake Mycoskie. When the media tells the stories of successful organizations, the emphasis is usually placed squarely on the remarkable passion and drive of their founders, as though they alone made the organizations work. The many prizes and fellowships given to founders from Echoing Green, the Draper Richards Kaplan Foundation, the Schwab Foundation, Ashoka, the Skoll Foundation and others, though certainly to be applauded, also contribute to the glamorization of founders. The effects are pernicious, fostering a "trying to be superhuman" syndrome among founders, and also leaving the crucial contributions of other staff out of the limelight. Every successful founder will tell you they couldn't possibly have made their idea work if it weren't for the incredible contributions of their staff.

There is no question that founders of social enterprises must be prepared to be the face of the organization, at least in the early growth phase. They've got to take a leading role in fashioning the message and spreading it, as well as in meeting with funders to build support. But they've also got to learn to distribute responsibility for building the organization and credit for doing so throughout all levels of staff. Early on, they've got to shift some of the weight from their own shoulders. And they've got to provide all those working for the organization with meaningful opportunities to contribute, and to see the difference their contributions are making. In a study of top-performing nonprofit organizations, Leslie Crutchfield and Heather McLeod Grant found that "wise CEOs recognize that they must share power if they are to unleash and magnify the potential of their organizations. They learn to let go to have greater impact."[1] Similarly, my study found that for early-stage organizations in particular, collective leadership is critical to allowing the CEO to focus on the fundraising and strategic planning efforts that fuel growth.

As the great leadership scholar Warren Bennis once said, "There are two ways of being creative. One can sing and dance. Or one can create an environment in which singers and dancers can flourish."[2] To distribute responsibility and to create an environment in which people feel empowered and appreciated, and where social creativity flourishes, leaders can draw on one of the most important innovations in business leadership in recent years: doing away with the rigid top-down hierarchical leadership model that came to dominate business in the twentieth century, and giving staff more autonomy and decision-making authority.

REVERSING THE PYRAMID

Many of the most dynamic organizations I studied are incorporating elements of the "reverse pyramid" leadership structure. The inverted leadership model was spearheaded by the Nordstrom department store chain because, as Jim Nordstrom says in *The Nordstrom Way*: "People will work hard when they are given the freedom to do their job in the way they think it should be done, when they treat customers the way they like to be treated. When you take away their incentive and start giving them rules, boom, you've killed their creativity."[3] Recognizing that an engaged sales staff that felt respected and empowered was the key lever to driving up revenue,

Customers

Sales and Support People

Department Managers

Store Managers, Buyers,
Regional Managers,
General Managers

Board of
Directors

The Nordstrom Reverse Pyramid Model Where Everyone in the Company Works to Support the Sales Staff. *Source*: Robert Spector and Patrick D. McCarthy, *The Nordstrom Way.*

Nordstrom leadership gave them more autonomy in their day-to-day work, and also asked for their views about potential improvements in the company.

This same reverse pyramid has been adopted by many technology companies in Silicon Valley, such as Netflix, because it makes them more nimble, able to adapt more readily to the rapid-fire changes they're constantly facing in their businesses. They can make decisions more quickly, and more good ideas for improvements to products and services are proposed by staff, because people understand that leadership will hear their voices and actually listen to them. What's more, employees are energized by a new sense of purpose, trust and appreciation.

Some of the social entrepreneurs I talked to also have put more decision-making responsibility in the hands of staff, at all levels, and they told me that doing so paves the way for fast growth. One of these is Premal Shah, who came on board as CEO of Kiva in 2006, after working as an executive at PayPal for several years. After Kiva founders Jessica Jackley and Matt Flannery appeared on the *Oprah*

Winfrey Show in 2007, Kiva went into growth overdrive. Shah says he felt he had no choice but to rely heavily on his frontline staff and volunteers to help steer the ship. He told me: "If I were to distill Kiva's leadership style down to its essence, now that we have a hundred staff and about five hundred volunteers at any point in time, it's all about ownership and allowing our staff to act like owners."

One way Kiva does this is to have employees decide on and manage their own metrics. They also allow staff to show those metrics in a very public way, such as at staff meetings or on their internal website, a wiki where anyone on the team can update it at any time, so the team can learn from how others are succeeding as well as failing. As Shah describes it: "It is a very low cost, and simple thing, but it's so essential to help equip people to learn from the past, preserve their institutional knowledge and feel like they have a resource to turn to when they feel over their head."

Some of the social entrepreneurs I talked to also have put more decision-making responsibility in the hands of staff, at all levels, and they told me that doing so paves the way for fast growth.

Another organizational leader who emphasizes the importance of staff developing its own metrics is Nick Ehrmann of Blue Engine, the teacher-mentoring program based in New York City. He says doing so is not just about empowerment; it's also a more effective way to gauge whether the programs are actually working. "I used to look at the data and come up with theories with our program director about why something was or wasn't working. Now it's upside down. Frontline staff are the experts; they're driving all of the theories up and determining what they think is happening and then I chime in after that." In addition to being a more accurate interpretation of an organization's performance, Ehrmann says this way of measuring success also builds a collective responsibility to learn and get better. When people are in charge of their own metrics, all of a sudden "the purpose of data isn't some kind of pure accountability mechanism to distinguish between people who fail and people who succeed. It's about how can we all succeed together."

Hand in hand with devolving authority, the leadership must also foster a sense of accountability and responsibility. As Nordstrom wrote on page 1 of the chain's employee handbook, that essentially comes down to inspiring people to "use good judgment."[4] One way to foster responsibility is by creating more mechanisms for transparency about operations and for giving feedback. Kiva has established structured feedback loops, not just top-down from the boss, but horizontally in every direction. One example of how they solicit feedback is a ritual they call Kiva Love: every month they pass a microfilm recorder around the entire office, and staff members praise each other for acts of courage and things they've done to be selfless, which might have affected their own metric negatively, but advanced the whole. According to Shah: "This horizontal accountability system appears to be much more impactful than our standard performance management system. Whatever we can do to continue to make it easier for people to see and recognize each other horizontally and support each other seems to support this notion that everyone is an owner and should act like an owner, and as Nordstrom would put it, 'use good judgment.'"

Technology provides many great ways to establish more transparency. One example is a method used by Watsi, a crowdfunding platform for people with health care needs around the world. Watsi was launched three years ago in the Y Combinator accelerator (an intensive coaching program for early-stage companies culminating in a Demo Day where they present their ideas to a by-invitation-only audience) and has now recruited 21,733 donors to fund life-changing health care for 10,789 people. To put as much information as possible in the hands of their staff, the organization has created group emails for each department, and every time a team member sends an email, internally or externally, they are required to bcc (blind carbon copy) the list. People of course don't read every single email, but anyone at the organization can subscribe to any list, and that way learn all about what each department is working on at any time. This radical transparency has been critical to empowering the staff at every level to feel connected to the work of everyone at the organization.

BE AN EGOLESS LEADER

A culture of collective leadership involves not only how the organization is structured and the allocation of responsibility, but also the style of leadership from the top. Here the key is what Harvard Business School professor Linda Hill dubbed "leading from behind." She was drawing on a phrase used by South African president and legendary leader of the movement against apartheid, Nelson Mandela. He wrote that a great leader "stays behind the flock, letting the most nimble go out ahead, whereupon the others follow, not realizing that all along they are being directed from behind." Hill argues that this leadership style is the best way to motivate people and to unleash their creative potential.

One founder who works hard to try to lead from behind is Rob Gitin of At The Crossroads. After Gitin's cofounder decided to leave the organization to attend medical school in 2001, Gitin found himself struggling to manage operations. He decided to build a culture of collective leadership in which everyone deeply understood the mission, was dedicated to furthering it, and was given responsibility and credit for the organization's success. My visit to the offices clearly conveyed how successfully he's fostered a spirit of engagement and empowerment. The energy in the room exuded wholehearted passion. Indeed, every desk and corner of the office displayed client mementos. Some of the staff have been with the team for ten years or more.

It's important to highlight that, as Linda Hill writes: "Leading from behind doesn't mean abrogating your leadership responsibilities." The heads of social startups absolutely do need to be public promoters. Appearing in media stories, speaking at conferences and generally presenting a charming, charismatic public face for the organization's larger mission are vital. Founders must usually also take primary responsibility for strategic planning and fund-raising, at least at the start. Funders usually expect to meet with founders, for example, rather than other staff.

Rob Gitin has certainly taken all his responsibilities as founder of At The Crossroads seriously. But being a strong leader who is the face and voice of an organization in no way rules out also putting the spotlight on others and attributing success to them. Gitin has often purposefully deflected attention from himself to the organization as a whole. "When you are a founder," he told me, "people identify you as the organization. I have been conscious that the less important I make myself, the stronger and more sustainable the organization is." Asked how he's done that, he offered a number of insights. "Part of it is using 'we' language rather than 'I' language, saying 'we are engaging in this process' rather than 'I am leading this process.'" That goes for communication outside the organization as well, such as in meetings with funders or even clients. For example, if a client says to someone on the team, "You are the only person that really cares for me," counselors are trained to respond, "Yes I do care about you, and there is an entire team of people at this organization that care about you too." Gitin acknowledged that it's important for founders and executive directors to build a high public profile, and that "you have to be comfortable using your status to open doors, but as soon as you walk through those doors, you start making the conversation about the organization."

Gitin is constantly creating ways to put his staff out in front so he can lead from behind. He tries to identify when he is the only one who has a relationship with a partner or a supporter and takes his staff members to meetings with that person so they too can develop their own relationship. When ATC publishes its biannual newsletter, Gitin makes sure the stories mention staff members other than himself, so readers can hear their voices and appreciate that it's not just him, but a whole team of experts making the organization work. For example, in a recent newsletter, ATC highlighted the story of a client named Bubbles, whose five children ended up in adoptive families after she became homeless due to drug addition. Bubbles has been working with ATC for sixteen years to transform her life. The newsletter highlights the work of ATC's program manager Shawn Garety to develop the relationship with Bubbles. As Shawn says, "Bubbles' profound wisdom, sharp wit and tenacity have kept me and ATC on our toes, laughing through and through. Over the years, we have been able to find humor in the darkest and brightest of our times together." By highlighting Garety's strong personal relationship with her clients, Gitin allowed her to take center stage, as opposed to hogging it for himself. He's realized that not only is this important from a morale perspective, to make the staff feel appreciated, but also from a practical perspective. He explains: "It's dangerous if I'm the only person talking to the outside world, because it creates a bottleneck." Now, instead of Gitin having a line of people waiting to meet with him, At The Crossroads accomplishes much more with multiple team members acting as the faces of the organization, including Garety.

Gitin is also continuously looking for opportunities to transfer responsibilities from himself to his staff. It's not easy to establish which responsibilities to retain and which to give up, and it's an evolving process. He says he's always recalibrating. For example, in 2012 when he took a seven-week sabbatical from the organization, he delegated his responsibilities to senior staffers. When he returned, he took back only about half the things he had delegated. He also told me that when he devised a new strategic plan with a key funder, his leadership team asserted their views about changes that should be made to it. "They came to me and they laid out all these things they felt we needed to do, and it was awesome."

Jim Collins sagely wrote in his business management classic *Good to Great*: "You can accomplish anything in life, provided that you do not mind who gets the credit." Rob Gitin and At The Crossroads are a great testament to that wisdom.

YOU CAN HAVE A LIFE

Leading from behind is important not only because it allows staff to take more ownership over the mission of the organization, but because it helps prevent exhaustion. One of the biggest problems I heard about in my survey of social enterprise leaders was that they felt burned out, or close to it. Tomás Alvarez, the founder of Beats Rhymes and Life, a hip-hop therapy organization that serves youth in West Oakland, told me that when he left his organization after ten years of working seven days a week, it took him a year of decompression to recover. He said that at the time it felt virtuous to work so hard to make his community a better place, but ultimately it was unhealthy. "When you're a social entrepreneur, the idea of prioritizing yourself feels so counterintuitive because the issues we're trying to solve are so pressing, and we don't want people to have to suffer. But because I didn't set boundaries, I ended up burning myself out." This is one of the great benefits of learning to diffuse responsibility. It allows you to make time in your life for family and friends and the other passions that energize you. You really can right-size your time commitment. Louise Langheier, for example, has maintained a great work life balance even as she's founded and built a highly successful collective management structure for Peer Health Exchange.

Founded fourteen years ago, Peer Health Exchange has an annual operating budget of $7.9 million, employs sixty people and has trained more than eighty-five hundred college student volunteers to deliver effective health education to more than 115,000 public high school students in New York City, Boston, Chicago, Los Angeles and the San Francisco Bay Area. In recent years, funding for wellness and sex education classes has been slashed, leaving teens vulnerable to unintended pregnancy, rape and sexual assault, drug addiction and other health-related problems. Through the strategic intervention of Peer Health Exchange, Langheier envisions a future "where health education is just a part of what a school provides its kids. Where it is required and funded and has a really high set of standards for what it teaches."

I visited Langheier at her office, located in a small San Francisco alleyway called Gold Street, the historical hub of the gold trade during California's gold rush era. I say "her office," but she doesn't actually have one. When I walked into the large, open-plan loft-style space, with nineteenth-century exposed brick walls and long rows of tables, she popped up from smack dab in the middle of the room, waving to greet me. The open space gives no indication as to who in the room is a manager and who is an assistant. The room bustles with activity, like the trading floor of an investment bank.

Right from the start, even before she created this office space, Langheier sought to share her leadership responsibility. She launched the pilot for Peer Health Exchange, alongside her peers, while she was a student at Yale University. When the school district cut funding for health education, a public high school teacher in New Haven, Connecticut, asked Yale students to teach health workshops, hoping college students would be more relatable than he was, as an older educator. Langheier and five other students took on the challenge, and enjoyed the experience so much that they began holding health workshops at many other high schools around New Haven. Langheier realized she found the work stimulating far beyond the scope of a simple extracurricular activity, so she decided to continue with it after she graduated. But she didn't want to do it all by herself. She convinced another student, Katy Dion, to join her as the cofounder of a nonprofit. Because she had a cofounder, she explains, she always felt accountable to someone else, and when they started the work of getting the company up and running, they established a practice of giving each other regular, no-holds-barred feedback.

As the organization took off, they extended their partnership outward and started sharing responsibility with the growing staff. "The cofounder model is part of our DNA," Langheier says. Every time they decided to bring in a new employee, they made the recruit feel like a team member, not someone coming in as a subordinate to an all-powerful founder. Langheier and Dion thought seriously about ways to divvy up responsibilities so they could give all their people a strong sense of ownership, whether over a new program or a fundraising campaign or a staffing decision.

The trust she's placed in her team has greatly motivated employees, and it's been a powerful recruiting tool. Highly talented applicants flock to openings at Peer Health Exchange because they know they will be given authority over high-level decisions, whereas in many other organizations planning is the domain of the founder or board. Many team members stay on for years, even though they have great prospects elsewhere. "Our VP of programs has been here for nine years," Langheier tells me proudly. "She could be doing anything because she's so talented, but she stays because she feels she owns this program."

The remarkable strength of the structure and culture is probably best demonstrated, though, by the decision Langheier made in 2004, only a year after the organization's inception. Peer Health Exchange was headquartered in New York at that time, and Langheier lived nearby. That year her mother, who lived in San Francisco, was diagnosed with cancer, and Langheier decided she wanted to spend as much of her time as possible enjoying her mother's company back in San Francisco. She commuted to the West Coast every weekend, doing her best to manage her responsibilities remotely when necessary.

As it turned out, because Dion and Langheier had shared many of their relationships with funders and other partners, Dion was able to seamlessly take over working with them when Langheier could not be there. For example, Dion and Langheier had written the curriculum and designed the trainings together, so Dion was able to pick up and run the health education programming. They had also participated together in many external meetings with board members and donors, so when Langheier's mom passed away and she could not be in those meetings because she was busy making funeral arrangements with her family, Dion could easily handle them.

When Langheier did return to New York full time, the organization was all the stronger because others had taken charge; they had become even more proficient managers of the mission.

In recent years, Langheier has established an enviable balance between her work and personal life, reserving her nights and weekends for sacred family time. "It doesn't even occur to me to work on a weekend," she says, "unless the organization is facing some crisis or we have a special program training I want to attend alongside our staff." She hasn't even come close to the burnout many social entrepreneurs struggle with, claiming that fourteen years later she still feels "genuinely excited to come in to work every day."

Of course, Langheier's less-controlling role within Peer Health Exchange is not without its challenges. She's met with some criticism for largely staying out of the media spotlight. Her board, for example, has suggested that she seek more press and emphasize her own story and role in interviews. Her staff has also sometimes told her they would like to get more direction from her about important decisions. Finding the sweet spot in delegating responsibility is always a challenge, and the right mix is a moving target. When an organization is launching a major new initiative, for example, the founder or executive director should undoubtedly play a prominent role in promoting it.

Langheier thinks the benefits of her approach have far outweighed any difficulties. And she constantly receives support for that conviction, both from inside and outside the organization. At a recent leadership summit where Langheier's senior team presented the organization's strategic plan to forty of Peer Health Exchange's top funders, they were thrilled to see the depth of the leadership bench. On her most recent maternity leave, Langheier left feeling confident the organization would continue to thrive in her absence, in the very capable hands of her five-person senior leadership team, which comprises a chief of sites, chief of shared services, vice president of programs and strategic partnerships, vice president of external affairs and vice president of finance, tech, and operations—and thrive it did.

SPEND QUALITY TIME ON HIRING

Of course, giving employees at all levels more responsibility requires they be well equipped to exercise that responsibility. It's vital that people have the right skills, and in nonprofit work the right degree of passion for the mission as well. Leaders must make hiring decisions carefully and strategically.

One of the biggest pitfalls early-stage organizations reported in my study was hiring people who weren't right for the job. Throughout my interviews, I heard story after story about hiring and staff development mistakes. Sarah Hemminger, the founder of Thread, which supports underperforming high school students through mentoring, succinctly stated that in the beginning she had "absolutely no clue how to hire the right people." Carolyn Laub, the founder of the Gay-Straight Alliance Network, ticked off her mistakes in rapid fire: "I made bad hires, I wasn't good at managing, I was losing members of my team, who were burned out."

Bad hiring decisions can be horribly costly. A *Harvard Business Review* study estimated that mistakes in hiring, such as a poor skills match, account for 80 percent of employee turnover; and research shows that for a nonprofit, the average cost of a single bad hire, whether the person remains with the company doing subpar work or needs to be replaced, is tens of thousands of dollars.[5]

To combat the disruption and expense of such mistakes, a hiring strategy is enormously helpful, not only in identifying the right people, but in communicating to them what their roles will be, precisely what your expectations are and your plans for continuing to grow the organization with their help. With a comprehensive and clearly communicated hiring strategy, expectations are clear on both sides, and great people are more likely to accept jobs, because they have confidence you've got a good growth plan.

One leader who learned this lesson the hard way is Thread CEO Sarah Hemminger. She got the idea for Thread from having watched a friend in his first year of high school. Once a varsity athlete and straight-A student, he began to struggle and missed more than thirty days of school after a devastating car accident left his mother temporarily paralyzed, unable to work, addicted to prescription medications and forced to move into public housing. Fortunately for him, his teachers intervened. "A group of them got together and said, 'Look, we're just not going to let this happen,'" Hemminger recalls. They began driving to his house, making sure he had breakfast, and driving him to school. Her friend, Ryan, turned his life around and was able to attend the U.S. Naval Academy. But the success story doesn't end there. Eventually, Hemminger convinced her friend to date her—they have been married for eighteen years.[6]

Thread began as an all-volunteer organization. Hemminger, who felt lonely and isolated after moving to Baltimore to pursue her PhD in biomedical engineering, was volunteering at a high school and met many students like Ryan: exceptional individuals in extraordinarily challenging situations. As she connected with these students, she quickly realized that forming genuine relationships might offer her the loving community she was missing and them the kind support that had helped Ryan years before. These students became the first cohort of Thread, which targets students academically performing in the bottom 25 percent of their freshman class, with an average GPA of 0.15 on a 4.0 scale, and who face significant barriers outside the classroom. As the program grew, Hemminger recruited volunteer mentors from her graduate school program. She asked them to conduct after-school tutoring sessions, and quickly had enough volunteers to assign just one mentee to each mentor, a great one-to-one model. As more and more people volunteered and they had more volunteers than students to counsel, they changed the model and paired multiple volunteers with each student, which is how the Thread concept of a "family" of support was born. Today, students are paired with up to five volunteers who do things like pack their lunches, give them a ride to school, tutor them and help them find a summer job. "Anything you would do for your own child is basically what we do for our children," Hemminger says.[7]

Although the program was booming, Hemminger soon realized that the model would be unsustainable unless they began hiring staff. Never having hired before, she started by dividing all the work she had been doing into new staff positions. "We had absolutely no clue how to really do a needs assessment or create job descriptions, let alone profile the right people for the right roles." As a result, Hemminger made some terrible hires. "It wasn't that these were bad people, it was just that we didn't know what we wanted or needed or how to select effectively." Once she realized that things weren't working, Hemminger went to her board, to her funders and to anyone who cared about the mission who had human resources expertise and was willing to advise her. With their guidance, Thread created processes to make sure they brought in people with the right skills and passion for the mission; that system has worked well as the organization has continued to grow.

Being strategic about hiring requires taking more time, which can be a difficult self-discipline. As Abby Falik of Global Citizen Year told me: "It can be so tempting to make quick hires because it relieves the pain of not having someone in a critical role." One of the best ways to evaluate whether someone is fit for a job is to ask them to do an assignment. Abby Falik advocated this practice and gave some great examples. "If the role is managing finance, you could ask them to build a financial model and present it in easy to understand terms to some members of your team. Or if you're hiring for a sales or fundraising role, you could have them develop a pitch and actually make it to a group of people on your team or your board. If the role is strategic planning, you could ask that they develop the rubric they would use for evaluating your program and presenting a new strategy to the board." This also allows you to spread responsibility for hiring to your team, getting valuable feedback from them about whether the person is the right match for the job.

Another piece of advice leaders gave is that it's vital to take the time while interviewing to evaluate whether or not someone is a good fit, not only according to skills but also for your organization's culture. That is of course easier said than done. One way of clarifying this is to talk very openly with candidates about your culture; include not only aspects that just about anyone would find appealing, such as that you emphasize collaboration and support of colleagues, but also those that might be challenging, like transparency. Some people might not like a culture that encourages subordinates to speak up with critiques.

Many leaders I interviewed told me they have developed one key question that helps them evaluate cultural fit, along the lines of the favorite question venture capitalist Peter Thiel says he likes to ask: "Tell me something that's true, that almost nobody agrees with you on." This helps him find employees who aren't afraid to speak their minds. Abby Falik always asks interview candidates to tell her about their first job ever, because "it's typically not on their resume, or a response they have practiced. The question is disarming and forces someone to drop into presenting something fresh and authentic about themselves. It helps me read whether this person can be vulnerable and also puts them in a more grounded, and less habitual, place for the rest of the interview." That's an important quality in staff, given that self-reflection is at the heart of Global Citizen Year's mission. She also asks candidates, "What would you do if you didn't have to work for money?" to see where their passions really lie.

Other leaders ask interview questions that get directly at whether someone is a team player. For example, Premal Shah of Kiva screens for optimism by asking a candidate: "How many bad days would you say you have in a given year?" As he reveals: "I'm looking for people who honestly struggle to come up with an answer or who would put it at a very few number of bad days a year, because our work is really hard so optimism is critical to creating the climate where we can get our work done." For Charles Best at DonorsChoose, his question is "Who are you most grateful for?" This question screens out a huge number of candidates: "You'd be shocked at the proportion of candidates who cannot list more than their mom when asked that question." For DonorsChoose this question is important because it's a very good proxy for humility and gratitude, and the kind of person you want to work with. "Don't you want to work with the person who can rattle off ten people they're grateful for, like their coach, their former teacher, the manager of their last job?"

CORRECT MISTAKES QUICKLY

Even after implementing these practices, you will almost inevitably discover that you've hired some people who aren't good fits. Don't fret about it; take action. The rule of thumb I've heard over and over from nonprofit leaders is that you must be "slow to hire and quick to fire." If someone isn't working out, you can give them a chance to improve, but drawing it out over several months when you know in your gut they aren't a match for your team isn't helpful to anyone. This is a hard rule for many nonprofit leaders to follow because they tend to be so empathetic and also to think of their staff as family. That sometimes makes letting people go very tough. Rob Gitin from At The Crossroads, who faced many early hiring challenges, ultimately realized that hiring and firing decisions must be only about the mission, not about making people happy. That realization was game changing for him. He told me: "Especially as a leader, one of the biggest things you can do in helping the organization accomplish the mission is to find a way to quickly transition people out when they're not the right fit. They can be amazing people, but that might not make them the right fit. Every single person on the staff has to have one reason for being there: to accomplish the mission."

PROVIDE OPPORTUNITIES FOR LEARNING AND BONDING

Once you have all the right people on board, you have to spend quality time helping them bond and develop their talents. Great teams don't just happen. They are the product of very deliberate team-building efforts. With such pressing workloads, taking time to focus on your people rather than your program and supporters can be a real challenge. As a result, many nonprofit leaders end up putting team building on the back burner. That's a big mistake. Providing opportunities for socializing with colleagues and for learning, taking people away from the daily grind for a respite, not only energizes and bonds people, but also helps prevent burn out.

Carolyn Laub, who started the Gay-Straight Alliance Network when she was barely out of college, told me: "Over and over I had staff leave that I desperately wanted to stay but they were

> Great teams don't just happen. They are the product of very deliberate team-building efforts.

burned out; clearly the pace of the work that I was willing to do was not the same that staff were expecting." Providing opportunities for your staff to learn and bond is also critical to developing a culture where people have each other's backs and feel connected to the organization, not just the cause, in an emotional way.

Rafael Alvarez, founder of Genesys Works, is a huge proponent of creating ways for his staff to socialize. Particularly important was bringing people from different offices together as the organization expanded. Alvarez started to see early signs of friction between his founding team and the new additions. "I knew I had to nip it in the bud," he said. He decided to invest in a three-day retreat for the entire team. The event was a huge success, and Alvarez told me that "it wasn't anything fancy, but had it not been for that retreat we would not exist today, I guarantee you that." The retreat has become a yearly event, even as the organization has grown much larger over the years.

Many other organizations I talked to hold similar annual retreats. Alan Khazei, the cofounder of City Year, talks about the organization's annual retreats as critical to building a common culture during its founding years. "We had an extremely diverse corps, from people who hadn't graduated from high school to Harvard graduates, so we realized early on that we had to build a very unique culture that would bring everyone together." Today, retreats and trainings are key to the effective delivery of City Year's service in more than three hundred schools nationwide.

Charity: water connects its staff to the cause by taking everyone on its staff, regardless of what department they work in, from accounting to engineering to product design, at least once on a one-week trip to visit its water projects around the world. As

CEO Scott Harrison says, "No one is going to get rich working for charity: water, so our job is to connect them to the mission, because that's the reason they're here."

Genesys Works, CityYear and charity: water are all large organizations that can afford these kinds of national and global all-staff retreats, but team-building does not have to be expensive. Global Citizen Year, for example, has borrowed from Acumen Fund to hold all-hands meetings on Mondays, when they bring in someone inspiring from the field to make a presentation. According to Abby Falik: "Because I'm in an external-facing role I spend a lot of my time getting inspired about the work from other people outside of our organization, but that's not true for most of our staff." Bringing the staff together once a week to learn from outside experts helps them to think in new ways about the organization's work, and to feel invested not only in the cause but also in the organization, because it is investing in their professional development.

Charles Best from DonorsChoose has developed an online system for his staff to connect using the tech platform Slack, through which staff can create conversation threads around common areas of interest. For example, they have a channel for parents, a channel for fitness buffs and a channel for inspirational projects where people can say, "Did you see this amazing project a teacher created?" This allows the staff to stay connected to each other and to continually be inspired by the organization's mission. Ultimately, he says, being engaged and feeling connected is what makes people stay.

In order to optimize the potential of these organizational and culture-building methods, founders and CEOs need the help of a strong executive team. Reversing the pyramid does not mean an organization should have no management structure at all; in fact, it works best when departments each have their own strong leaders to guide them. We'll see in the next chapter how a number of leaders have built strong executive teams and benefited hugely from being able to delegate so much responsibility to them.

CHAPTER 11

Bringing in
Senior Leadership Early

Transmitting responsibility and autonomy throughout an organization does not require a radically "flat" management structure. In fact, in order to diffuse responsibility widely, you must have the right expertise in the right key senior positions, at the right time. Think of these managers as the tent poles that allow you to keep widening the tent and inviting others into the management team. You'll need to exercise astute judgment about who you can ask to take charge of what. If you've got an experienced program director, for example, they can figure out how responsibilities for particular parts of projects can be apportioned without overloading staff, and can also make sure they get the right training and guidance. Someone with less expertise in developing programs won't know about certain pitfalls and may make bad decisions about giving people responsibility. Rob Gitin, for example, in the early days of bringing on staff made the mistake of giving counseling responsibility to some people who weren't appropriately matched for street outreach. Initially, he thought that someone's passion about the work would be enough to make them a strong counselor. But he quickly realized that their having certain important traits, such as self-awareness, was essential. For example, one of his early counselors took criticism very personally and had a hard time implementing feedback. This might have been fine for a structured organization, but it did

164

not work for At The Crossroads, where street outreach was very unstructured and required its counselors to hold themselves accountable.

Bringing in people with expertise for certain roles frees a founder to focus on the most important work he or she should be doing, which in the early growth phase is generally building relationships with major funders and figuring out overall strategic planning. Too many founders get so swamped by attending to the day-to-day operations that they don't have time to think about the big picture.

YOU CAN'T CHANGE THE WORLD ALONE

Jim Collins famously wrote in *Good to Great* that CEOs who took their companies to a higher "great" level of performance "first got the right people on the bus, the wrong people off the bus, and the right people in the right seats."[1] He stressed that these CEOs prioritized getting the senior people they needed in place *before* they focused on developing the strategy for taking the organization to the next level. In my study, I interviewed several founders who told me they prioritized this way, and that it made all the difference in scaling up faster.

One such founder is Laura Weidman Powers, who started Code2040. Early on, the company had a hard time keeping up with fundraising. "By the end of 2013, we were headed to running out of cash," Powers recalls. "I realized that if I didn't turn 100 percent of my time to fundraising, we would run out of money." She hired two senior managers, a vice president of programs and a vice president of operations, so she could devote herself entirely to that mission. "I left the program in the hands of my capable staff. Six months later, we had raised a million and a half dollars, and by the end of the year we closed on $2.5 million." Meanwhile, the operations of the organization hadn't suffered.

When she brought her focus back to the operations side of things, Powers saw that her vice president of programs had done an excellent job of keeping the fellowship program afloat while she was preoccupied. She realized that fundraising had been occupying too much of her time, when what she really needed to do was focus on external relations and strategy. By permanently handing over the bulk of the programming work and hiring additional fundraising staff, Powers has freed up an enormous amount of her time, allowing her to focus on high-level fundraising and partnership development with tech companies. The shift in roles has also given her the space to think more strategically about how to address the larger problem of diversity in the tech industry, rather than having to spend so much time in the weeds of internal management systems. Code2040, meanwhile, is flourishing; by 2017 it had grown to an annual budget of $8 million with a staff of thirty-two, which has matched over 250 fellows with seventy-five tech companies since its inception.

While some organizations may require senior staff to boost their programming, nonprofits with a technology angle may require senior staff to lead their tech platform. Another founder who invested early in hiring senior leadership is Rey Faustino, who started One Degree in 2012. Faustino's $80,000 in seed money came from an Echoing Green fellowship he won for his plan to develop an innovative technology platform. The platform bridges the gap between social services agencies and the myriad people who need those services, but don't access them; on the site people can easily find local offerings, such as food banks, medical clinics, after school activities and counseling.

As he began to put the grant to work, Faustino understood that the development of an efficient and appealing website was crucial to One Degree's success. But he had little experience in information technology, so he decided to bring in a chief technology officer. "I could have brought on someone with basic engineering expertise to just build whatever I told them to build," he told me. "Or I could have outsourced it. But I knew I wanted a version of me, but technical. Someone who was visionary, who could build the architecture of this product and the future product while I built other parts of the organization, whether on the operations side or on the fundraising side."

Hiring a talented person for the role required the majority of his $80,000 funding, so Faustino paid himself very little and lived largely off ramen noodles for the first year. But by the end of that year, his chief technology officer had rebuilt their entire product, developing stronger feedback loops within the site to figure out who was visiting it and how best to serve their customers. By 2017, he'd brought the organization to $1.2 million in annual revenue.

Of course, not every founder realized the wisdom of bringing on senior managers so quickly. In fact, the number one mistake founders identified in looking back at their organizations' trajectories was failing to delegate to qualified senior staff early on. Carolyn Laub is one of them. She started the Gay-Straight Alliance Network when she was just twenty-three years old, having come out as bisexual in college; shortly afterward she founded a support group for lesbian, gay, bisexual, transgender, queer and questioning (LGBTQ) youth in high school. As a young adult, she joined a youth-driven effort to advocate for a California statewide school nondiscrimination law and experienced firsthand the power of young people advocating for themselves. While running the support group, she got inspired by a young woman group member who had started a Gay-Straight Alliance extracurricular student club at a Palo Alto high school that was vigorous in standing up for LGBTQ students. When teachers failed to protect LGBTQ students from their peers' harassment, the group asked for and won the opportunity to train all the teachers on how to intervene in incidents of bullying. Emboldened by the group's success, Laub decided to create a formal organization and work to grow it to national scope. But she can see now that for years growth was hampered by her failure to build a strong upper management team. For many years, the only staff she brought in were organizers to work directly with student groups. She hired no one to help with fundraising or communications or staff development, taking all those responsibilities on herself.

The result was that by the time the Gay-Straight Alliance Network was seven years old, although it was doing good work, she had only been able to raise enough funding to hire six staff members, and she was still doing nearly all the high-level work herself. To scale the California-based program nationally, on the one hand she knew she needed support staff for the fundraising, marketing and communications work, but on the other hand she could not afford to hire people. It wasn't until 2005, when she created a national plan for growth with the help of a consultant, that she realized she needed to hire a national program manager to manage the programming as well as the development and communications staff, which would allow her to focus on her personal strengths for fundraising and strategy. Within a year, Gay-Straight Alliance Network's revenue began to take off, and the program expanded into dozens of states and eventually become a nationwide organization.

In addition to assuring an organization has the needed expertise and freeing up the founder or CEO's time, there is another important reason to bring in senior managers early. Research on startups shows that their growth has a "path dependent" nature, meaning the early nature of an organization tends to become fixed in its DNA, and that can make changing the style of management down the road quite difficult. In fact, studies show this is a key reason why many organizations go through difficult growing pains, sometimes to the point of threatening their continued existence. Say that for the first few years, the founder hires no senior managers and takes direct responsibility for all the key management functions. All the staff are direct reports, and build trust and respect for the founder as a supervisor. Now, if the founder brings in someone to take over direct management of staff, staff may resent getting less face time with the founder. Their antipathy toward the new boss, and to the new procedures, or changes in programming, may undermine their sense of belonging and commitment. That resentment can in turn make the new senior manager's job a good deal harder. Often, valuable employees leave at this juncture, taking vital organizational knowledge and camaraderie with them. By setting up a strong management structure early, you avoid this shock to the system.

CREATE A VISION FOR YOUR
IDEAL SENIOR LEADERSHIP TEAM

Senior positions, and the responsibilities they entail, should be tailored specifically to each organization and founder, and designed to complement the founder's strengths and weaknesses. There is no standard template leaders can follow to make these decisions; each organization must develop a specific hiring strategy. As we saw in the examples above, while Laura Powers benefited most from hiring a high-level program administrator to take charge of running workshops and training classes, Rey Faustino really needed a chief technology officer to help him launch One Degree. We all tend to have some biases about our own abilities, so making the assessment requires a founder to engage in an honest analysis of his or her own strengths, as well as those of the existing staff. Spending time to develop a plan for what you want your senior leadership team to look like is key to success.

One founder described an especially helpful method for doing this. Abby Falik developed her idea for Global Citizen Year while she was still a student at Harvard Business School. Her inspiration for the organization came from her experience after graduating from high school, when she wished she could have taken some time before starting college to travel and get experience out in the world. She entered the Harvard Business School Pitch for Change competition, outlining her vision of a bridge year before college. When she won first place, she immediately began raising seed capital. Global Citizen Year, now in its sixth year of operation, has assisted hundreds of fellows to raise the money to take a bridge year.

Falik lacked experience in hiring and developing staff, but realized early on that she needed to be strategic about it. She quickly began working with a pro bono leadership coach, who assigned her an interesting exercise. "He told me to take a week and map out everything I did with my time that gave me energy, and then to note the things that depleted me or took my energy. At the end of the week, I took it back to him and he said, 'Your job is simple: build a team that sets you up to be doing exclusively the things that give you energy.'" He encouraged her to write job descriptions for all the work that depleted her and hire people who were instead energized by those tasks. Through this analysis process, Falik realized that what she really loved was being a "professional inspirer," working with people to spread the message of the organization. Yet most of her time was being sucked up by internal operations and management, which she dreaded. She developed a plan she says has been her "North Star" as she has grown the organization over the last five years.

Her first step was to bring in an executive administrative assistant to support her. While this might seem like a luxury for a founder in the early growth phase, Falik reports that it allowed her to do much more of the work she's best at, in particular, freeing her to do more fundraising. She realized: "If I'm paying someone $4,000 a month in an executive administrative role, that might pay for itself, if I'm able to take a couple of extra donor meetings a year." Looking at other young social startups, Falik says that many starve themselves, failing to think boldly and hire the expert team they need to

You can be creative with job descriptions and titles. Don't get restricted by traditional titles like "chief financial officer" or "development director"; instead, learn how to embrace people's unique qualities and let that translate into the titles you give them.

drive strong growth. "By definition you have to be a risk taker," she reflected, and part of that is spending the money to hire the right people earlier than you may be entirely comfortable with.

So how does an early-stage organization craft a clear hiring plan for its senior team? First, examine your own strengths and weaknesses. As Falik constantly tries to do, be honest about what you are good at and what gives you energy. Bring in people who can complement your strengths and compensate for your weaknesses. Many organizational leaders hire management coaches to help them with this process. New leaders in particular can benefit from a management coach who knows how to work side by side with them to develop a great hiring plan. You can be creative with job descriptions and titles. Don't get restricted by traditional titles like "chief financial officer" or "development director"; instead, learn how to embrace people's unique qualities and let that translate into the titles you give them. For example, Beth Schmidt from Wishbone wanted to hire a development director, but when she posted the job description using that title she had a hard time getting great candidates for the job. After she changed the title to "director of partnerships" she attracted a lot of people from the business world who had been in business development roles.

LEARN TO LET GO

Even once you have a great senior team in place, one of the hardest things to do, especially for the founder of an organization, is to let go of trying to have their hands in everything that is happening. Even Premal Shah, CEO of Kiva, who managed an enormous team of staff almost from the start, constantly struggles with how to let go of micromanaging. He learned a good discipline from Meg Whitman, CEO of Hewlett Packard: at the start of every month he writes down everything he is doing and examines the list to see what he can uniquely do best, where he is the most valuable. He asks himself, What are the things other people could do? and finds ways to shift those tasks off his plate. This has allowed both him and his senior leadership team to flourish.

Abby Falik of Global Citizen Year learned a similar lesson from Michael Brown, the cofounder of City Year. He told her that as a founder your inclination is to hold on tightly to everything, to want to control it all. At some point as you hire senior people specialized in the areas where they work, it becomes natural to start letting go and delegating, because you know the organization can only thrive when you do so. That said, Brown's instruction to her was to always know the three things you're going to be obsessive about, the three things you're never going to let fully out of your control. According to Falik: "For me it's been around our vision, our external branding and messaging, and our hiring. I just know that I can't take my eye off those three functions at any level, but if it doesn't fall within those parameters, I need to be willing to let it go."

Even when people know they have to let go, it can be very hard to do so. In fact, some weren't able to until circumstances, such as going on maternity leave, forced their hand. Leaders can achieve this by design by taking a sabbatical, as Rob Gitin did at At The Crossroads. "By taking that time off I had to identify which of my responsibilities would lay fallow during that time versus which ones would be taken up by others." As Gitin recalls in hindsight: "If we've built a place that relies on us too much, ultimately it will fail." Having the courage and the skill to let your senior staff succeed without you, even if only temporarily, just might be the most important thing you can do as a leader.

CHAPTER 12

Building an Active Board

Another way the fast-growth organizations I studied leveraged talent was by appointing highly engaged board members with valuable connections and expertise, and drawing actively on that expertise. Too often, nonprofit leaders describe building a relationship with their boards as a waste of time. They report that preparing for board meetings, attending committee gatherings and meeting one on one with board members fails to yield significant payoffs. Many also look to their boards exclusively for fundraising assistance, selecting members purely for their marquee value in impressing donors, and their ability to tap their networks for funds. This leads to frustration because while some board members are vigorous in offering this assistance, many are not. In fact, only 15 percent of survey respondents reported their boards were involved in fundraising, with 66 percent saying they wished their board would help more on fundraising. This is a huge disconnect.

One reason this happens is that many early-stage social entrepreneurs take the "friends and family" approach to building their boards, rather than putting in the work to find board members with relevant expertise. By contrast, many of the founders who scaled their organizations quickly made great use of their boards, recognizing that the right board members could offer invaluable advice as well as provide important introductions and, yes, help significantly with fundraising too. These founders appointed board members with accounting expertise to help create a financial model for

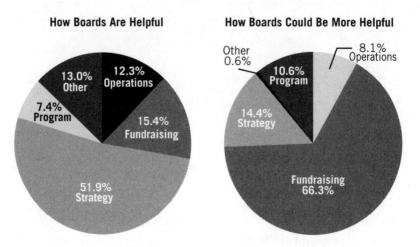

How Boards Are Helpful

13.0% Other

12.3% Operations

7.4% Program

15.4% Fundraising

51.9% Strategy

How Boards Could Be More Helpful

Other 0.6%

8.1% Operations

10.6% Program

14.4% Strategy

Fundraising 66.3%

Areas Where Nonprofit Leaders Say Boards Offer Helpful Input versus Areas Where Nonprofit Leaders Would Like Boards to Be More Helpful

growth, as well as members with experience in entrepreneurship and hiring, who were willing to work their connections. In particular, a strong working relationship between the board chair and executive director can be a huge catalyst for growth.

How do nonprofit leaders get the most out of their boards? It all starts with recruiting the right people.

RECRUITING STRONG BOARD MEMBERS

Only about half of the respondents to the survey reported that they thought their board members had the expertise the organization needed to meaningfully contribute to its growth. This failure to access talent on boards is thwarting the potential of the entire sector.

Nonprofit leaders face three primary challenges when it comes to recruiting strong boards. First, despite being connected to the communities they serve, leaders may feel they don't have access to the caliber of people who can help them raise money. Second, nonprofit leaders may not be sure of exactly what kind of expertise is needed for their organization's board. And finally, it can take a long time to recruit new board members; the process of finding the right people, meeting with them to assess interest and waiting for a board meeting to officially vote on them can take several months.

A common myth is that the people able to recruit strong board members just happen to be more connected than the rest of us. My experience is that this isn't always the case; there are a lot of

Many of the founders who scaled their organizations quickly made great use of their boards, recognizing that the right board members could offer invaluable advice as well as provide important introductions and, yes, help significantly with fundraising too.

nonprofit leaders out there who hustle to find people who can be useful to them. Ellen Moir, the founder of New Teacher Center, came from humble roots. Her mom didn't graduate from high school and her father barely did, spending his life scraping by selling men's clothing. She started her organization as a former teacher and based it in the sleepy tree-lined downtown heart of Santa Cruz, where her office was sandwiched between the Sockshop and Awesome Granola. She did not have opportunities to hobnob with nonprofit power brokers there. But she didn't let that stop her, spending many of her early days driving over the hill to Silicon Valley where she could network with tech executives. At one point, when the organization already had a relatively large budget of $10 million, Moir received a $100,000 grant from Silicon Valley Social Ventures (SV2), a network of engaged philanthropists who donated their time and talents as well as their treasure. Moir's team gave her grief about spending time on what they saw as a small grant in comparison to their budget. But Moir understood that the grant was about much more than money. "It was about the intellectual and social capital," she told me.

Sure enough, at an SV2 networking event she was invited to, Moir sat down with Lance Fors, a technology entrepreneur who was immediately drawn to her story. As Moir remembers: "He told me we were at a real 'inflection point' . . . I didn't know what that meant, but I did know that we were on what I would call 'a roll' and that

Lance really wanted to help us." Fors was elected board chair shortly thereafter and helped the organization spin off from the University of California at Santa Cruz, where it was based at the time. He has continued to work side by side with Moir to scale New Teacher Center to the $40 million organization it is today. Moir says she has relied heavily on Fors, in the beginning calling him multiple times a week, even sometimes multiple times a day, to work through opportunities and challenges the organization was facing, from fundraising to human resources. Although Moir certainly believes it was luck that she sat next to Fors at the event, she stresses that the serendipity of the meeting was a direct result of her avid networking.

The first step in recruiting strong board members is to identify your needs. Too often conversations about board recruitment start with "Who do we know?" as opposed to "Who do we need?"[1] Jan Masaoka from Blue Avocado talks about how an organization should ask two questions: (1) What are the three most important things for our board to accomplish this year? and (2) Do we have the right people on the board to make that happen? Your answers will give you the clarity with which to write good job descriptions to show to potential candidates. A board matrix to assess current board members' skills and roles that you would like to fill can also be a great way to home in on who you are looking for. This way, instead of reaching out to your contacts and asking, "Do you know anyone who would like to join our board?" you can be more specific and say, "Do you know of any Latina women in the fundraising business who would like to join our board?"

Another powerful resource for finding board candidates is LinkedIn, which has an excellent function that lets you type in the skills you are looking for and spits out results from your own network of people who have them.[2] You can also ask current board members, senior staff and existing funders who are, after all, already invested in the success of the organization, to suggest potential candidates.

Once you have some potential candidates in the hopper, you should go through a due diligence process. I always create projects to test potential board members; the exercise not only illuminates their skills and level of commitment but also allows them to discover their own level of interest in the organization. One mistake organizational leaders often make is trying too hard to encourage a board member to join, without having a clear sense of whether they are going to step up and get to work. For example, you could informally ask a potential board member to help review a marketing piece and provide comments, help cohost an event or even ask them to serve on a committee. In the months leading up to her organization's launch, Beyond 12's Alexandra Bernadotte recruited advisors on everything from organizational finances to strategy, whom she planned to later invite to join as board members. She saw her advisors as a key part of the process of devising her concept and crafting her model, and she made sure they had skills that complemented her own. Because she engaged them so early on in the development process, she was able to get enormous buy-in from them, so that by the time she invited them to become board members they were already highly invested in the organization's success. Keep in mind that it's a lot harder to fire a board member than to hire one, so the extra work to assure a good fit will spare you much anxiety.

CREATING CLEAR EXPECTATIONS

It doesn't matter who you have on your board; if you don't have a framework for what you want them to accomplish, you won't achieve anything together. This was a struggle that Emily Arnold-Fernandez experienced firsthand when she started her organization, Asylum Access, which advocates globally for better treatment of refugees. In 2005, she had been part of a working group brainstorming opportunities to support legal refugee aid, particularly in Egypt and Uganda. She was in her twenties, and recalls that she didn't really know any of the others in the group well, but that, like her, they all seemed young and passionate about the refugee issue. They decided to start the organization and agreed she should be the executive director, and the rest would make up the board of directors. Looking back, while she deeply respected these people on a professional level, she didn't know them well or have a strong relationship with them. And most important, like many other organizations that begin with a "starter board," none of them had board experience.

She remembers how green she was in the early days: "I didn't even know what a board was supposed to do, and no one knew what decisions were my decisions versus board decisions." She also struggled with the fact that the board wasn't invested in the same way she was. For example, when it came time to grow the organization, she would plead with them: "If we don't get some money we're going to have to shut this down. I can't keep doing this for free." Sometimes they were responsive, but other times she felt like they just didn't have the same kind of skin in the game. And they had a huge reluctance to do the fundraising; this made Arnold-Fernandez feel extremely resentful, since she was putting herself on the line in all her relationships by asking for money, whereas her board was not doing the same.

In hindsight, Arnold-Fernandez realizes that tensions stemmed from a lack of clear expectations. There were no guidelines about how much the board should be fundraising, and none of them had any experience raising money. Ultimately, she determined she had to create a whole new board. "I needed to bring on people with more capacity to write checks and fundraise, but we couldn't do that if we were not requiring our existing board members to do the same." She geared herself up for some hard conversations, but when she actually sat down with each of them, it wasn't that bad. In talking with them, she realized they too had been feeling bad that they hadn't met her expectations. For a couple of board members who really wanted to stay, she made sure they committed to the new fundraising requirements.

The transition to a high-performing board involved some fits and starts. She brought on a couple of new board members who had strong giving capacity and/or connections, but found she didn't feel comfortable telling them what to do. One board member came on and actually took too much control, making inappropriate requests of Arnold-Fernandez and her team, and criticizing staff in front of funders, creating a toxic environment for the rest of the board members. The problem got so bad that Arnold-Fernandez lost a major funder she had been quite close with, who sent a note saying they could no longer fund the organization because it was not "well run." Arnold-Fernandez felt this was an unfair characterization: the problem wasn't with the quality of the work itself, for which she had won numerous awards. It was just that she didn't know how to run a board.

It wasn't until Arnold-Fernandez engaged an executive coach in 2012 that she realized her board would never work properly until she created a clear set of expectations, not just around fundraising but all aspects of board membership. "I had just assumed that a board member would know what they should be doing because they had been a C-level officer in a company. Obviously this wasn't the case, but it took me a long time to learn this lesson." She realized that developing clearer roles would change everything, and it did. She had one of her interns do a literature review on how to run a board and also read a lot of the fundamental texts, turning to Board Source, a clearinghouse of best practices for nonprofit boards. Then the board created a committee to develop a governance structure, and came up with multiple policies, including a board policy, which laid out more clearly the members' roles and responsibilities. She now has a small but active group of five board members who are clear about their goals and support her in all the ways she had always dreamed, including as strategic advisors and fundraisers. The organization has expanded into Africa, Asia and Latin America and is a leader in global refugee policy.

In their book *Governance as Leadership*, which reframed the way nonprofits think about board management, Richard Chait, William Ryan and Barbara Taylor set forth a board's three modes of governance: fiduciary, strategic, and generative modes. As they say, "When organizations reframe governance as leadership, the board becomes more than a fiduciary of tangible assets and more than

Three Modes of Board Governance

1. Fiduciary Mode
  Accounting assessments
  Ensuring legal and tax compliance
  Prepare for audits
  Create board committees
  Oversee executive director's annual review

2. Strategic Mode
  Strategic-plan focused
  Identify key metrics of success
  Track progress toward goals
  Monitor programmatic outcomes
  Establish strategic priorities

3. Generative Mode
  Understand the broader ecosystem
  Focus on organizational learning
  Foster collaboration with partners
  Make data-driven decisions
  Focus on the endgame

Source: Based on the modes established in Richard Chait, William Ryan and Barbara Taylor, *Governance as Leadership.*

management's strategic partner, as vital as those functions are. The board also becomes a crucial and generative source of leadership for the organization."[3]

Nonprofit leaders should be asking themselves in which of these three categories their board has skills, and then fill those gaps. Maybe you have a board that is meeting its fiduciary responsibilities, but you wish they were asking more hard questions about your long-term strategy. That is the sort of analysis you should do.

Before you can engage your board members, you must have "jobs" to assign them. This starts with establishing a strong committee structure. At a minimum, every board should have (1) a governance committee to recruit new board members, maintain the policies of the organization and oversee the executive director review process; and (2) a finance committee to oversee the budget process and long-term financial planning. As the board grows and needs evolve, you may also decide to set up other committees, such as an audit committee, strategic planning committee or fundraising committee. By requiring that board members sit on at least one committee, with chairs managing them, the board will naturally take on the governance role Chait, Ryan and Taylor describe.

Finally, the most critical element of successful board engagement is the board policy. A good board policy should be succinct and clearly lay out roles and responsibilities, including but not limited to the following:

- commitment to the mission of the organization;
- term of service;
- fiduciary duties (including the obligation, if any, to make a personal financial contribution, introduce potential donors to the organization, etc.);
- commitment to active involvement (including meeting attendance and committee participation requirements);
- board meeting practices; and
- board-staff interactions.

Each board member should have a clear understanding of the expectations laid out in the board policy before they agree to serve and should sign the policy every year to renew their commitment. This not only presents the board expectations in one place so that people know what they are signing up for, but also gives you a clear accountability mechanism for letting go of board members who are not meeting expectations. Annual board self-assessments are also a great way to allow board members to reflect on whether they feel they are meeting expectations and, if not, you can look into what you can do to help them, or perhaps relieve them of their positions.

DEVELOPING ENGAGEMENT TAKES TIME

Effective board engagement requires a lot of nurturing and follow-up. You should work hard to involve members in ways both interesting to the board members and useful to the organization. One way you can create this kind of win-win relationship is by developing an annual board engagement plan. Tiffany Cooper Gueye, CEO of BELL in Boston, loves board engagement plans so much that she sits down with each of her fourteen board members at the beginning of every year and creates an individualized, written plan for what they hope to accomplish. When I commented on how much time this must take, she responded that it's absolutely worth it. "Before we did [the reviews], people weren't clear on whether they were even being useful, or how they could be more helpful." The plans have helped her find ways for everyone to contribute, no matter what their skills. She noted: "One of my board members, for example, doesn't have deep pockets or deep networks, but he comes into the office on Saturdays to help frame our strategic choices and create slide presentations."

When developing your board engagement plan, you should consider not only how the board member can help the organization, but also how they can grow personally from the experience. After all, it's a two-way street; it's not just about what they will give but what board members will get out of serving.

Another way to encourage your board members to be more active is by providing opportunities for them to constantly learn about the substance of the work. Board members not only need to know about the issues you're working on in order to make effective decisions for the organization, but to help them feel more connected to the cause. You can do this by taking them on trips to see your work locally or around the world, share relevant articles and set aside a few minutes at the beginning of a board meeting to reflect on a substantive discussion prompt.

Board meetings should not simply be reporting sessions from the CEO; they should be interactive-learning meetings that draw on the skills and experience of members. The key to making your board meetings substantive is to use a "consent agenda"; in it you include all the substantive organizational updates in the board packet, which you provide in advance. This way, during the meeting you can focus the discussion on substantive issues. IDEO.org, for example, spends the first thirty minutes of their board meetings talking about an article they assign in advance. This helps board members feel the organization is using them for their strategic advice, not just their network and fundraising.

Finally, the best boards I've seen know the importance of being social. Creating opportunities for board members to get to know each other outside the board room is critical to developing the camaraderie that inspires more active engagement and the commitment to have your back when you need it. Some boards go for dinner after every meeting or go on a hike or an offsite visit once a year. Getting your board together once or twice a year outside the boardroom can make a huge difference.

Whether you are just starting an organization or already in the thick of growth, it is critical that you constantly take stock of your board to ensure they are bringing you the resources you need for scaling.

BENCHMARKS FOR SOCIAL STARTUP SUCCESS: LEADING

✓ Does your organization create ways for staff to operate with autonomy and decision-making authority?

✓ Does your staff have clear metrics for success within their roles, which, ideally, they help to create?

✓ Does your organization have processes to give horizontal feedback?

✓ Do you use "we" as opposed to "I" language when talking about the organization?

✓ Does your organization create opportunities for all team members to act as the face of the organization in some capacity?

✓ Do you create boundaries between your work and personal life to avoid burnout?

✓ Do you have strong processes in place for hiring and firing?

✓ Do your interview questions assess whether potential candidates fit your organizational culture?

✓ Does your organization provide opportunities for learning and bonding?

✓ Do you have a vision for your ideal senior leadership team based on your personal strengths and weaknesses?

✓ Do you have a strategy to allow other staff to assume organizational duties that are not dependent on you?

✓ Do you have a strong recruitment process to bring on board members with relevant expertise?

✓ Do you create ways to "test" board members before they commit to joining the organization?

✓ Do you have a committee structure in place to engage board members?

✓ Do you have a board policy in place to create clear expectations for your board?

✓ Do you create opportunities for your board to be social with each other outside the boardroom?

PART 5

TELLING COMPELLING STORIES

Marketing expert and best-selling author Seth Godin famously said, "Marketing is no longer about the stuff that you make, but the stories that you tell." The nonprofit community has embraced the wisdom of telling a good story, and also the bounty of new means of telling them, from streaming video to the more recently harnessed immersive storytelling power of virtual reality. The short virtual reality film *Clouds Over Sidra* was created under the auspices of the United Nations and directed by UN advisor Gabo Arora and Hollywood filmmaker Chris Milk. It paints an indelible portrait of the life of a twelve-year old Syrian girl living in the Zaatari refugee camp in Jordan along with 130,000 other Syrians who fled their country's civil war.[1] Viewers have reported that the experience was so vivid, they felt they could smell the bread baking in the makeshift ovens and feel the heat of the dry desert wind.

Yet many nonprofit leaders have not taken full advantage of the opportunities to tell a more compelling story about the work they're doing. Andy Goodman, an expert in the field of public interest communications and the author of *Why Bad Presentations Happen to Good Causes*, conducted extensive research, traveling around the country listening to presentations by nonprofit leaders to answer the question "Why are so many of our colleagues—decent, well-educated, well-intentioned folks—so good at being so boring?"[2] His research uncovered three primary reasons: (1) people didn't prepare enough: 53 percent of people said they spent less than two hours preparing for a speech, and only 10 percent said they had a "significant amount" of training; (2) people were in denial about the quality of their presentation abilities: 49 percent claimed they were delivering good-to-excellent presentations, while 82 percent said they were not seeing good-to-excellent presentations; and (3) most people imitated the style of presenting they'd seen at non-profit conferences rather than crafted their own distinctive style.[3]

It may seem that some people are just born storytellers and that most of us can't expect to truly wow an audience. I would have said that myself before I conducted my research for this book. But what I discovered by talking with many organizational leaders who were powerful storytellers was that it's more the product of a whole lot of preparation and practice than of an innate talent.

A great case in point is Nadine Burke Harris, founder of the Center for Youth Wellness. Her TED talk titled "How Childhood Trauma Affects Health Across a Lifetime" has been viewed over 2.5 million times, and counting.[4] That's an astounding accomplishment for a talk about such a serious subject with which the public has so little familiarity, and in which she does not shy away from imparting a great deal of medical information, even using the rarefied language of medicine to educate her listeners. She explains, for example, about the hypothalamic-pituitary-adrenal axis and how it controls the fight-or-flight response, which accounts for the long-term damage of childhood trauma. She also does not employ the common device of telling a particular child's story to tug at the hearts of her listeners. How did she make the talk so compelling? She worked hard at learning the techniques of storytelling and public speaking. As she told me, she realized that "I could be speaking the gospel coming straight from the Lord, but if I say it in a way that is boring, no one is going to invite me to speak." She made it her mission to get better at public speaking, and says, "I see myself as a professional athlete, but my sport is public speaking." She is constantly pushing herself to speak in situations where she might be scared, worried that she's out of her league. She also studies other people's presentations, live at conferences and on video, the way sports coaches study tape of games.

The good news about the work required is that there is so much great expertise for learning techniques to turn to: many good books, rich online resources and a host of workshops. In the next chapter I will offer highlights from leading experts about the elements of a great story and introduce practices adopted by some organizations to develop great storytelling talent in their staff and also empower their beneficiaries to be compelling storytellers.

CHAPTER 13

Creating a Compelling Narrative

Powerful storytelling matters so much that in her exponential fund-raising class, Harvard professor Jennifer McCrea devotes an entire section to storytelling techniques. She brings in Marshall Ganz, a professor at the Harvard Kennedy School of Government, a specialist in the methods of promoting social movements, including how people can craft a strong "public narrative."[1] Ganz was a leader in developing methods of organizing and protest in the civil rights movement in the 1960s; he also played an important role in the farmworkers' rights movement, working alongside Cesar Chavez. Ganz writes that "all stories have three elements: a plot, a protagonist, and a moral."[2] Many stories also have an antagonist, which is a great device for making them more emotionally gripping, adding dramatic tension and inspiring listeners to engage with the fight. Who doesn't love to see a villain vanquished? For nonprofits, the problems we combat are the chief antagonists.

Thinking about the key message we want to convey is enormously helpful in crafting a presentation. While the plot of certain stories is relatively easy to fashion, such as the many stories of particular beneficiaries told so well on so many organizations' websites and in so many fundraising campaigns, sometimes seeing a plot in the information we have to impart is more challenging. That was the case for Nadine Burke Harris when she was creating her TED talk. She could have started by telling a heart-wrenching story of how an early trauma led to debilitating health problems for a particular person. Doing so would have been very effective. But instead she led with hard information:

> In the mid-1990s, the CDC and Kaiser Permanente discovered an exposure that dramatically increased the risk for seven out of ten of the leading causes of death in the United States. In high doses it affects brain development, the immune system, hormonal systems and even the way our DNA is read and transcribed.[3]

She quickly proceeded to explain that this "exposure" was not to toxic chemicals, as might be expected, but to childhood trauma. With that opening salvo, she had introduced her antagonist, and she had succinctly and potently conveyed how nefarious it was. As her talk proceeded, she continued to introduce a wealth of medical information, truly teaching her audience about the problem, and she managed to do so in a way that was both intellectually and emotionally engaging throughout.

When I asked her how she had crafted her talk, she told me the process of developing and giving it was transformational to her style of speaking, because she learned how to incorporate the elements of storytelling. "Prior to TED, I would get up there and say, 'Here's a great big idea. And it's wonderful, and here's why.'" The team at TED taught her that her talk should include all these characteristics, much in keeping with what Ganz advises, but put in somewhat different terms: a narrative arc, a protagonist and a challenge; that she should share about herself and her vulnerabilities; and she should make the audience part of the solution. Her protagonist was herself; she used her personal story of digging into the problem of early trauma to open up about herself and introduce her vulnerabilities, namely her inability for some time to figure out what was wrong with some of the children she was trying to diagnose. As she said, "Somehow I was missing something important." Her narrative arc was a journey of discovery, recounting step by step how she learned about key findings that led to understanding the magnitude of the problem of early trauma and its many horrible longer-term effects.

For including the audience in the solution, she closed with a rous-
ing call to action: "The single most important thing that we need
today is the courage to look this problem in the face and say this is
real and this is all of us. I believe that we are the movement." The
result was so powerful that she received an offer to write a book on
the subject, which will of course help her continue to reach out to
the public and build the movement.

Another helpful insight Marshall Ganz offers about telling a great
story is to think of three stories within our overarching story: the
story of self, what is unique about each of us, the challenges we've
faced and how we've overcome them in our own lives; the *story of us*,
describing an experience common to all of us; and the *story of now*,
conveying the urgency of the problem. He advises that as part of the
story of now, we should address the question of whether the problem
can be solved, and to "answer that question in the spirit of hope."[4]

As Jennifer McCrea and her coauthor Jeffrey Walker point out in
their book *The Generosity Network*, President Obama followed this
model in his 2004 Democratic National Convention speech.[5] He told
the story of self by recounting his unusual family history: the son
of a Kenyan father and an American mother who decided to name
their son Barack. He told the story of us by declaring that his story
was the "American story," describing how we all share the value of
hope. And finally he told the story of now by saying, "We have more
work to do." He put a fine point on that spirit of inclusion with his
rallying cry during the 2008 election: "Yes we can." That was a brilliant piece of oratory, strategically designed to engage all his follow-
ers in the solutions to the social problems he was fighting for.

KNOW YOURSELF

Many social entrepreneurs are hesitant to talk about themselves
and their personal journeys because they feel that promoting the
mission shouldn't be about them; it should be about the cause. But
opening up about ourselves, being vulnerable and telling our story,

and importantly, why we became devoted to the cause, creates a personal connection with our audience. As part of telling her personal story, Nadine Burke Harris talks about growing up in Palo Alto, raised by her Jamaican father, who was a chemist, to love science. That isn't integral to informing her audience about childhood trauma, but it helps create a spirit of intimacy.

> Opening up about ourselves, being vulnerable and telling our story, and importantly, why we became devoted to the cause, creates a personal connection with our audience.

Jennifer Pitts, former managing director of communications and development for Tipping Point, explained to me that another reason many social entrepreneurs don't tell their own stories is that "most people don't know what is interesting about themselves; people don't get into the work of nonprofits because they're so fascinated by their own story." Pitts works with nonprofit leaders to help them with self-discovery, and she finds that everyone has a personal narrative relevant to promoting the cause, whether it's about how they grew up, the lessons their parents taught them or perhaps the conversations they had at the dinner table. She argues that organizational leaders should feel no discomfort about getting help in telling their personal stories, saying, "If you can hire a speechwriter or a communications expert to help you develop your story, that doesn't make you any less of a leader." If you feel uncertain about how much of your story to tell and which aspects, getting expert advice is well advised. As Pitts also points out: "Making really clear choices about the stories you tell is critical, because they are all opportunities for connection or disconnection."

GETTING TO KNOW YOUR AUDIENCE

Most people who sit down to prepare a presentation ask themselves, "What do I want to say?" as opposed to "What does my audience need to hear?" Andy Goodman recommends that you get to know your audience in advance, such as by interviewing the conference organizer who scheduled your session, or finding someone on the inside of the organization where you'll be speaking to provide insight.[6] Here is a key set of questions he suggests:

- Who will be in the audience?
- What do they know or believe that I can build on?
- What do they know or believe that I have to overcome?
- By the end of my presentation, what do I want them to have learned?
- By the end of my presentation, what do I want them to feel?

Knowing the answer to these questions will allow you to tailor your remarks so you can bring your audience along with you more powerfully.

It's also important to be cognizant that people have different learning styles, in particular that some people will be most engaged and impressed by hard data while others will be more receptive to emotionally engaging storytelling. You should combine the styles and speak to both the head and the heart. Jennifer Pitts keeps this in mind by envisioning two people in the audience: "One is the grumpiest, most analytical numbers person in the room and the other is the bleeding heart, the crier. I know that if I can make the crier think and the thinker feel, I've covered everyone in between."

Erin Ganju, cofounder and CEO of Room to Read, swears by the magic of combining the head and the heart: "Every presentation has to have great data for the analytic types who are going to be skeptics. You have to put those critics to bed, but then it's all about following up with the heart." For example, when she tells the story of their reading programs, she'll talk about the 781 million people on the planet who are illiterate, but she knows the number would fall on deaf ears without telling a story to go along with it, such as "the one child, in a community in rural Nepal, whose father passed away, whose mother is illiterate, who has three brothers and sisters, whose school was insufficient and who wasn't learning to read until Room to Read came to the village, started a library program, trained their grades one and two teachers, and now a year later he's one of the best readers in the school and he checks out a book every day from the library." As Andy Goodman says, "Nobody ever marched on Washington because of a pie chart." The story is an important bridge between the data and people's hearts, to inspire action.

It's also important to be cognizant that people have different learning styles, in particular that some people will be most engaged and impressed by hard data while others will be more receptive to emotionally engaging storytelling.

CONNECT THE STORY TO THE POPULAR NARRATIVE

In looking for ways to tell the story of now, of why taking action is urgent *now*, it's important to harness the power of news coverage related to your mission. One of the most powerful ways to create a sense of urgency is to connect your message to a current issue in the news; in other words, craft a "news hook," which will also help you immensely with your pitches to get coverage from the media. As journalist David Henderson once said, "Just because you are worthy, doesn't mean you are newsworthy."[7]

Wendy Kopp did a masterful job of connecting her mission to the broader public narrative about the education problem when she started Teach For America.[8] She had been inspired to start the organization when she learned about the inequities in educational outcomes that persisted on racial and economic lines. But that didn't mean that her first pitch for support was met favorably. As part of her undergraduate thesis at Princeton, she had created a plan and put together a budget, requiring $2.5 million to launch, and she decided to see if she could get federal support. She wrote to President George H. W. Bush suggesting he create the new teacher corps she was proposing, but received only a rejection letter in return. When she read in *Fortune* that the magazine had hosted a summit where corporate leaders expressed their commitment to education reform, she reached out to all those quoted in the article, sending them a copy of her proposal and a letter requesting a meeting. The CEO of Union Carbide, which had just formed a task force to explore education reform, responded to her proposal and offered her donated space and connections to other executives. Mobil Oil awarded her $26,000 in seed money, and before long she was off and running. She had seized an opportunity to take advantage of a new public narrative. As she says, "These executives had committed themselves to taking on education reform but didn't yet know what to do."

STAYING ALERT FOR NEWS HOOKS IS VITAL

Few of the organizations I studied had an in-house public relations team. Instead, the leaders themselves constantly kept their tentacles out in the news stream, also crowdsourcing the effort to all staff, who contributed relevant news links to platforms like a Slack channel as they found them. We covered how Laura Weidman Powers of Code2040 pounced on the news that Google had released abysmal diversity numbers. Her first step was to write an opinion piece, accepted by the San Jose *Mercury News*, in which she challenged Silicon Valley to bring more blacks and Latinx into the tech industry.[9] The larger news coverage of the problem was also integral to her ongoing presentations about the organization to funders and the public. When Abby Falik of Global Citizen Year saw that Bill Gates had written in his annual letter that the Gates Foundation would be "focused on global citizens," or that Malia Obama had decided to take a bridge year before attending Harvard, she used those stories to help promote her message that an immersive global year between high school and college is not remedial or a "gap," but an aspirational next step for our country's emerging leaders.[10] The more topical you can make a presentation or a pitch, the more convincing your call to action will be. And following the news cycle this way will help you to get a good deal more press. On that note, the OpEd project, founded by Katie Orenstein to increase the range and quality of voices we hear in the media, offers invaluable resources and workshops for learning the art of getting this kind of coverage.[11]

STRENGTHEN YOUR STORYTELLING MUSCLES

Practice is critical to making a truly captivating presentation. Nadine Burke Harris practiced her fifteen-minute speech for six months. Looking back, she laughs, saying, "By the time I gave the talk, I had practiced it so many times I am sure my husband had it memorized and could have given it for me." Jennifer Pitts recommends that her clients practice in front of a neutral audience "again, and again, and again" in the two weeks before they deliver.

Practice is critical to making a truly captivating presentation. The work here should involve not only gaining a command of your content, but also honing your style of delivery. In *Why Bad Presentations Happen to Good Causes*, Andy Goodman provides a wealth of tips on how to improve your delivery, such as how to connect with the audience through eye contact, how to modulate your voice for dramatic effect and how to use body language to help hold people's attention. I highly recommend the book and his downloadable booklet as well.[12]

TEACH ALL YOUR PEOPLE TO TELL THE STORY

Many of the organizations I studied created opportunities not only for their CEOs, but also for their staff to practice storytelling on a regular basis. IDEO.org cofounder Patrice Martin told me the organization has held storytelling workshops with their entire team, helping them craft a personal story about why applying design thinking to remediate poverty matters. Another interesting way the skills are built is with what they call "Storytelling Roulette." At every weekly staff meeting, a member of the communications team spins a wheel with everyone's name on it, and whoever's name it lands on is tasked with telling a story at the next meeting, about a project the communications team has picked. This practice has had the added benefit of creating institutional memory. As Martin told me: "Because we have grown so quickly, many of the staff who weren't here two years ago don't know how we talk about our work. We need to make sure that everyone on our staff can talk about all of the stories of IDEO.org, not just the projects that individuals happen to work on. We view everybody here as a brand ambassador."

D-Rev also regularly practices storytelling with their staff. Staff rotate organizing what they call "TED Talk Thursdays," collectively watching a TED talk relevant to their work and analyzing not only the substance of the talk but the details of delivery. Krista Donaldson, the CEO, also works regularly with a speaking coach to help her practice her skills, and because of all of the coaching she has received, she is now able to coach staff members herself. When people tell her what a good speaker she is, she always chuckles a bit to herself, and tells them: "You have no idea how much coaching I've had!"

It is also important to make sure that your board is well practiced in delivering the story of the organization so that they too can be ambassadors of your cause. At Accountability Counsel, we have brought in outside friends of the organization to listen as each of our board members makes a two-minute pitch, as if they were meeting someone new at a cocktail party and telling them about the organization's work. Our board members report that these practice sessions have made them better at advocating for the organization in front of potential partners, funders, board members and beyond.

ASK YOUR BENEFICIARIES TO TELL THEIR STORIES

The other people you should engage in telling your story are your beneficiaries. Many organizations of course tell stories about their beneficiaries, but having them tell their own stories is a powerful practice.

The cofounders of City Year, Michael Brown and Alan Khazei, did a great job of this and were able to get Bill Clinton's support largely because he was so impressed by hearing the stories of their participants. In 1992, during his first presidential campaign, then-governor Clinton planned a visit to the offices of City Year to explore the idea of creating a federal policy to support national service across America. Although no one could have predicted with just 3 percent of the democratic primary polls at that point that Bill Clinton would eventually become president, Khazei and Brown knew this was a huge opportunity to infuse their mission into the national dialogue. They pulled out all the stops to get the right people in the room. Mitt Romney, then CEO of Bain and Company and a City Year supporter, mayor of Boston Ray Flynn, and Hubie Jones, one of the top social justice leaders in Boston, agreed to attend and help promote City Year's work. Also seated at the table were a number of corps members who told their stories of participating in the program. According to Khazei, who wasn't even at the table himself, instead sitting in the back of the room, these corps members were the key to convincing Clinton. Khazei told me: "What really turned Clinton on was listening to these young people from all these diverse backgrounds serving together." Once Clinton became president he established AmeriCorps, using City Year as a model, by signing the National and Community Service Trust Act of 1993.[13] Since that time, more than one million young people have participated in AmeriCorps, contributing over 1.4 billion hours of public service.[14]

The corps members were so effective at telling their stories, in fact, that City Year began to showcase them more and more with the media and with other visitors to the organization. As Khazei said, this was also helpful for the movement-building component of the organization: "No one knew what national service was at the time; it really didn't exist except in small pilot programs. So we made it part of the corps members' responsibility to advance the cause of national service, asking them to go out, tell their story, what they learned, how they've grown, what's been hard and where they made a difference."

While asking your beneficiaries to speak on your behalf can be enormously powerful, doing it well also requires careful thought and preparation. There are ethical issues involved. You must assure that they are willingly consenting to speak, not feeling coerced, and that they not only feel comfortable doing so but are well prepared and in good mental and physical shape for coping with the stress of public appearances. It is also critical to set them up for success by making sure they are sufficiently prepared to tell the story well.

SELECTING AND PREPARING YOUR SPOKESPEOPLE

When selecting beneficiaries to speak on an organization's behalf, Jennifer Pitts advises a rigorous selection and preparation process, beginning with a set of in-depth interviews in which you talk with a range of beneficiaries. It's best to consider people who have been out of the program for a good period of time, to prevent the possibility of retraumatization, and because they can speak to the longer term impact of the program.

The conversations should be kept strictly confidential, and Pitts says it's important to let beneficiaries own the interview process and reveal only the parts of their story they want to reveal. She makes it clear that they are not required to talk about anything they don't feel comfortable sharing. With that condition, she guides the interviews with a set of basic questions: "What was your life like before you found this program? What did you like about the program? How does it compare to other programs like it? How has your life changed since starting this program? And most importantly, what would be different for you if you hadn't found this program?"

Pitts also argues that it's helpful to ask for permission to record the conversations so she can recall details, and assure they are speaking in their own words if they're going to be giving speeches.

She argues that it's important to help them craft their stories, but imperative that they speak truly in their own voices.

Jennifer Pitts also recommends that organizations assist beneficiaries with crafting speeches. Helping them to be prepared is in their best interest as well as yours. "They are an expert on their story," she says. "You are the expert on the audience." Many organizations are so honored that a beneficiary has agreed to share their story that they feel it's contrived or disrespectful to ask what the person plans to share. But the biggest mistake you can make is to put someone on stage to represent your organization without a clear idea of what they plan to say. A particular problem is that organizations also often fail to give time constraints and then allow practice time to ensure the time limit has been met. The impact of a story is watered down when it goes on too long or fails to include the right details.

You should also help beneficiaries with their delivery, which must include preparing them for exactly how an event will unfold. Pitts says, "It's important that you cover every detail with them so that you are not putting someone in a situation where they are surprised or caught off guard by the room, the audience or how much money you're trying to raise." Even make sure they don't need help getting appropriate clothing or a ride to the event.

While Tipping Point has an internal communications team that helps prepare their beneficiaries to speak at their annual events, you can also hire outside consultants or speaking coaches to help them through the process. Or as Accountability Counsel once did, bring in friends of the organization to listen to your beneficiaries speak and provide advice for free.

Storytelling isn't just about raising money or courting supporters; it is about building a movement for change. You cannot build a movement without lighting a fire in the people who are poised to spread your message, whether it's donors, partner organizations, media or policy makers. As Steve Jobs brilliantly said, "The most powerful person in the world is the storyteller. The storyteller sets the vision, values and agenda of an entire generation that is to come." We all have the power within us to be great storytellers for the causes we care about; we just have to work hard to bring those talents out.

BENCHMARKS FOR SOCIAL STARTUP SUCCESS: STORYTELLING

✓ Do you have a clear sense of the key message your organization needs to convey?

✓ Have you developed a *story of self* that connects you to a cause and creates intimacy with the audience?

✓ Have you developed a *story of us* that connects the audience to the cause?

✓ Have you developed a *story of now* that conveys the urgency of the problem?

✓ Do you follow the news cycle intentionally to find ways to connect the problem you're addressing to current events?

✓ Do you create opportunities for your staff to practice their own stories?

✓ Do you create opportunities for your beneficiaries to tell stories on behalf of the organization?

✓ When beneficiaries tell their stories on behalf of the organization, do you work with them to help them practice in a way that is respectful and honors their story?

CONCLUSION

Conducting the research for this book has been an incredible journey. I've been able to spend time with so many inspiring leaders who wake up every day charged up to make our world a better place. I have been so impressed with their ingenuity in leveraging all the assets they can find to impact as many lives as possible. I had loads of admiration for social entrepreneurs before I embarked on this journey, but learning more about their work and watching them in action up close has made me respect them all the more.

The journey has also made me even more keenly aware of how many nonprofits are operating on a month-to-month basis, scrambling to raise money to sustain themselves. While so much innovation has occurred in the nonprofit world in recent decades, my conversations with organizational leaders and my observations of their daily routines have impressed upon me how considerable the challenges any nonprofit faces are, no matter how innovative its model or impactful its services. I have often looked back to nights I spent around my family's dinner table, when my parents would talk about the many organizations they were involved with, and how the organizations were barely squeaking by and could hardly serve all the people who needed their services.

I grew up in the small town of Napa, California, the daughter of a community banker and a schoolteacher. As Irish Catholics, we did our best to make it to church every week, but more often on Sundays you could find my sisters and me tagging along with our parents to serve meals at the homeless shelter or checking people into the free health clinic. My parents were always attending non-profit board meetings or collecting auction items for an upcoming fundraiser. My dad was known around town as the "cleanup guy" for struggling nonprofits, the one they begged to join their board to help them get their house in order when they were on the brink of failure. I hope the lessons I've shared from the modern nonprofit community will help organizations avoid the tough straits my dad helped so many nonprofits recover from.

But it's not just organizations seeking to scale that can benefit from these lessons. We can all find better ways to support causes for social good using the tools in this book. Bill Drayton, the founder of Ashoka and often called the "godfather" of social entrepreneurship, lives by the mantra that "everyone is a change maker." I hope the stories I've told will inspire support for social change organizations. Busy as we are, we can all find some way to contribute. Students tell me all the time: "I really love social entrepreneurship and I want to make a difference in the world, but first I'm going to get some corporate work experience." I thought the same way when I was in college. I didn't understand that the two paths are not mutually ex-clusive until I cofounded Spark while also practicing corporate law. When I think back to my parents' community activities, I realize I should have seen that it was possible to have a thriving career and also be involved in social causes—and find it extremely fulfilling. I had regretted choosing the corporate path after law school, and thought I'd sold out because I didn't go to work for the ACLU or Hu-man Rights Watch. But in founding Spark, I saw that just as my dad was able to use his skills as a community banker to help nonprofit boards, I too could use my professional skills and connections to rally my peers for our cause.

We all have something we can give to make this world a little bit better. I hope the profiles of the creative and determined leaders I've shared, and the stories of the remarkable impact they are hav-ing, will encourage you to seek organizations you can spend time supporting.

ACKNOWLEDGMENTS

First and foremost, I am profusely indebted to my collaborator in writing this book, Emily Loose. Emily, you have been by my side since the infancy of this project and remained an extraordinary thought partner throughout. You knew when to push me hard to produce my best, and when to cheer me on to keep me going. Your skillful hand in editing these pages has helped me find my voice and structure my thinking in a way that can be useful to the world. I am eternally grateful for all of your support.

Thank you to my phenomenal agent, Lisa DiMona at Writer's House, who truly understood what I wanted to achieve with this book and has been a fountain of innovative ideas about how to turn my vision not only into an incredible book, but also a movement. Thank you also to her amazing colleague Nora Long, whose early editing vastly improved my proposal and sample chapters. And I am so thankful to my editor, Dan Ambrosio at DaCapo Press, for taking a chance on me and believing in this book every step of the way, and to the rest of the Da Capo team Miriam Riad, Kevin Hanover, Matthew Weston and Raquel Hitt for supporting this book in so many ways. Thank you to Christine Marra and her highly capable team at Marrathon Production Services for making this finished product such a beautiful work of art. And to the team at Digital Natives, thank you for all that you have done to set this digital immigrant up for success.

This project never would have existed without the founding of Spark, which taught me so much about how to be an activist, a risk taker, a team player, a fundraiser and a social entrepreneur. It has been such an amazing adventure since one of my oldest friends Maya Garcia Lahham sat me down over a glass of wine in 2004 to tell me about this "idea" she had for an organization to support women's empowerment, and I have been so lucky to be on this journey along with cofounders Fiona Hsu, Rohini Gupta, Nealan Afsari,

Karen Hennessy and Mona Motwani, as well as so many other Spark leaders who have kept the organization alive and thriving, including Shannon Farley, Jackie Rotman, Amanda Brock, Jamie Allison Hope, Gayle Karen Young, Carlo DaVia and so many more.

I am so grateful to Valerie Threlfall for teaching me how to navigate the art of survey design, along with Meredyth Sneed and Elizabeth Kelley for helping me to lead the most comprehensive survey of seed stage social entrepreneurs ever conducted. Thank you also Echoing Green, especially Cheryl Dorsey, Teresa Vasquez, Andrea Davila and Janna Oberdorf; and Silicon Valley Social Ventures, especially Jen Ratay and Elizabeth Dodson, for opening up your portfolios to us for the social entrepreneurship survey and for being such steadfast supporters of this project every step of the way. And of course this survey would not have been possible without the participation of the hundreds of social entrepreneurs who took time out of their busy schedules to fill out the questions—I am so appreciative of them.

So many other funders of social entrepreneurship were helpful during the survey and other research for this book, including Scott Thomas and Sammy Politziner of Arbor Brothers; Bill Drayton, Michael Zakaras and Clair Fallender at Ashoka; Christy Chin, Stephanie Khurana and Robin Richards of Draper Richards Kaplan Foundation; Kevin Starr and Laura Hattendorf at Mulago Foundation; Vanessa Kirsh and Kim Syman at New Profit; Jayson Morris at Peery Foundation; Sally Osberg at Skoll Foundation and Anne Marie Burgoyne and Beth Schmidt at Emerson Collective.

I am also grateful to the people who inspired me to believe that writing a book was even possible, such as Peter Sims, whose kind introduction to Emily Loose kicked off this whole project, and Courtney Martin, an incredible cheerleader who forced me to open my first Twitter account to jump into the conversation.

Each and every person that I interviewed for this book has been a huge source of information, opening their hearts and their minds to my research and being so eager to help in so many ways. It is one thing to lead a successful organization, but it is quite another to be so thoughtful about the strategies that lead to its success, so thank you for taking the time away from your work to reflect with me. Although I could not feature every single organization whose representatives I interviewed in the book, each and every story certainly influenced my thinking and framing of the concepts herein.

I am eternally grateful for all of the opportunities that Stanford University has provided me to be able to do the social change work that I care about so deeply. In particular, Larry Diamond, Deborah Rhode, Tom Schnaubelt,

Megan Swezey Fogarty, Luke Terra and Julie Reed have all been such fierce champions of the Program on Social Entrepreneurship in partnership with the Haas Center for Public Service and the Center on Democracy Development and the Rule of Law. The Program on Social Entrepreneurship never would have happened without the brilliant vision of Kavita Ramdas and the ongoing commitment of Sarina Beges, both of whom have also been such staunch supporters of this book throughout its writing. My teaching assistants—Gilat Bachar, Erin Raab, Sarah Shirazyan and Shea Streeter—have made it possible for me to teach every year; you blow me away with your thoughtfulness, diligence and commitment to the work you do. And Deborah Rhode, you have been such an amazing mentor to me since I started teaching at Stanford Law School ten years ago. The Program on Social Entrepreneurship would not exist without your guiding light, and I cherish the words of wisdom that you provide on our long walks around the Stanford campus.

To the team at Stanford's Center for Philanthropy and Civil Society, especially Laura Arrillaga-Andreessen, Rob Reich, Paul Brest, Lucy Bernholz, Kim Meredith, Annie Rohan and Cristina Alfonso, thank you for your trail-blazing vision and deep commitment to developing an entire field in academia dedicated to strengthening philanthropy and civil society. The world is a better place because of your work. And to the staff at the Stanford Social Innovation Review, in particular Eric Nee, Johanna Mair and Jenifer Morgan, thank you for paving the way for academic research on social entrepreneurship, including my own.

Thank you to those who took the time to read drafts of my chapters, and for pushing me to make them better—Ayesha Barenblat, Louise Langheier, Heather McLeod Grant, Alexa Cortés Culwell, Jennifer Pitts, William Jackson, Sarina Beges, Jackie Rotman, Emily Dillon, Kendall Romaine, Tashrima Hossain, Ayushi Vig and Sofia Filippa.

My student research assistants never cease to amaze me; they were instrumental in helping to develop a comprehensive literature review of the social entrepreneurship field, and transcribed hundreds of pages of interviews. Thank you for all the hard work—Devanshi Patel, Marly Carlisle, Sophia Jaggi, Jacqueline Wibiwo, Emily Dillon, Kendall Romaine, Carly Hayden, Tashrima Hossain, Ayushi Vig, Anna Wohl, Sofia Filippa, Delaney Overton and Miriam Natvig. Thank you also to Sheeroh Murenga, my partner halfway across the world who also transcribed so many other interviews for me.

When people ask me who my closest mentors are, I always give the same reply: my girl squad. You are my biggest inspirations, and I am eternally grateful to my dearest friends for always being my mirror, helping me to see my blind spots, supporting me through challenging times and rooting for me every step of the way—Sarah Ray, Kirsten Green, Akshata Murty, Carolyn Cassidy, Anja Manuel, Nadine Burke Harris, Natalie Fields, Lateefah Simon, Jennifer Siebel Newsom, Alexandra Wolfe, Liv Mills Carlisle, Jennifer Bennett, Caroline Cameron and so many others.

This book might not have happened were it not for the support of my beloved writers' group, Anja Manuel, Kori Schake, Sarah Thornton and Ana Homoyoun, who have provided meaningful and constructive feedback in the absolute nicest and most supportive way over the past three years. I always looked forward to our monthly dinners and feel so lucky to count each of you as a colleague and friend.

I have given birth to three babies since deciding to write this book. As such, none of this would have been feasible without the amazing childcare providers who love my children as if they were their own and make it possible for me to do all of the work I love—Alyssa Jennings, Evelyn Sagastume, Mica Crittendon, Laura Pedley and Gabriela Boff, not to mention all of the phenomenal teachers and staff at Cow Hollow School.

I am also indebted to the always positive and effusively kind staff at Saint Frank Coffee for keeping me sufficiently caffeinated and providing an inspiring space where I wrote much of this book.

It is said that one of the greatest gifts in life is to be surrounded by unconditional love. I am so blessed to have received this gift in abundance in my life. My parents, Brian and Maggie Kelly, have always believed in me, modeling and teaching me from a young age that I could accomplish anything in life with hard work. I cannot imagine life without my sisters, Megan and Jen, and their families, Manuel, Todd, Lolo, Alex, Lucas, Carolina, Jordan, Taylor, Carter and Rita, as well as my husband's family, Ted, Bill, and Teresa.

My own children, Lara, Eleanor and Teddy, are the lights of my life and already impress me daily with their kindness and generosity toward each other and the world. I hope that I can instill in you the value of citizenship and the importance of giving back that my parents gave to me.

Last but not least, to my dearest Ted: my dreams came true the day I met you. I never knew it was possible to be fulfilled in so many ways by a single person. I am so lucky to get to spend my life with you by my side. Table 51 forever.

APPENDIX A
Cast of Characters

Accountability Counsel, founded by Natalie Bridgeman Fields, defends
the environmental and human rights of marginalized communities
around the world.
Year Founded: 2009
Issue Area: Human Rights/Environment
HQ: San Francisco, California
Current Budget: $2 million
Number of Staff: 14
Impact: Directly supported nearly a million people in thirty-seven countries
around the world to challenge abuse; advocacy improved global ac-
countability policy at multilateral development banks, federal agencies
and institutions.
Website: www.accountabilitycounsel.org

Aspire Schools, founded by Don Shalvey and led by Carolyn Hack, seeks
to grow the charter school movement by opening small, high-quality
charter schools in low-income neighborhoods.
Year Founded: 1998
Issue Area: Education
HQ: Oakland, California
Current Budget: $200 million
Number of Staff: 2,006
Impact: Serves 16,000 students grades TK through 12 across California and
Tennessee, with 100 percent of high school graduates accepted into a
four-year university.
Website: www.aspirepublicschools.org

Asylum Access, founded by Emily Arnold-Fernandez, is an innovative international nonprofit dedicated to making human rights a reality for refugees.
Year Founded: 2005
Issue Area: Human Rights
HQ: Oakland, California
Current Budget: $3.5 million
Number of Staff: 85
Impact: Legal assistance to over twenty thousand refugees annually; policy change impacting over 2 million to date.
Website: www.asylumaccess.org

At The Crossroads, founded by Rob Gitin, reaches out to homeless youth and young adults and works with them to build healthy and fulfilling lives.
Year Founded: 1997
Issue Area: Poverty/Homelessness
HQ: San Francisco, California
Current Budget: $1.6 million
Number of Staff: 17
Impact: 90 percent of counseling clients achieve one or more of their life goals, including getting into stable housing, building a healthy community, managing substance use issues or finding employment.
Website: www.atthecrossroads.org

BELL, founded by Earl Phalen and under the leadership of CEO Tiffany Cooper Gueye, seeks to transform the academic achievements, self-confidence and life trajectories of children living in underresourced communities.
Year Founded: 1992
Issue Area: Education
HQ: Boston, Massachusetts
Current Budget: $22 million
Number of Staff: 58
Impact: Students attending BELL programs demonstrate improved achievement in reading and math, as opposed to suffering summer learning loss, outpace their peers in gaining academic skills and demonstrate improved social-emotional skills. BELL's impact has been validated and continuously improved through two randomized control trial studies to date.
Website: www.experiencebell.org

Benetech, founded by Jim Fruchterman, is a nonprofit that empowers communities in need by creating scalable technology solutions.
Year Founded: 2000
Issue Area: Human Rights/Technology
HQ: Palo Alto, California
Current Budget: $17 million
Number of Staff: 74
Impact: Benetech has driven large scale change in education, human rights and the environment, including delivering over 10 million accessible books to more than half a million people with disabilities such as dyslexia or blindness, with more than 535,000 titles in thirty-two languages.
Website: www.benetech.org

Beyond 12, founded by Alexandra Bernadotte, uses technology and student coaching to give students the academic, social and emotional support they need to succeed in higher education.
Year Founded: 2009
Issue Area: Education
HQ: Oakland, California
Current Budget: $4.2 million
Number of Staff: 25
Impact: In partnership with K–12 and higher education institutions, tracking the progress of more than fifty thousand students; coaching close to two thousand students on 180 college campuses, 82 percent of whom have persisted to their third year of collage compared with 59 percent of first-generation college students nationwide.
Website: www.beyond12.org

Blue Engine, founded by Nick Ehrmann, partners with schools to unlock human potential by bringing together teams of teachers working in historically oppressed communities to reimagine the classroom experience for all students.
Year Founded: 2009
Issue Area: Education
HQ: New York, New York
Current Budget: $6 million
Number of Staff: 26
Impact: Currently supporting eighty-six Blue Engine teaching assistants and sixteen hundred students, students achieve an additional seven to nine months of learning per year, leading to spikes in pass and college-ready rates on state exams; 40 percent of alumni base currently teaching.
Website: www.blueengine.org

Braven, founded by Aimée Eubanks Davis, is a semester-long credit-bearing course followed by a post-course experience that lasts until college graduation for underrepresented university students, which builds the skills, mindsets, experiences and networks necessary to excel in the workforce.

Year Founded: 2013

Issue Area: Education and Workforce

Staff: 19

HQ: Chicago, Illinois

Current Budget: $4.1 million

Impact: 540 fellows, nearly two times as likely to obtain a strong internship in comparison to peers; 66 percent land strong, first jobs post-college within six months, in comparison to 49 percent of their peers within twelve months.

Website: www.bebraven.org

CareMessage, founded by Vineet Singal and Cecilia Corral, creates a powerful communications channel between health care organizations in medically underserved areas and the patients they serve.

Year Founded: 2012

Issue Area: Health

HQ: San Francisco, California

Current Budget: $8.9 million

Number of Staff: 40

Impact: Reached more than 1.2 million patients through relationships with two hundred health care organizations in more than thirty-five states and exchanged nearly 15 million messages with those patients.

Website: www.caremessage.org

Center for Youth Wellness, founded by Nadine Burke Harris, fights against adverse childhood experiences and toxic health by preventing, screening and healing.

Year Founded: 2010

Issue Area: Health

HQ: San Francisco, California

Current Budget: $7.9 million

Number of Staff: 27

Impact: Developed an ACEs (adverse childhood experiences) screening tool that has been shared with over fifteen hundred clinicians in twenty-four countries; launched a practice community of a thousand pediatricians to screen 300,000 children for ACEs; and operates a community-based

clinic screening nine hundred children annually for ACEs, treating three
hundred through intensive integrated care.
Website: www.centerforyouthwellness.org

charity: water, founded by Scott Harrison, seeks to solve the water crisis in
our lifetime.
Year Founded: 2006
Issue Area: Access to Clean Water
HQ: New York, New York
Current Budget: $40 million
Number of Staff: 75
Impact: 22,936 water projects funded; 7 million people get clean water work-
ing with twenty-five local partners in twenty-four countries.
Website: www.charitywater.org

City Year, cofounded by Michael Brown and Alan Khazei, seeks to help
students in high-poverty communities reach their potential through
individualized support.
Year Founded: 1988
Issue Area: Education
HQ: Boston, Massachusetts
Current Budget: $152,000,000
Number of Staff: 998
Impact: A national study showed that schools partnered with City Year are
two times more likely to improve on state English assessments and up to
three times more likely to improve proficiency rates in math.
Website: www.cityyear.org

Coalition for Queens (C4Q), founded by Jukay Hsu and David Yang,
fosters the Queens tech ecosystem to increase economic opportunity
and transform the world's most diverse community into a leading hub
for innovation and entrepreneurship.
Year Founded: 2011
Issue Area: Job Development
HQ: Long Island City, New York
Current Budget: $4.3 million
Number of Staff: 30
Impact: In under a year, graduates go from making $18,000 to over $85,000
post-program, shifting from poverty to the middle class in the process,
and working at leading companies such as Pinterest, Kickstarter,
LinkedIn, Jet and JPMorgan Chase. Participants are representative of the

diversity of the New York City community with over 50 percent women, 60 percent African American or Hispanic, 50 percent immigrant and 50 percent without a college education.
Website: www.c4q.nyc

Code2040, founded by Laura Weidman Powers and Tristan Walker, creates pathways to success for blacks and Latinx in the innovation economy.
Year Founded: 2012
Issue Area: Economic and Racial Equity
HQ: San Francisco, California
Current Budget: $8 million
Number of Staff: 32
Impact: 250+ Fellows matched with 75+ tech companies and a community of 5,000 students, allies, volunteers and supporters.
Website: www.code2040.org

D-Rev, led by Krista Donaldson, a nonprofit medical device company focused on closing quality healthcare gaps for underserved populations.
Year Founded: 2009
Issue Area: Health
HQ: San Francisco, California
Current Budget: $2.1 million
Number of Staff: 11
Impact: With Brilliance, D-Rev's newborn jaundice product, 225,000 babies have been treated, averting three thousand deaths and disabilities; and with Re-Motion Knee, D-Rev's amputee mobility product, 7,501 amputees have been fitted with the knee, reporting an 86 percent satisfaction rate.
Website: www.d-rev.org

DonorsChoose, founded by Charles Best, is an online platform where anyone can help a classroom in need, moving toward a nation where students in every community have the tools and experiences they need for a great education.
Year Founded: 2000
Issue Area: Education
HQ: New York, New York
Current Budget: $14 million
Number of Staff: 92
Impact: Vetted and fulfilled over 890,000 classroom projects across the nation ranging from butterfly cocoons to robotics kits to *Little House on the Prairie*.
website: www.donorschoose.org

Embrace, founded by Jane Chen, integrates appropriate technology with training and monitoring to support health workers and facilities in low-resource settings.
Year Founded: 2008
Issue Area: Health
HQ: San Francisco, California
Current Budget: Private company
Number of Staff: 5
Impact: Helped over 250,000 babies
Website: www.embraceglobal.org

Genders and Sexualities Alliance Network (GSA Network, previously Gay-Straight Alliance Network), founded by Carolyn Laub, is a next-generation LGBTQ racial and gender justice organization that empowers and trains queer, trans and allied youth leaders to advocate, organize, and mobilize an intersectional movement for safer schools and healthier communities.
Year Founded: 1998
Issue Area: LGBTQ
HQ: San Francisco, California
Current Budget: $2.3 million
Number of Staff: 20
Impact: In California, GSA Network has grown the network of GSA clubs from forty to over nine hundred clubs, impacting more than 1.1 million students in 61 percent of California's public high schools and a growing number of middle schools; nationally, GSA Network has united over forty statewide organizations supporting GSAs to accelerate the growth and impact of the GSA movement in four thousand schools nationwide.
Website: www.gsanetwork.org

Generation Citizen, founded by Scott Warren, works to ensure that every student in the United States receives an effective action civics education, which provides them with the knowledge and skills necessary to partici-pate in our democracy as active citizens.
Year Founded: 2008
Issue Area: Civic Engagement
HQ: New York, New York
Current Budget: $2.6 million
Number of Staff: 30
Impact: 10,500 students impacted
Website: www.generationcitizen.org

Genesys Works, founded by Rafael Alvarez, transforms the lives of disadvantaged high school students through skills training, meaningful internships and impactful relationships.
Year Founded: 2002
Issue Area: Job Training
HQ: Houston, Texas
Current Budget: $25 million
Number of Staff: 130
Impact: 94 percent of program alumni go on to college, of which 71 percent persist. Five years after program completion, 74 percent of alumni are working full time earning a median annual income of $45,000.
Website: www.genesysworks.org

GiveWell, founded by Elie Hassenfeld and Holden Karnofsky, is dedicated to finding outstanding giving opportunities and publishing the full details of their analyses to help donors decide where to give.
Year Founded: 2007
Issue Area: Philanthropy
HQ: San Francisco, California
Current Budget: $2.4 million
Number of Staff: 17
Impact: More than $100 million to top charities in 2015
Website: www.givewell.org

Global Citizen Year, founded by Abby Falik, is reinventing the "gap year" between high school and college as America's launch pad for global leaders.
Year Founded: 2010
Issue Area: Education
HQ: Oakland, California
Current Budget: $4.4 million
Number of Staff: 40
Impact: 530 alumni
Website: www.globalcitizenyear.org

Global Women's Water Initiative, founded by Gemma Bulos, is building a movement of local women water experts to address the issue that affects them most: water.
Year Founded: 2011
Issue Area: Gender Equality/Water
HQ: Oakland, California

Current Budget: $650,000
Number of Staff: 5
Impact: Invested in twelve teams of rural African women and trained them
  in water, sanitation and hygiene techniques that will result in clean
  water and sanitation for 40,600 people.
Website: www.globalwomenswater.org

Hot Bread Kitchen, founded by Jessamyn Rodriguez, is a workforce
  development and business incubation program that seeks to train low-
  income women in food careers, supporting its programming through
  bread sales and kitchen rentals.
Year Founded: 2008
Issue Area: Gender Equality/Job Development
HQ: New York, New York
Current Budget: $5 million
Number of Staff: 15 admin, 50 production/trainees
Impact: Since moving to East Harlem in December 2010, Hot Bread Kitchen
  has trained 156 low-income women from thirty-six countries and graduated sixty-six into full-time jobs with benefits. Its culinary incubator has
  provided commercial kitchen space and technical assistance to support
  the growth of 169 food businesses. Hot Bread Kitchen has created over
  two hundred jobs in a neighborhood with one of the highest rates of
  joblessness in New York City.
Website: www.hotbreadkitchen.org

IDEO.org, founded by Jocelyn Wyatt and Patrice Martin, designs prod-
  ucts, services and experiences to improve the lives of people in poor and
  vulnerable communities with a practice of human-centered design.
Year Founded: 2011
Issue Area: Poverty Alleviation
HQ: San Francisco, California
Current Budget: $13.25 million
Number of Staff: 65
Impact: 434,570 people impacted through its sixty-four design projects in
  twenty-three countries in sectors as varied as water and sanitation to
  financial opportunity, agriculture and reproductive health.
Website: www.ideo.org

Kiva, founded by Premal Shah, Jessica Jackley and Matt Flannery, works
  with microfinance institutions on five continents to provide loans to
  people without access to traditional banking systems.

Year Founded: 2005
Issue Area: Economic Empowerment
HQ: San Francisco, California
Current Budget: $16 million
Number of Staff: 105
Impact: To date, Kiva has facilitated nearly a billion dollars in loans to 2.3
  million microentrepreneurs across ninety countries. The repayment rate
  is 97 percent and the average loan size is $800.
Website: www.kiva.org

Last Mile Health, founded by Raj Panjabi, delivers care in the world's most
  remote communities.
Year Founded: 2007
Issue Area: Health
HQ: Boston, Massachusetts
Current Budget: $9.7 million
Number of Staff: 100
Impact: Trained over three hundred community health professionals, bring-
  ing health care to over two hundred remote communities and fifty thou-
  sand people and increasing, for example, access to diarrhea (by 48%),
  malaria (by 29%) and pneumonia (by 53%) treatment among children.
Website: www.lastmilehealth.org

Living Goods, founded by Charles Slaughter, supports "Avon-like"
  networks of microentrepreneurs empowered with their Smart Health
  app who go door-to-door selling life-changing products such as simple
  treatments for malaria and pneumonia, fortified foods, family planning,
  clean cook stoves and solar lights.
Year Founded: 2007
Issue Area: Health
HQ: San Francisco, California
Current Budget: $16.3 million
Number of Staff: 206
Impact: Supports over sixty-five hundred community health promoters,
  serving a population of 5 million. In 2016, Living Goods supported
  213,000 pregnancies and treated 681,000 children under five years old
  for deadly diseases. A randomized control trial showed Living Goods
  is cutting child mortality by over 25 percent and reducing stunting by
  7 percent.
Website: www.livinggoods.org

New Door Ventures, under the leadership of Tess Reynolds, provides
  skills training, meaningful jobs, education assistance and personal sup-
  port to help disconnected youth get ready for work and life.
Year Founded: 1981
Issue Area: Job Training
HQ: San Francisco, California
Current Budget: $6.45 million
Number of Staff: 50 (or 250 including youth interns)
Impact: 89 percent of program graduates from 2012 to 2016 were attached to
  next-jobs or continued education six months after program completion
  (after previously not working nor in school). Of those with backgrounds
  of homelessness, 94 percent retained stable housing six months after
  program completion. Of those with prior justice-system involvement,
  96 percent did not reoffend by the six-month follow-up.
Website: www.newdoor.org

New Teacher Center, founded by Ellen Moir, is dedicated to accelerating
  student learning by improving teacher effectiveness through mentoring
  and new teacher induction programs.
Year Founded: 1998
Issue Area: Education
HQ: Santa Cruz, California
Current Budget: $40 million
Number of Staff: 209
Impact: NTC operates in thirty-three states and roughly six hundred school
  districts. In fiscal year 2016, NTC reached over forty thousand teachers
  and seventy-five mentors and coaches, thereby impacting over 3.4 mil-
  lion students.
Website: www.newteachercenter.org

One Acre Fund, founded by Andrew Youn, battles hunger and poverty by
  increasing the productivity of smallholder farmers in East Africa.
Year Founded: 2006
Issue Area: Food Security/Economic Development
HQ: Bungoma, Kenya
Current Budget: $83 million
Number of Staff: 5,000
Impact: One Acre Fund has served 310,000 farm families in East Africa, whose
  incomes have risen by $135 and who paid back loans at a rate of 99 percent.
Website: www.oneacrefund.org

One Degree, founded by Rey Faustino, is a nonprofit technology-driven
   organization revolutionizing the way low-income families access com-
   munity resources.
Year Founded: 2012
Issue Area: Poverty Alleviation
HQ: San Francisco, California
Current Budget: $1.2 million
Number of Staff: 8 full time, 14 part time
Impact: 185,000 people in the San Francisco Bay Area have used OneDegree,
   or one in six people in need.
Website: www.1degree.org

Peer Health Exchange, founded by Louise Langheier, empowers young
   people with the knowledge, skills and resources to make healthy deci-
   sions by training college students to teach a skills-based health curricu-
   lum in underresourced high schools across the country.
Year Founded: 2003
Issue Area: Health
HQ: San Francisco, California
Current Budget: $6.5 million
Number of Staff: 50
Impact: Statistically significant positive results on knowledge, skills and
   help-seeking behavior, particularly in sexual and mental health and use
   of health resources.
Website: www.peerhealthexchange.org

Room to Read, founded by John Wood, Dinesh Shrestha and Erin Ganju,
   seeks to transform the lives of millions of children in developing coun-
   tries by focusing on literacy and gender equality in education.
Year Founded: 2000
Issue Area: Education
HQ: San Francisco, California
Current Budget: $54 million
Number of Staff: 1,400
Impact: Impacted more than 10 million children by developing literacy skills
   and a habit of reading among primary school children and by support-
   ing girls to complete secondary school with strong life skills.
Website: www.roomtoread.org

Row New York, founded by Amanda Kraus, is teaching young people in underresourced communities the sport of competitive rowing—and through it, the values of teamwork, tenacity and commitment to self and others.
Year Founded: 2002
Issue Area: Education
HQ: New York, New York
Current Budget: $3.4 million
Number of Staff: 23 full time, 19 part time
Impact: 100 percent of students who completed the Row New York program in 2016 graduated from high school in four years and 92 percent matriculated to college.
Website: www.rownewyork.org

San Francisco Child Abuse Prevention Center, led by Katie Albright, prevents child abuse and its devastating impact.
Year Founded: 1998
Issue Area: Children, Youth and Families
HQ: San Francisco, California
Current Budget: $7 million
Number of Staff: 51
Impact: The Prevention Center seeks to end child abuse and reduce its devastating effects by providing evidence-informed family support and education to more than twelve thousand children, parents, caregivers and community members annually and by working with public and private partners to improve the abuse prevention and response system.
Website: www.sfcapc.org

SIRUM, founded by Kiah Williams, Adam Kircher and George Wang, uses an innovative technology platform to save peoples' lives by allowing health facilities, manufacturers, wholesalers and pharmacies to donate unused medicine rather than destroy it.
Year Founded: 2011
Issue Area: Health
HQ: Palo Alto, California
Current Budget: $1 million
Number of Staff: 5
Impact: Since its inception, SIRUM has repurposed over $7 million of medicine, enough for over 150,000 prescriptions.
Website: www.sirum.org

Springboard Collaborative, founded by Alejandro Gac-Artigas, closes the reading achievement gap by coaching teachers, training family members and cultivating reading habits so that our scholars have the requisite skills to access life opportunities.
Year Founded: 2013
Issue Area: Education
HQ: Philadelphia, Pennsylvania
Current Budget: $7 million
Number of Staff: 13 full time, 134 seasonal staff
Impact: By training parents and teachers to collaborate, Springboard more than doubles students' annual reading progress and puts them on track to close the reading achievement gap by fourth grade, which is among the strongest predictors of high school completion, college graduation and earning potential.
Website: www.springboardcollaborative.org

Teach For America, founded by Wendy Kopp, finds, develops and supports a diverse network of leaders who expand opportunity for children in classrooms, schools, and every sector and field that shapes the broader systems in which schools operate.
Year Founded: 1989
Issue Area: Education
HQ: New York, New York
Current Budget: $287,000,000
Number of Staff: 1891 full time, 31 part time
Impact: More than 53,000 corps members and alumni are on the leading edge of expanding opportunity for children in urban and rural communities.
Website: www.teachforamerica.org

Thread, founded by Sarah Hemminger, engages underperforming high school students confronting significant barriers outside of the classroom by providing each one with a family of committed volunteers and increased access to community resources.
Year Founded: 2004
Issue Area: Education
HQ: Baltimore, Maryland
Current Budget: $4.14 million
Number of Staff: 35 full time, 12 part time

Impact: Weaving together 303 students and alumni, 850-plus volunteers and 350-plus collaborators, doing whatever it takes to help students realize their potential.
Website: www.thread.org

Watsi, founded by Chase Adam, enables individuals to directly fund low-cost, high-impact medical care for people in need.
Year Founded: 2012
Issue Area: Health
HQ: San Francisco, California
Current Budget: $2 million
Number of Staff: 16
Impact: In its first three years, 16,700 donors have contributed over $5.5 million on Watsi's platform to fund care for nearly seven thousand patients in twenty-two countries.
Website: www.watsi.org

Wishbone, founded by Beth Schmidt, sends low-income high school students from Connecticut, New York City, Los Angeles and the San Francisco Bay Area to extracurricular programs.
Year Founded: 2012
Issue Area: Education
HQ: San Francisco, California
Current Budget: $2.3 million
Number of Staff: 7
Impact: Since 2012, they have helped 1,582 students raise over $3 million in funding for summer programs.
Website: www.wishbone.org

APPENDIX B
Methodology

PHASE 1: THE LITERATURE REVIEW

In the first phase of my research, over the course of 2013 through 2015, I worked with several of my student research assistants to pull together hundreds of articles related to best practices in the nonprofit world, to learn what experts were saying about the path to scale. During that process, we discovered about a dozen key strategies at the heart of nonprofit growth, from impact measurement to funding to innovation. We also realized through our research that very little actual data existed about how organizations grow, especially in the early stages. This led me to administer my own survey to collect relevant data to better understand the key elements of nonprofit scale.

PHASE 2: THE SURVEY

The second phase of my research was to test several variables we had uncovered in Phase 1 to determine which strategies were most important in the early path to scale. To download the full results of the survey, "Scaling the Social Startup: A Survey of the Growth Path of Top-Performing Social Entrepreneurs," go to www.kathleenjanus.com/resources. The survey had two primary objectives: First, we wanted to understand the practices and tools used by social entrepreneurs at different stages of organizational progress. Secondly, we wanted to gather social entrepreneurs' perspectives on the key supports and challenges they had encountered along their path to building multimillion-dollar organizations.

Survey Instrument Development

Our initial survey was developed over a multimonth period in late 2014. Survey experts Valerie Threlfall and Elizabeth Kelley of Threlfall Consulting led the survey drafting, while I provided strategic guidance and ongoing feedback to instrument development. As part of the process, I consulted many practitioners and funders of social entrepreneurial organizations including:

- Andrea Davila, Echoing Green
- Christy Chin, Draper Richards Kaplan
- Elizabeth Dodson, Silicon Valley Social Ventures
- Fay Twersky, William and Flora Hewlett Foundation
- Heather McLeod Grant, coauthor of *Forces for Good*
- Johanna Mair, Stanford University
- Katie Albright, San Francisco Child Abuse Prevention Center
- Kim Syman, New Profit
- Lance Fors, Social Venture Partners Network
- Lindsay Louie, William and Flora Hewlett Foundation
- Michael Lombardo, Reading Partners
- Paul Brest, former president of the William and Flora Hewlett Foundation
- Reshma Saujani, Girls Who Code
- Shannon Farley, Fast Forward

In 2016, we removed select questions from our survey and added some additional demographic questions, based on our survey experience in 2015.

Survey Administration

We administered our core survey to two separate samples in 2015 and 2016.

Echoing Green and Silicon Valley Social Ventures (SV2) Portfolios

- In 2015, we surveyed social entrepreneurs who received either an Echoing Green fellowship or an SV2 grant. We selected recipients from these portfolios, as both selecting organizations have thoughtful selection criteria, which place a premium on innovation and preliminary evidence of effectiveness. Echoing Green or SV2 administered the survey to the members of their portfolios in January 2015.
- Of the 597 people surveyed, 147 responded for a 25 percent overall response rate across the two portfolios. Respondents represent 141 orga-

nizations, 124 of which are Echoing Green fellowship recipients and 17 of which are SV2 grantees.
- Survey respondents received multiple reminders from their sponsoring organization, Echoing Green or SV2, during the period of survey administration. Respondents were also eligible to receive a $25 gift card for successful completion of the survey.

Additional Social Entrepreneurial Portfolios
- In 2016, we built a convenience sample of high-performing social entrepreneurs affiliated with eight major grant portfolios whose contact information was available through network outreach and/or Internet research. It's important to note that in 2016, we did not conduct outreach in affiliation with the sponsoring organizations like we did in 2015. We contacted chief executive officers/executive directors of organizations from the following portfolios:
  - Arbor Brothers
  - Ashoka US
  - Blue Ridge Foundation
  - Draper Richards Kaplan
  - Echoing Green (only those who had not responded to prior survey)
  - Fast Forward
  - Mulago Foundation
  - New Profit
  - Peery Foundation
  - Skoll Foundation
  - SV2 (only those who had not responded to prior survey)
- The goal of adding these individuals was to explicitly increase the number of participating organizations in our survey. We selected respondents from these well-recognized grant/award portfolios so we could learn from the best practices of some of the most successful leaders and organizations.
- Convenience sampling is a nonprobabilistic, nonrandomized sampling methodology that leverages available contacts and is commonly used in exploratory work and/or when there is no way to access an entire eligible survey population.
- In September 2016, we administered a survey to these individuals, knowing that our method of convenience sampling would likely result in a lower response rate. Of the 685 respondents contacted, 239 had been asked to complete the 2015 survey, but had not responded. Three

hundred sixty-one emails bounced and there were 72 responses for a response rate (net of bounce-backs) of 22 percent.

- Survey respondents received multiple reminders from Kathleen Kelly Janus during the period of survey administration. Respondents were also eligible to receive a $25 gift card for successful completion of the survey.

Survey Sample

- Overall, our aggregate combined sample includes 219 individuals from 210 organizations.
- Of the 685 respondents contacted in 2016, 239 had been asked to complete the 2015 survey, but had not responded. This means that across the two administrations, we contacted 727 unique individuals. With 219 total responses, we had an overall response rate of 30 percent.
- The attributes of these individuals and their organizations are summarized below:
  - As the overall portfolios included some original founders who may no longer be with their organizations, we only included feedback from individuals who are still with their organizations in our analysis. Ninety-two percent of respondents are the original founders of social entrepreneurial organizations (still with their organizations).
  - Survey respondents represent organizations across our target budget spectrum of $500,000 to $3,000,000.[1] (Organizational annual budgets range from $15,000 to $50,000,000 with a median budget of $1,000,000. Organizations surveyed have been in operation for varying amounts of time, ranging from zero to fifty-one years, with a median tenure of ten years in operation. Organizations report having between zero to twenty-five hundred full-time employees, with a median of twelve full-time employees.)
  - Only respondents who indicate their organization is a 501c3 non-profit, a 501c3 hybrid (a 501c3 organization with a for-profit arm), or another type of nonprofit organization (e.g., an international non-profit) are included in the sample. Respondents who indicate their organization is a for-profit, for-profit hybrid or a 501c4 are excluded from the analysis.
  - Survey respondents represent a spectrum of geographic focus areas, with 24 percent reporting a local (U.S.) focus, 18 percent reporting a regional (U.S.) focus, 28 percent reporting a national (U.S.) focus, and 30 percent reporting an international (non-U.S.) focus.

Below are some charts describing our final sample in greater detail.

Survey Sample: Field of Focus

Field of Focus	Percentage of Respondents[2]
Arts/Culture	7%
Civil Rights	19%
Community Improvement	23%
Education	48%
Employment	16%
Environment	14%
Global Development	15%
Health	22%
Housing	7%
Human Services	12%
Public Benefit/Advocacy	15%
Youth Development	26%
Other	31%

Survey Sample: Target Geography

Target Geography	Percentage of Respondents
International (non-U.S.)	30%
Local (U.S.)	24%
National (U.S.)	28%
Regional (U.S.)	18%

Survey Sample: Grant Portfolio Affiliation[3]

Portfolio	Percentage of Respondents
Arbor Brothers	7%
Ashoka	35%
Blue Ridge Foundation	4%
Draper Richards Kaplan Foundation	22%
Echoing Green	67%
Fast Forward	7%
Mulago Foundation	7%
New Profit	10%
Peery Foundation	4%
Silicon Valley Social Ventures	12%
Skoll Foundation	8%
Stanford Social Entrepreneurs in Residence	3%

Characterization of Sample Based on Organization Annual Budget

Organization Size	Count of Organizations in Segment	Proportion of All Organizations	Average Number of Years in Operation
Less than $500K	44	21%	4
$500K–$2MM	54	26%	12
$2MM+	54	26%	11

What We Can (and Cannot) Say from This Dataset

This dataset allows us to understand the most common practices and approaches used by social entrepreneurs, as well as dominant perspectives from social entrepreneurs about issues such as growth and scaling. However, it is hard to elicit "best practices" from the dataset, beyond being able to document how the practices of larger organizations differ from those of smaller organizations, given the lack of data about comparative social impact among respondent organizations. While we do believe there is some opportunity to assume that the organizations presented in our survey population are among the most successful, given the fact that they met the selection criteria of these competitive grant or award processes, we cannot assume they are all high-performers.

In addition, while we cannot assume that scaling or an increase in organizational budget is a proxy for organizational impact, we believe this dataset allows us to elicit the most common practices used by organizations as they sought to become sustainable multimillion-dollar organizations. We believe that providing *descriptive* data about these practices is useful for the field, given the lack of comprehensive data about social entrepreneurs' practices; however, the data by itself should be used cautiously to make *normative* statements about best practices.

PHASE 3: THE INTERVIEWS

Between May 2015 and March 2017, I interviewed nearly one hundred social entrepreneurs, academics, funders and other experts, asking them a simple question: "What is the key to nonprofit success?" Their stories helped shed light on some of the data we found in the survey and led me to develop the five primary strategies that tended to come up again and again in the interviews as critical to scale: testing, measuring, funding experimentation, leading collectively and storytelling. A complete list of the interviews I conducted for this book is as follows:

Social Entrepreneurs

Adam, Chase	Watsi
Albright, Katie	San Francisco Child Abuse Prevention Center
Alvarez, Rafael	Genesys Works
Arnold-Fernandez, Emily	Asylum Access
Bernadotte, Alexandra	Beyond 12
Best, Charles	DonorsChoose
Bulos, Gemma	Global Women's Water Initiative
Burke Harris, Nadine	Center for Youth Wellness
Corral, Cecilia	CareMessage
Donaldson, Krista	D-Rev
Ehrmann, Nick	Blue Engine
Eubanks Davis, Aimée	Braven
Falik, Abigail	Global Citizen Year
Farley, Shannon	Fast Forward
Faustino, Ray	One Degree
Fields, Natalie Bridgeman	Accountability Counsel
Forti, Matt	One Acre Fund
Fruchterman, Jim	Benetech
Gac-Artigas, Alejandro	Springboard Collaborative
Ganju, Erin	Room to Read
Gitin, Rob	At The Crossroads
Gueye, Tiffany Cooper	Bell
Harrison, Scott	charity: water
Jackley, Jessica	Kiva.org
Janah, Laila	Samasource
Karnofsky, Holden	GiveWell
Kassalow, Jordan	Vision Spring
Khazei, Alan	City Year
Kirsch, Vanessa	Public Allies
Kopp, Wendy	Teach For All
Langheier, Louise	Peer Health Exchange
Laub, Carolyn	Gay-Straight Alliance
Lublin, Nancy	Crisis Text Line
Martin, Patrice	IDEO.org
Moir, Ellen	New Teacher Center
Nesbit, Josh	Medic Mobile

Panjabi, Raj	Last Mile Health
Powers, Laura	Code2040
Reynolds, Tess	New Door Ventures
Rodriguez, Jessamyn	Hot Bread Kitchen
Schmidt, Beth	Wishbone
Shah, Premal	Kiva.org
Shepard, Lisbeth	Green City Force
Simon, Lateefah	Center for Young Women's Development
Singal, Vineet	CareMessage
Slaughter, Chuck	Living Goods
Warren, Scott	Generation Citizen
Williams, Kiah	SIRUM
Wyatt, Jocelyn	IDEO.org
Yang, David	Coalition 4 Queens
Youn, Andrew	One Acre Fund

Academics and Experts

Bornstein, David	Author, *How to Change the World*
Brest, Paul	Stanford Law School
Cortés Culwell, Alexa	Open Impact
Fors, Lance	Social Venture Partners (SVP)
Foster, William	The Bridgespan Group
Mair, Johanna	Stanford Center on Philanthropy and Civil Society
McCrea, Jennifer	Author, *The Generosity Network*
McLeod Grant, Heather	Author, *Forces for Good*
Meehan, Bill	Stanford Graduate School of Business
Seelos, Christian	Stanford Center on Philanthropy and Civil Society
Rodriguez Heyman, Darian	Nomi Foundation
Shah, Sonal	Georgetown Beeck Center for Social Impact
Wexler, Rob	Adler & Colvin

Funders

Burgoyne, Anne Marie	Emerson Collective
Chin, Christy	Draper Richards Kaplan
Davila, Andrea	Echoing Green
Dorsey, Cheryl	Echoing Green
Drayton, Bill	Ashoka
Farley, Shannon	Fast Forward
Hattendorf, Laura	Mulago Foundation
Kher, Renuka	Tipping Point

Kirsch, Vanessa	New Profit
Klein, Matt	Blue Ridge Foundation
Khurana, Stephanie	Draper Richards Kaplan
Lurie, Daniel	Tipping Point
Morris, Jayson	Peery Foundation
Niklaus, Andrew	Tipping Point
Osberg, Sally	Skoll Foundation
Pitts, Jennifer	Tipping Point
Politziner, Sammy	Arbor Brothers
Ratay, Jennifer	Silicon Valley Social Ventures (SV2)
Starr, Kevin	Mulago Foundation
Syman, Kim	New Profit
Thomas, Scott	Arbor Brothers
Walker, Darren	Ford Foundation

APPENDIX C
Additional Resources

GENERAL

Arrillaga-Andreessen, Laura, *Giving 2.0: Transform Your Giving and Our World* (Jossey-Bass, 2012).

Bornstein, David, *How to Change the World: Social Entrepreneurs and the Power of New Ideas* (Oxford University Press, 2007).

Bornstein, David, and Susan Davis, *Social Entrepreneurship: What Everyone Needs to Know* (Oxford University Press, 2010).

Dees, Gregory, Jed Emerson and Peter Economy, *Enterprising Nonprofits: A Toolkit for Social Entrepreneurs* (Wiley, 2001).

———, *Strategic Tools for Social Entrepreneurs* (Wiley, 2002).

Janus, Kathleen and Valerie Threlfall Consulting, *Scaling the Social Startup: A Survey of the Growth Path of Top-Performing Social Entrepreneurs*, available at www.kathleenjanus.com/resources.

Kanter, Beth and Allison Fine, *The Networked Nonprofit: Connecting with Social Media to Drive Change* (Jossey-Bass, 2010).

Keohane, Georgia Levenson, *Social Entrepreneurship for the 21st Century: Innovation Across the Nonprofit, Private and Public Sectors* (McGraw Hill, 2014).

McLeod, Grant, Heather and Leslie Crutchfield, *Forces for Good: The Six Practices of High-Impact Nonprofits* (Jossey-Bass, 2012).

Meehan, Bill and Kim Starkey Jonker, *Engine of Impact: The Essentials of Strategic Leadership in the Nonprofit Sector* (Stanford University Press, 2017).

Osberg, Sally and Roger L. Martin, *Getting Beyond Better: How Social Entrepreneurship Works* (Harvard Business Review Press, 2015).

WEBSITES AND BLOGS

Blue Avocado blog, www.blueavocado.org.

Board Source, www.boardsource.org.

Bornstein, David. *New York Times* "Fixes" Column, www.nytimes.com/ column/fixes.

(The) Bridgespan Group, Transformative Scale Resource Center, www.bridgespan.org/insights/initiatives/transformative-scale/ transformative-scale-resources.

The Chronicle of Philanthropy, www.philanthropy.com.

Compass Point, www.compasspoint.org.

Harvard Business Review—Ideas and Advice for Leaders, www.hbr.org.

Huffington Post, Huffpost Impact, http://www.huffingtonpost.com/impact/.

Inside Philanthropy, www.insidephilanthropy.com

Kanter, Beth, *Beth's Blog: How Nonprofits Can Use Social Media*, www .bethkanter.org/welcome/.

LinkedIn for Good, LinkedIn blog, http://blog.linkedin.com/topic/ linkedin-for-good/.

Nonprofit Quarterly, www.nonprofitquarterly.org.

Stanford Social Innovation Review, www.ssir.org.

PART 1: TESTING

Brown, Tim & Jocelyn Wyatt, "Design Thinking for Social Innovation," *Stanford Social Innovation Review*, Winter 2010.

Brown, Tim, *Change by Design: How Design Thinking Transforms Organizations and Inspires Innovation* (HarperBusiness, 2009).

Chesborough, Henry, *Open Innovation: The New Imperative for Creating and Profiting from Technology* (Harvard Business Review Press, 2005).

Design Kit: The Human-Centered Design Toolkit, IDEO.org, 2015, downloadable at www.designkit.org.

Drucker, Peter F., "The Discipline of Innovation," *Harvard Business Review*, August 2002.

Farson, Richard and Ralph Keyes, "The Failure Tolerant Leader," *Harvard Business Review*, August 2002, available at https://hbr.org/2002/08/the -failure-tolerant-leader.

Lean Impact: Lean Principles for Nonprofits and Social Enterprises, www .leanimpact.org.

Levitt Cea, Joanna and Jess Rimington, "Creating Breakout Innovation," *Stanford Social Innovation Review,* Summer 2017.

Ries, Eric, *The Lean Startup: How Today's Entrepreneurs Use Continuous Innovation to Create Radically Successful Businesses* (Crown Business, 2011).

Seelig, Tina, *inGenius: A Crash Course on Creativity* (HarperOne, 2012).

Tantia, Piyush, "The New Science of Designing for Humans," *Stanford Social Innovation Review,* Spring 2017.

PART 2: MEASURING

B Analytics Compare Software, http://b-analytics.net/products/benchmark-and-report.

Brest, Paul, "The Power of Theories of Change," *Stanford Social Innovation Review,* Spring 2010.

Developing a Theory of Change (revised March 2014), NPC and Clinks.

Epstein, Marc J. and Kristi Yuthas, *Measuring and Improving Social Impacts: A Guide for Nonprofits, Companies and Impact Investors* (Berrett-Koehler Publishers, 2014).

Hunter, David E. K., *Working Hard—and Working Well* (Hunter Consulting LLC, 2013).

McKinsey on Society, *Social Impact Assessment Portal,* http://mckinseyonsociety.com/social-impact-assessment/.

Morino, Mario, *Leap of Reason: Managing to Outcomes in an Era of Scarcity* (Venture Philanthropy Partners, 2011).

Mulgan, Geoff, "Measuring Social Value," *Stanford Social Innovation Review,* Summer 2010.

Outcome Focused Grantmaking: A Hard-Headed Approach to Soft-Hearted Goals, William and Flora Hewlett Foundation, March 2012.

Snibbe, Alana Conner, "Drowning in Data," *Stanford Social Innovation Review,* Fall 2006.

"Theory of Change Basics: A Primer on Theory of Change," Act Knowledge, March 2012.

Theory of Change Community Library Resources, http://www.theoryofchange.org/library/.

Tools and Resources for Assessing Social Impact (TRASI), Foundation Center, http://trasi.foundationcenter.org.

PART 3: FUNDING

Battilana, Julie, Matthew Lee, John Walker and Cheryl Dorsey, "In Search of the Hybrid Ideal," *Stanford Social Innovation Review,* Summer 2012.

Bell, Jeanne, Jan Masaoka and Steve Zimmerman, *Nonprofit Sustainability: Making Strategic Decisions for Financial Viability* (Jossey-Bass, 2010).

Foster, William, Ben Dixon and Matthew Hochstetler, "In Search of Sustainable Funding: Is Diversity of Sources Really the Answer?" *Nonprofit Quarterly,* March 21, 2007.

Foster, William, Peter Kim and Barbara Christiansen, "Ten Nonprofit Funding Models," *Stanford Social Innovation Review,* Spring 2009.

McCrae, Jennifer and Jeffrey Walker, *The Generosity Network: New Transformational Tools for Successful Fund-Raising* (Deepak Chopra Books, 2013).

Panas, Jerold, *Asking: A 59-Minute Guide to Everything Board Members, Volunteers and Staff Must Know to Secure the Gift* (Emerson & Church, 2013).

Rodriguez Heyman, Darian, *Nonprofit Fundraising 101: A Practical Guide with Easy to Implement Ideas and Tips from Industry Experts* (Wiley, 2016).

Tierney, Thomas J. and Joel L. Fleishman, *Give Smart: Philanthropy That Gets Results* (PublicAffairs, 2012).

Wexler, Robert, "Effective Social Enterprise—A Menu of Legal Structures," *Exempt Organization Tax Review,* June 2009.

PART 4: LEADING

Brinckerhoff, Peter, *Mission-Based Management: Leading Your Not-for-Profit in the 21st Century* (Wiley, 2009).

Chait, Richard, William Ryan and Barbara Taylor, *Governance as Leadership: Reframing the Work of Nonprofit Boards* (Wiley, 2004).

Collins, Jim, *Good to Great* (HarperBusiness, 2011).

———, *Good to Great and the Social Sectors: A Monograph to Accompany Good to Great* (HarperCollins, 2005).

Drucker, Peter, *Managing the Nonprofit Organization* (HarperBusiness, 2006).

Kotter, John, "What Leaders Really Do," *Harvard Business Review,* December 2001.

Letts, Christine et al., *High-Performance Nonprofit Organizations: Managing Upstream for Greater Impact* (Wiley, 1999).

Light, Paul, "Reshaping Social Entrepreneurship," *Stanford Social Innovation Review,* Fall 2006.

Masaoka, Jan, *Best of the Board Café: Hands-On Solutions for Nonprofit Boards* (Fieldstone Alliance, 2009).

Rodriguez Heyman, Darian, *Nonprofit Management 101: A Complete and Practical Guide for Leaders and Professionals* (Jossey-Bass, 2011).

PART 5: STORYTELLING

Aaker, Jennifer and Andy Smith, *The Dragonfly Effect: Quick, Effective and Powerful Ways to Use Social Media to Drive Social Change* (Jossey-Bass, 2010).

Duarte, Nancy, *HBR Guide to Persuasive Presentations* (Harvard Business Review Press, 2012).

Ganz, Marshall, *Why David Sometimes Wins: Leadership, Organization and Strategy in the California Farm Worker Movement* (Oxford University Press, 2010).

Goodman, Andy & Cause Communications, *Why Bad Presentations Happen to Good Causes: And How to Ensure They Won't Happen to Yours*, available for download at http://www.thegoodmancenter.com/resources/.

The OpEd Project, www.theopedproject.org.

NOTES

INTRODUCTION

1. Brice S. McKeever and Sarah L. Pettijohn, "The Nonprofit Sector in Brief 2014: Public Charities, Giving and Volunteering," Urban Institute, 2014.

2. For a full list of the cast of characters, along with their organizational information, see Appendix A.

PART 1—TESTING IDEAS

Chapter 1: The Discovery Phase

1. Eric Ries, *The Lean Startup: How Today's Entrepreneurs Use Continuous Innovation to Create Radically Successful Businesses* (Crown Business, 2011).

2. Tim Brown, *Change by Design: How Design Thinking Transforms Organizations and Inspires Innovation* (HarperBusiness, 2009).

3. Henry Chesbrough, *Open Innovation: The New Imperative for Creating and Profiting from Technology* (Harvard Business Review Press, 2005).

4. *Design Kit: The Human-Centered Design Toolkit,* IDEO.org, 2015; downloadable at www.designkit.org.

5. Bryan Stevenson, *Just Mercy: A Story of Justice and Redemption* (Spiegel & Grau, 2015).

6. "Bryan Stevenson Urges USCA Audience to 'Get Proximate,'" Black AIDS Institute blog, 2015; available at https://www.blackaids.org/news-2015/2527 -bryan-stevenson-urges-usca-audience-to-qget-proximateq.

7. "Gates Foundation Commits More than $500 Million to Tackle the Burden of Infectious Disease in Developing Countries," November 2, 2014; available at http://www.gatesfoundation.org/Media-Center/Press-Releases/2014/11/ ASTMH-Address.

8. Jill Tucker, "Oakland Preschool on Wheels Seeks to Bridge Access Gap," *San Francisco Chronicle,* November 27, 2015; available at http://www.sf chronicle.com/education/article/Oakland-preschool-on-wheels-seeks-to -bridge-6660902.php.

9. Sam Milbrath, "Co-creation: 5 Examples of Brands Driving Customer-Driven Innovation," Vision Critical blog, August 5, 2016; available at https://www.visioncritical.com/5-examples-how-brands-are-using-co-creation/.

10. "How Childhood Trauma Affects Health Across a Lifetime," TEDMED 2014; available at https://www.ted.com/speakers/nadine_burke_harris_1.

11. *The Accountability Resource Guide*; available at http://www.account abilitycounsel.org/resources/arg/.

Chapter 2: Engaging All Stakeholders

1. Carole Cadwalladr, "The Guy Behind the *Kony 2012* Video Finally Explains How Everything Went So Weird," *Business Insider*, March 3, 2013; available at http://www.businessinsider.com/the-guy-behind-the-kony-2012-video -finally-explains-how-everything-went-so-weird-2013-3.

2. Polly Curtis and Tom McCarthy, "*Kony 2012*: what's the real story?" *Guardian*, March 8, 2012; available at https://www.theguardian.com/politics/ reality-check-with-polly-curtis/2012/mar/08/kony-2012-what-s-the-story.

3. *Kony 2012,* video available at https://invisiblechildren.com/kony-2012/.

4. Samantha Grossman, "'*Kony 2012*' Documentary Becomes the Most Viral Video in History," *Time*, March 12, 2012; available at http://newsfeed.time.com /2012/03/12/kony-2012-documentary-becomes-most-viral-video-in-history/.

5. Polly Curtis and Tom McCarthy, "*Kony 2012*: what's the real story?"

6. Michael Deibert, "The Problem with Invisible Children's '*Kony 2012*,'" *Huffington Post* blog, March 7, 2012.

7. Lauren Raab, "'*Kony 2012*' Group Invisible Children Is Shutting Down," *Los Angeles Times*, December 15, 2014; available at http://www.latimes.com/ local/lanow/la-me-ln-invisible-children-kony-2012-20141215-story.html.

8. Jim Fruchterman, "Landmine Detector Project Lessons Learned," *Bene-blog: Technology Meets Society*, December 2, 2007; available at http://benetech .blogspot.com/2007/12/landmine-detector-project-lessons.html.

9. More information is available at https://www.nationalservice.gov/ programs/americorps.

Chapter 3: Reframing Failure as Learning

1. Richard Farson and Ralph Keyes, "The Failure Tolerant Leader," *Harvard Business Review,* August 2002; available at https://hbr.org/2002/08/the-failure -tolerant-leader.

2. Ibid.

3. *Design Kit: The Human-Centered Design Toolkit,* www.designkit.org.

4. Krista Donaldson, "Failure, Design & Impact," LinkedIn, September 10, 2015; available at https://www.linkedin.com/pulse/failure-design-impact -krista-donaldson.

5. Tanya Raukko, "8 Questions with: Garrett Spiegel/D-Rev," *Imprint,* March 24, 2014; available at http://www.imprintlab.com/8-questions-with-garrett -spiegel-d-rev/.

6. Garret Spiegel, "Learning from Comet: rural clinics and home-care aren't ready for phototherapy," D-Rev blog, October 21, 2014; available at http://d-rev.org/2014/10/learning-comet-rural-clinics-home-care-arent-ready -phototherapy/.

7. "Raj Panjabi: Post Conflict Health," PopTech, 2010; available at https:// poptech.org/popcasts/raj_panjabi_postconflict_health.

8. Jonny Price, "Kiva Zip Pilot in Kenya Winding Down," Kiva blog, September 16, 2015; available at https://borrow.kiva.org/blogs/200, accessed May 25, 2017.

9. "Our Mistakes," Givewell.org; available at http://www.givewell.org/ about/our-mistakes.

10. "GiveWell and Good Ventures," *The GiveWell Blog,* June 28, 2012; available at http://blog.givewell.org/2012/06/28/givewell-and-good-ventures/.

11. Laurie Michaels and Judith Rodin, "Embracing Philanthropy's Risky Business," *Stanford Social Innovation Review,* Summer 2017.

PART 2—MEASURING IMPACT

1. Tris Lumley, "Raising the Bar on Nonprofit Impact Measurement," *Stanford Social Innovation Review,* July 10, 2013.

2. The Robin Hood Poverty Tracker is available at http://povertytracker .robinhood.org/#home. For information about how the foundation streamlines the impact metrics of its grantees, see also Michael M. Weinstein and Ralph M. Bradburd, *The Robin Hood Rules for Smart Giving* (Columbia University Press, 2013).

3. "The State of Data in the Nonprofit Sector," EveryAction and Nonprofit Hub, 2016.

4. Peter Buffett, "The Charitable-Industrial Complex," *New York Times*, July 26, 2013.

Chapter 4: Crafting a Compelling Theory of Change

1. John Sawhill and David Williamson, "Measuring What Matters in Non-profits," *McKinsey Quarterly*, May 2001.

2. Cathy James, "Theory of Change Review, a report commissioned by Comic Relief," September 2011.

3. "Developing a Theory of Change," NPC and Clinks, revised March 2014; available at http://www.clinks.org/sites/default/files/TheoryofChangeGuide.pdf.

4. James P. Connell et al., "New Approaches to Evaluating Comprehensive Community Initiatives," Aspen Institute, 1995.

5. Available at http://www.theoryofchange.org.

6. Mario Morino, *Leap of Reason: Managing to Outcomes in an Era of Scarcity* (Venture Philanthropy Partners, 2011).

7. David E. K. Hunter, *Working Hard—and Working Well* (Hunter Consulting , 2013).

Chapter 5: Maximizing Use of Data

1. G. T. Doran, "There's a S.M.A.R.T. Way to Write Management's Goals and Objectives," *Management Review* 70, no. 11, 1981, 35–36.

2. Allison Gauss, *The SMART Way to Create Fundraising Goals*, Classy blog, https://www.classy.org/blog/the-smart-way-to-create-fundraising-goals/; and Mike Morrison, *History of SMART Objectives*, RapidBi (June 22, 2010), https://rapidbi.com/history-of-smart-objectives/.

3. See, for example, Maria A. May, "RCTs: Not All That Glitters Is Gold: A look at the limitations of randomized control trials," *Stanford Social Innovation Review* blog, August 28, 2012; and Peter York, "Fueling Nonprofit Innovation: R&D Vigor Trumps Randomized Control Trial Rigor: Research and development can help more nonprofits learn, innovate, and reach goals faster and for less money," *Stanford Social Innovation Review* blog, August 16, 2011.

4. Mae Wu et al., "Dosed without Prescription: Preventing Pharmaceutical Contamination of our Nation's Drinking Water," NRDC White Paper, December 2009.

5. Becky Briesacher et al., "Out-of-Pocket Burden of Health Care Spending and the Adequacy of the Medicare Part D Low-Income Subsidy," *Med Care*, 2010 June; 48(6): 503–9, available at https://www.ncbi.nlm.nih.gov/pmc/

articles/PMC3084515/; and Dan Mangan, "Medication Costs Fuel Painful Medical Debt, Bankruptcies," CNBC.com article, May 28, 2014.

6. *My Stomach Hit the Floor*; video available at http://leapofreason.org/video-gallery/video-nick-ehrmann-my-stomach-hit-the-floor/.

Chapter 6: Making Your Data Tell a Story

1. Alana Conner Snibbe, "Drowning in Data," *Stanford Social Innovation Review,* Fall 2006.

2. *From 89 Indicators to 4*, video available at http://leapofreason.org/video-gallery/video-mike-duggan-from-89-indicators-to-4/.

PART 3—FUNDING EXPERIMENTATION

1. William Foster and Jeffrey L. Bradach, "Should Nonprofits Seek Profits?" *Harvard Business Review,* February 2005.

2. William Foster, Peter Kim and Barbara Christiansen, "Ten Nonprofit Funding Models," *Stanford Social Innovation Review,* Spring 2009.

3. William Foster, Ben Dixon and Matthew Hochstetler, "In Search of Sustainable Funding: Is Diversity of Sources Really the Answer?" *Nonprofit Quarterly,* March 21, 2007.

Chapter 7: Laying the Foundation to Experiment with Earned Income

1. "2016 Snapshot: For-Profit and Hybrid Echoing Green Fellowship Applications"; available at http://www.echoinggreen.org/pubs/Echoing-Green-Snapshot-For-Profit-Hybrid-2016.pdf.

2. Robert Wexler, "Effective Social Enterprise—A Menu of Legal Structures," *Exempt Organization Tax Review,* June 2009.

3. Julie Battilana, Matthew Lee, John Walker and Cheryl Dorsey, "In Search of the Hybrid Ideal," *Stanford Social Innovation Review,* Summer 2012.

4. Wexler, "Effective Social Enterprise—A Menu of Legal Structures." See also Robert Wexler and David Levitt, "Using New Hybrid Legal Forms: Three Case Studies, Four Important Questions, and a Bunch of Analysis," *Exempt Organization Tax Review,* January 2012; and John Tyler and Robert Wexler, "Update on Hybrids and Social Enterprise Organizations," 32nd Annual Representing and Managing Tax-Exempt Organizations, April 23, 2015.

5. "Embrace: Deciding on a Hybrid Structure, Global Health Innovation Insight Series Case Study," Stanford Graduate School of Business, 2013.

6. Julie Battilana, Matthew Lee, John Walker and Cheryl Dorsey, "In Search of the Hybrid Ideal," *Stanford Social Innovation Review,* Summer 2012.

Chapter 8: Testing Earned-Income Strategies

1. "Developing Viable Earned Income Strategies," in *Strategic Tools for Social Entrepreneurs: Enhancing the Performance of Your Enterprising Nonprofit*, eds. Greg Dees et al. (Wiley, 2002).

2. See https://www.nationalservice.gov/programs/americorps/current-members/americorps-week/americorps-week-2017#third.

3. Ibid.

Chapter 9: Optimizing Fundraising Efforts

1. John Kania and Mark Kramer, "Collective Impact," *Stanford Social Innovation Review*, Winter 2011.

2. "Is Grantmaking Getting Smarter?" Grantmakers for Effective Organizations, November 19, 2014.

3. Alex Neuhoff, Katie Smith Milway, Reilly Kiernan and Josh Grehan, "Making Sense of Nonprofit Collaborations," Bridgespan Group and Lodestar Foundation, December 2014.

4. Alex Neuhoff and Katie Smith Millway, "Collaboration-palooza," *Stanford Social Innovation Review*, December 17, 2014.

5. Kania and Kramer, "Collective Impact."

6. Chris Rabb, *Invisible Capital: How Unseen Forces Shape Entrepreneurial Opportunity* (Berrett-Koehler, 2010).

7. Ben Beers and Lindsay Booker, "Data Evolution: What We Learn from Fellowship Applicants," Echoing Green, blog, April 19, 2016; available at http://www.echoinggreen.org/blog/data-evolution-what-we-learn-fellowship-applicants.

8. Jennifer McCrea and Jeffrey Walker, *The Generosity Network* (Deepak Chopra Books, 2013).

PART 4—LEADING COLLABORATIVELY

Chapter 10: Cultivating Collective Leadership

1. Leslie R. Crutchfield and Heather McLeod Grant, *Forces for Good: The Six Practices of High-Impact Nonprofits* (Jossey-Bass 2012).

2. Warren Bennis, *On Becoming a Leader* (Basic Books, 2009).

3. Robert Spector and Patrick D. McCarthy, *The Nordstrom Way: The Inside Story of America's #1 Customer Service Company* (Wiley, 1996). For more on the inverted pyramid of management and how it applies in the nonprofit sector, see Peter C. Brickerhoff, *Mission-Based Management: Leading Your Not-for-Profit in the 21st Century* (Wiley, 2009).

4. Spector and McCarthy, *The Nordstrom Way.*

5. Laurie Bassi and Daniel McMurrer, "Maximizing Your Return on People," *Harvard Business Review,* March 1, 2007.

6. Edwin Warfield, "A Video Conversation with Sarah Hemminger, CEO and Co-Founder of Thread—Part I," Baltimore citybizlist, May 11, 2016; available at http://baltimore.citybizlist.com/article/350685/a-video-conversation -with-sarah-hemminger-ceo-and-co-founder-of-thread-part-i.

7. Edwin Warfield, "A Video Conversation with Sarah Hemminger, CEO and Co-Founder of Thread—Part II," Baltimore citybizlist, May 16, 2016; available at http://baltimore.citybizlist.com/article/350686/a-video-conversation -with-sarah-hemminger-ceo-and-co-founder-of-thread-part-ii.

Chapter 11: Bringing in Senior Leadership Early

1. Jim Collins, *Good to Great: Why Some Companies Make the Leap . . . and Others Don't* (HarperBusiness, 2011).

Chapter 12: Building an Active Board

1. Jan Masaoka, "Ditch Your Board Composition Matrix," *Blue Avocado: A Magazine of American Nonprofits*; available at http://blueavocado.org/content/ ditch-your-board-composition-matrix.

2. LinkedIn for Nonprofits, http://nonprofit.linkedin.com/content/me/ nonprofit/en-us.

3. Richard Chait, William Ryan and Barbara Taylor, *Governance as Leadership: Reframing the Work of Nonprofit Boards* (Wiley, 2004).

PART 5—TELLING COMPELLING STORIES

1. Mike Butcher, "UN Launches Powerful, First Ever, VR Film following Syrian Refugee Girl," *TechCrunch,* January 23, 2015.

2. Andy Goodman and Cause Communications, *Why Bad Presentations Happen to Good Causes: And How to Ensure They Won't Happen to Yours,* available for download at http://www.thegoodmancenter.com/resources/.

3. Ibid.

4. Nadine Burke Harris, "How Childhood Trauma Affects Health Across a Lifetime," filmed September 2014, available at https://www.ted.com/speakers/ nadine_burke_harris_1.

Chapter 13: Creating a Compelling Narrative

1. McCrea and Walker, *The Generosity Network.*

2. Marshall Ganz, "What Is Public Narrative?" 2008, chutzpahportfolio
.yolasite.com/resources/WhatIsPublicNarrative08.pdf.

3. Harris, "How Childhood Trauma Affects Health Across a Lifetime."

4. McCrea and Walker, *The Generosity Network*.

5. Ibid.

6. Goodman and Cause Communications, *Why Bad Presentations Happen to Good Causes*.

7. David Henderson, *Making News: A Straight-Shooting Guide to Media Relations* (iUniverse Star, 2006).

8. For more on the Teach For America story, see Wendy Kopp, *One Day, All Children . . . the Unlikely Triumph of Teach For America and What I Learned Along the Way* (PublicAffairs, 2001).

9. Laura Weidman Powers, "Google and Diversity: Be Careful What You Say About It," *Mercury News,* June 9, 2014.

10. See, for example, Abigail Falik, "Malia's Decision to Take a Gap Year Isn't Just Good for Her—It's Good for the Country, Entrepreneur Says," *Washington Post,* May 2, 2016.

11. Available at www.theopedproject.org.

12. Goodman and Cause Communications, *Why Bad Presentations Happen to Good Causes*.

13. See https://www.nationalservice.gov/about/who-we-are/our-history.

14. See https://www.nationalservice.gov/programs/americorps.

APPENDIX B. METHODOLOGY

1. For purposes of this analysis, we define small organizations as organizations having less than $500,000 in annual budget; medium organizations are organizations with a $500,000 to $2 million annual budget, and large organizations are those that have an annual budget greater than $2 million.

2. Respondents were able to select multiple answers to this question, with the result that responses do not total to 100 percent.

3. Thirty-nine percent of survey respondents report being part of multiple portfolios.

INDEX